Congress Declares War

ALSO BY ROLAND H. WORTH, JR.
AND FROM MCFARLAND

*Alternative Lives of Jesus: Noncanonical Accounts
through the Early Middle Ages* (2003)

World War II Resources on the Internet (2002)

Biblical Studies on the Internet: A Resource Guide (2002)

*Secret Allies in the Pacific: Covert Intelligence and Code Breaking
Cooperation Between the United States, Great Britian, and
Other Nations Prior to the Attack on Pearl Harbor* (2001)

*Church, Monarch and Bible in Sixteenth Century England:
The Political Context of Biblical Translation* (2000)

*No Choice but War: The United States Embargo Against Japan
and the Eruption of War in the Pacific* (1995)

*Pearl Harbor: Selected Testimonies, Fully Indexed, from
Congressional Hearings (1945–1946) and Prior Investigations
of the Events Leading Up to the Attack* (1993)

Bible Translations: A History Through Source Documents (1992)

Congress Declares War

December 8–11, 1941

Roland H. Worth, Jr.

McFarland & Company, Inc., Publishers
Jefferson, North Carolina, and London

LIBRARY OF CONGRESS CATALOGUING-IN-PUBLICATION DATA

Worth, Roland H., 1943–
    Congress declares war : December 8–11, 1941 / Roland H. Worth, Jr.
        p.   cm.
    Includes bibliographical references and index.

    ISBN 0-7864-1804-4 (softcover : 50# alkaline paper)

    1. World War, 1939–1945—Causes. 2. World War, 1939–1945—Diplomatic history. 3. World War, 1939–1945—United States. 4. United States—Politics and government—1933–1945. 5. United States—Foreign relations—1933–1945. I. Title.
D742.U5W67   2004
940.53'11—dc22   2004010998

British Library cataloguing data are available

©2004 Roland H. Worth, Jr. All rights reserved

No part of this book may be reproduced or transmitted in any form or by any means, electronic or mechanical, including photocopying or recording, or by any information storage and retrieval system, without permission in writing from the publisher.

Manufactured in the United States of America

On the cover: *Top photograph:* ©2004 Clipart
Bottom photograph: ©2004 Photospin

McFarland & Company, Inc., Publishers
   Box 611, Jefferson, North Carolina 28640
       www.mcfarlandpub.com

For Michael Alexander Worth,
my grandson
(born April 16, 1996)

Wherever chance and good fortune take you,
you are always in my hopes and prayers

Contents

Preface   1

Introduction   5

1. Congress, Bureaucrats, Press and Public Opinion Anticipate Action   9

2. The Presidential Address and Senatorial Action: Declaring War on Japan   35

3. The House of Representatives Responds to War with Japan   54

4. Germany and Italy Join the War   99

5. The Senate: Declaring War on Germany and Italy   127

6. The House of Representatives Responds to War with Germany and Italy   136

Notes   153
Bibliography   171
Index   177

Preface

The initial research for this volume began about 10 days after America's initial twenty-first century "Pearl Harbor"—the hijacking and crashing of three nearly fully fueled jetliners into the Pentagon and the World Trade Center. In 1941, Americans had few firsthand accounts of the Pearl Harbor attack, and those usually were as relayed by the local press via the trans–Pacific cable. Even what the White House released was being funneled to it through often equally slow mechanisms. Photographs were few and not immediately available and when they *were* released, censorship limited both their number and the depiction of the horror of what had transpired.

On September 11, 2001, millions worldwide saw terrorist attacks in real time, uncensored.

However history ultimately judges the course and results of the war that began on that date, the day will come when historians will find it useful to analyze from a safe distance in time how America and its political leadership reacted to the crisis. It does take time to understand the balance between self and national interest that motivates politicians, not to mention how well grounded their decisions actually turn out to be and how effectively they carry out the policies they had embraced. Here we attempt to apply a very similar analysis to an earlier generation's defining moment, asking how the American political system reacted to the news, examining the debates that followed, and scrutinizing the declaration of World War II.

As in my other World War II research, I once again owe a debt of gratitude to the Boatwright Library of the University of Richmond in Richmond, Virginia. Its ample collection has done much to make this book feasible. It is a tad illogical, I confess, to feel that the *Congressional Record* of 1941 is any more impressive merely because it was printed at

1

the time of the debates it records. Yet on a psychological level there is something to the "feel" of the paper and even the impact of the words that a reprint or a microfilm can rarely provide.

In researching this work a word of appreciation is also due to the County of Henrico Public Library system, which proved extremely helpful in obtaining microfilm of contemporary newspapers that were not available locally. Although the immediate reporting of events inevitably has its failures, it also provides the record of the very human foibles and quibbles that do not always make it into the formal history books, yet help us gain an insight into the attitudes then present in the various participants. This is, as radio commentator and newsman Paul Harvey would put it, "the rest of the story." Or, at least, part of it.

In summarizing the comments of the various House and Senate members I have sometimes rearranged the internal order of some of the remarks made by various speakers. The order in which they spoke is faithfully maintained, but I have tried to squeeze their comments into more concise terms so that the reader can more quickly grasp the major points of emphases and the most intriguing comments made by each participant. As a responsible news reporter and commentator would do, I have tried to treat their intent and purpose, fairly.

On the other hand, more than once I have found it irresistible to contrast implicitly some of their reactions to the rhetoric that followed the World Trade Center attack of 2001. Whether those differing reactions is tribute to a greater national maturity today—or the self-destructive ideological construct of twenty-first century anti–American paranoia—we must leave to the individual reader.

Although the members of Congress had the opportunity to revise their remarks prior to publication in the next day's *Record*, it seemed best to use the text that they wished to appear in the formal journal. Even though slightly more polished, these thoughts came on the same day, and are as contemporary to the date of the debates as if actually spoken on the House or Senate floor.

This approach also permits us to hear the contemporary opinions of more individuals. The day of the House debate concerning war with Japan, only eight House members spoke,[1] though additional members gained permission to add their own thoughts to the record and, as noted, some who did speak added to their original material. By examining the entire permanent record we gain access to more individuals and obtain a significantly more comprehensive sense of the emotions, logic, and attitudes at play on that fateful day than if we limited our analysis to just the direct participants.

For a similar reason I have also liberally quoted both what legislators said off the House or Senate floor and the remarks of other political and social leaders in the days between the Pearl Harbor attack and the declarations of war that began the following day: In the things they said they both clarified their own positions and helped shape the views of both the political class of the nation and the public at large.

In dealing primarily with what people said rather than what they did, the words of an endless array of Congressmen and women have a potential for numbing the mind. Therefore I have attempted to analyze what a number of the speakers said about the attitudes that were present, and provide at least passing information on the backgrounds and accomplishments of many of them. This should help them appear not as mere names but as real, flesh-and-blood creatures. It should also help the reader gain a better comprehension of the views they were implying but not always making explicit.

In the interest of brevity I have abbreviated citations of the *Congressional Record* as "CR."

Roland H. Worth, Jr.
Spring 2004

1

Introduction

Hundreds of books have been written about Pearl Harbor and the events immediately preceding the attack. I myself have published three: the first is a compilation of the best of the testimony garnered by the various U.S. government investigative committees; the second is a study of the economic embargo of Japan in the summer of 1941 as one of the precipitating causes of the war; and the third is an analysis of the covert inter–Allied cooperation in intelligence gathering in the Pacific prior to the attack. Others have summarized the events leading up to the war, the attack itself, or the reasons it was possible for it to be launched and carried out with such minimal Japanese losses.

What normally gets lost in the shuffle are the political aspects of the American reaction, the formal declaration of war, and the discussions and interactions that were required to make it a reality. War is never solely a military act; it is inevitably a political one as well. No member of Congress, cabinet member, or even the president of the United States can totally divest himself of a consideration of the practical political ramifications of any international crisis or tragedy. Even the most idealistic has to package a policy in a form that can be sold to Congress and to the broader American public, especially when he or she is carrying the baggage of past comments and commitments.

For the interventionists of the day, that baggage was, in part, that they had seemingly totally missed the potential danger in the Pacific. They had become so obsessed with demanding American intervention in Europe and pillorying their critics for opposing such a course, that they paid little attention to where actions were ultimately to occur that were to compel U.S. involvement.

Similarly, the isolationists had problems of their own. If the interventionists had so stressed European intervention that involvement anywhere else verged on secular sacrilege, isolationists had so stressed opposition to war that even one in the Pacific could easily seem a repudiation of the principles for which they had long fought.

In the language of the debates before Congress about formally declaring war, we see the first efforts of both sides to reconcile their past rhetoric with present reality. A disaster had been thrust upon one and all and its nature was so unexpected in its specific location and intensity that none was prepared for it.

If it had been a mere declaration of war by Japan, it would not have been all that surprising. Relations were brittle; it would have taken little to move the conflict from the negotiating table to the battlefield. But what came was a surprise attack; a massive surprise attack; a successful massive surprise attack. That it targeted America's citadel of the Pacific was enough to shock everyone.

In this volume I concentrate on the American political system in crisis: how it reacted to word of the attack, how it debated what should be done, and how it handled itself in the formal proceedings that led to a declaration of war. Within this context I examine public reaction and that of the opinion-molding mass media of the day and how the media both helped shape—but also reflected—the quickly evolving opinion of the political establishment in Washington.

Those supporting a European war in the House and the Senate had a war handed to them ready-made—but not the war they wanted. This one was half a world away and against a very different enemy. Would it divert attention from the war they so passionately believed essential to U.S. long-term security interests? Would it divide America too much to urge a simultaneous two-war strategy? In the light of the scope of the disaster at Pearl Harbor, was it even practical to urge such a course?

Those opposing participation in Europe's bloodbath had no problem with vigorously supporting a Pacific war for in this one there was no question that America had been directly and overtly attacked. The isolationists' problem was one of not becoming politically compromised by earlier opposition to a war in a different part of the world, one they were still opposed to. Furthermore, might not the current conflict be used as a pretext to expanding it to Europe as well?

The president had fundamental questions of politics and prudence to resolve as well. Should he seek a declaration of war against Japan alone or urge a similar course toward Germany? Was war politically feasible? Was there enough support for a two-front war? And, even if (as Roosevelt believed) war with Germany was inevitable, was it more prudent to wait for overt German action instead of taking the initiative?

Hence the political leadership had to face serious and difficult problems, and answer them within a matter of about 24 hours—from the attack the morning of December 7th to the meeting of Congress to discuss the matter the early afternoon of the next day. In these early years of the twenty-first century, we routinely emphasize rapid responses. The mindset was far different in that earlier and slower-paced society.

But war waits for no one, and fundamental war-and-peace decisions had to be made, promptly. How and why Congress made those decisions and how it justified them both to itself and others is the major subject of this book. I shall also consider how the foreign policy decisions of Germany changed the playing field yet again when mid-week was reached following the Pearl Harbor attack, and how a two-front war (or two simultaneous wars a world apart) became inescapable no matter what one's political preferences might have been.

1

Congress, Bureaucrats, Press and Public Opinion Anticipate Action

The danger of involvement in the European war was clearly great in the early days of December, 1941: Interventionists thought such participation essential; anti-interventionists opposed it as hostile to the nation's interests. But both factions shared the perception that involvement grew ever nearer. In regard to the Far East the passions were muted. There both factions wanted to avoid a war. Yet here, too, quietly but ever more firmly, war seemed to be edging ever nearer.

Most Americans could sense this drift warward in the actions, rhetoric, and proposals being presented in the negotiations between the U.S. and Japan. Indeed, in the abstract there was a consensus that hostilities were waiting in the near future: In a Gallup poll whose survey was completed on the 6th, 52 percent "thought war would break out soon"; 21 percent were uncertain.[1]

In one sense insiders both in government and the press were even more well aware that the situation was actually far worse, that the weekend of December 6–7 represented an extremely high risk of seeing the passage from diplomatic saber-rattling into the cannon fire of overt international conflict. As the journalist Harrison E. Salisbury later recalled, "The fact that both Churchill and [American ambassador to Britain] Winant expected the Japanese to attack that weekend is natural. The weight of public information pointed to a weekend attack."[2]

But such were mere opinions and intellectual calculations. Nothing more. When war came it came with the loudness and alarm of a thunderbolt—striking where no one expected,[3] to a degree no one expected,[4] and with a success that was utterly horrifying to all levels of American civil and political authority. Even in the ambiguous form that quickly spread throughout the nation, it was clear that nothing short of a major military disaster had occurred.

Even those who felt themselves experts and knew the probabilities were shocked by what they heard. Perhaps the columnist Dorothy Thompson summed it up best in her musings on President Roosevelt's address to Congress on the 8th requesting a declaration of war:

> There was even something of an anticlimax about it—and something idiotic. No variation. Just like Holland—and we were the Great United States. Just like Russia—and we were thousands of miles away....
> A friend, sitting next to me at the radio, said, "Well, at least, you are not shocked."
> "No," I said. "I am not shocked."
> Yes, but I was. Odd that one never gets over being shocked. Over and over again the same pattern and always the surprise—the silly surprise. And I felt it, too. "Not to us, they can't do that to us." Even when I'd known all the time that they could, and they would. Known it in the bones, where one knows things best. But still the surprise.[5]

The first news reached the listening public via an announcer with the Mutual Broadcast System reading a United Press bulletin with the White House announcement. At 2:26 P.M. the bulletin interrupted a football game. At 2:30 the other two major radio networks broke the story.[6]

The three networks and many local stations promptly shifted to a format of sharing every piece of breaking data they could obtain, including domestic and foreign reactions, and even reports—live—from both the Philippines and Hawaii. One NBC reporter was standing on the roof of a local newspaper when he noted that "one of the bombs [just] dropped within fifty feet of the KGU [radio] tower. It is no joke; it is a real war."[7] Later he added the vague words that were, perhaps, just as ominous as specific numbers would have been: "We have no statement as to how much damage has been done, but it has been *a very severe attack*."[8] Sometimes what one does not know is even more frightening than what one does. An unspecified calamity was out there—the human imagination filled in the rest.

The situation was still fluid and subject to change by the hour—or even more often[9]—and that concerned only what was being issued to the press for public consumption. Press Secretary Stephen T. Early issued the latest news releases from his office as the data became available and the decision was made to release various specific pieces of information to the public.[10]

At the 4:40 P.M. press conference it suddenly dawned upon Early that it was grimly inappropriate to be releasing data to Japanese correspondents and he enquired whether there were any such present in the large crowd. (Things were so hectic the thought simply had not yet occurred to anyone to pull the press credentials of Japanese reporters.) Although Early was reassured by the negative response, he was later learned that a Japanese correspondent had been present for a short while earlier in the day but had left.[11] In the highly emotional situation, this departure was an act of common prudence at the very least.

If the Pearl Harbor strike had blind-sided the military, the press, the politicians, and the public at large, there was always the danger that something else could occur before the president rose to address the Congress. "Every few minutes" some type of new information seemed to arrive and was carefully examined by both the president and key advisers, remembered cabinet member Frances Perkins.[12] Through it all, the president seemed a calm island in a sea of chaos.[13] When his son, Elliott, finally got through on the telephone, Roosevelt pumped his son for information as to how the military personnel were reacting where Elliott was stationed and what they were hearing. He then hung up before his son could press too hard about what he himself was hearing from Hawaii.[14]

With all the constantly changing data, no one felt it wise to venture to the press more than the most broadly worded opinion, since events might undercut anything overly specific. The White House itself was acutely aware of this, and released a statement at 11 PM Sunday stressing, "It should be emphasized that the message to Congress has not yet been written and its tenor will, of course, depend on further information received between 11 o'clock tonight and noon tomorrow. Further news is coming in all the time."[15] (Actually, a draft had been prepared by the president earlier in the day.[16] Grace Tully had taken the dictation about 5 P.M. that evening.[17] Either the press spokesman was unaware of this, simply did not wish to admit it and open the door to questions about what it contained, or did not wish it to seem that the president would overlook late-breaking data.)

Whether a formal declaration of war would be requested was a carefully guarded secret. The president declined to be too specific even with the congressional leaders he met with that evening, because he "knew that if he stated it to the conference that it would be all over town in five minutes because it is perfectly foolish ever to ask a large group of Congressmen to keep a secret."[18] The restraint, of course, also provided Roosevelt the opportunity to modify his plans if something dramatic occurred in the meantime.

Theoretically there were at least three options open: Declare war on Japan alone; declare war on all the Axis powers; or don't officially declare war at all but simply pass a resolution noting that a state of war exists. At least one important senator Tom T. Connally, had suggested the last option might be the most prudent approach.[19]

Not declaring (or at least not recognizing the existence of) war was absent from the list. Not only had an American territory been assaulted, but one of its most important naval bases had, as well. True, there had been troublesome incidents in the past. The most infamous was the attack on the U.S. gunboat *Panay* in China which, from the standpoint of what was admitted or provable, might or might not have been carried out as an intentional act upon orders from higher Japanese authority. In contrast, as Admiral William D. Leahy thought at the time, "Pearl Harbor was no local incident."[20] There was simply no way the attack of Dec. 7th could have been launched without permission at the highest levels.[21] Earlier events might be swept under the rug; this one was too blatant, too clear-cut, and too disastrous to treat in such a manner.

In the horror of the moment, few people could note the absurdity in what was happening—it was humorous in a grim sort of manner, if one could mentally step back a few feet from the onrush of events. One of the few who did was, of all people, Archbishop Michael J. Curley, of Baltimore, who feared that readers of his words in print might not catch the macabre humor he intended:

> We might as well have a war in the Pacific. We're out looking for war, aren't we? We're out looking for war in the Atlantic, so why not in the Pacific? In fact, we've got a war in the Atlantic. We've had one there ever since the order to shoot on sight went out. We're not satisfied. We're looking for war, so I see no reason why we should not have a war in the Pacific, or all of the seven seas and everywhere.[22]

His was probably a manifestation of the "either laugh or cry" phenomenon: the psychologically pressing need to mock a situation lest it totally overwhelm the emotions.

When the newspapers went to press the night of December 7th, it was clear that the Congress would balk at little, if anything, the president asked. Speaker Sam Rayburn was pressed as to whether there would be a request for a declaration of war. He responded that though he had not explicitly been given the answer to that question, that he would press for such a course: it was the one matter on which he was confident there would be full agreement by everyone."[23] The other side of the political spectrum concurred. Minority Senate leader Charles L. McNary stressed, "The Republicans will all go along in my opinion, with whatever is done."[24] The House Minority Leader, Joseph W. Martin, Jr., concurred, "There is no politics here. There is only one party when it comes to the integrity and honor of the country."[25]

Only if the European War were dragged into this equation was there the potential danger of this consensus breaking down. Some calculated that events would take care of themselves. For example, Sen. Tom T.

1. Congress, Bureaucrats, Press and Public Opinion

Connally of Texas, chairman of the Foreign Relations Committee, thought that events in Europe would decide the matter for the U.S., rather than the U.S. having to take the initiative.[26] (The president had already embraced this policy of delay, though without announcing it.)

Former Presidents and Presidential Candidates Embrace War

In the traditional, rallying around the president phenomena, former presidents and presidential candidates promptly concurred that Roosevelt's hand had been forced. Among those opponents, Alf M. Landon concurred that "The Japanese attack leaves no choice. Nothing must be permitted to interrupt our victory."[27] The more recent foe Wendell L. Wilkie told the press, "I have not the slightest doubt as to what a United America should and will do."[28]

As former President Herbert Hoover summed it up, "American soil has been treacherously attacked by Japan. Our decision is clear. It is forced upon us. We must fight with everything we have."[29] In a stance similar to that of many others, he bluntly refused to recant any of his prior opposition to Roosevelt's foreign policy. In light of the clear challenge to America it had to be one of the "matters to be threshed out by history." In the short term future there was now only one option: to "fight" and "defeat" Japan in any and all places that it could be beaten.[30] As he said the following day after Roosevelt had sought and obtained the declaration of war, "The President took the only line of action open to any patriotic American."[31]

However much Hoover recognized that, militarily, there was no option but war, in private he was considerably skeptical of the wisdom of America's diplomacy that preceded it. In his judgment, the American diplomatic note of November 26th was nothing less than an ultimatum, and he believed that Secretary of State Cordell Hull had sent it fully recognizing that war would occur if the U.S. refused to modify its contents.[32] "Continuous putting pins in rattlesnakes finally got this country bitten," he wrote to one correspondent.[33]

Anti-Interventionist Interpretations of the Attack

Isolationists were as angered as interventionists over what had happened. Senator Arthur H. Vandenberg stressed that there was a vast difference between opposing war and avoiding war under these circumstances: when war is initiated by a foreign foe, one could do nothing but deliver the fastest and most powerful "answer."[34] And that answer? "The answer so far as I am concerned is victorious war with every resource at our command."[35]

Congressman Hamilton Fish was ranking minority leader on the House Committee on Foreign Affairs, which normally would have jurisdiction on any war resolution. The resentment between him and the president was so great and tenacious that he was conspicuously not invited to the White House Sunday night conference, but even he stressed that he would recommend unity on the House floor when it came his turn to speak.[36]

A peaceful resolution had now been ruled out by the other side: "The unwarranted, brazen, and senseless attack by the Japanese navy and air forces while negotiations were in progress and in defiance of President Roosevelt's late letter to the emperor of Japan forces us into a war in defense of our own possessions."[37] This was far different situation, as Fish saw it, from a European war in which America would be involved in defense of British interests rather than its own. As an indication of his commitment to the policy he recommended, he expressed readiness to move from his reserve status in the Army to active combat duty.[38]

Similar declarations of outrage were coming from members of both the House and Senate whether they were in Washington or scattered around the country.[39]

Senator Burton K. Wheeler could not comprehend any rationale behind the Japanese attack. "They must have gone crazy," he suggested to the press. The blame was wholly upon them. "War seldom, if ever, settles anything and it is inconceivable to me that the Japanese Government would be foolish enough to want war with this country." On the other hand the attack certainly had occurred, and as repeated reports indicated, there was but one option: "The only thing now is to do our best to lick hell out of them."[40] Wheeler received the word of the attack while in his native Montana, and quickly grabbed the first available train back to Washington.[41]

In a combination of racial prejudice and blatant, unrealistically low evaluation of Japanese fighting ability, there was general over-optimism about how quickly the war would be over, some thinking of mere months. Unlike many senators and representatives, Wheeler quickly came to a recognition that the distances involved in waging the war destroyed that possibility (adding a dig at the interventionist Euro-centrism in the process): "We are not going to be able to lick the Japs in thirty or sixty days or six months like some people think. It's going to be difficult for us to get at them. And because we have been giving away so much of our equipment [to Britain] we haven't got as much as we should have. Make no mistake. This is no pink tea [easy and comfortable task]. The sooner every one realizes this, the better."[42]

Fellow isolationist Sen. Bennett C. Clark (Democrat, Missouri) took the common stance that the attack left no room for further argument. So far as he was concerned he would vote in the affirmative "on any recommendation he [the president] might make either for a declaration of war or the prosecution of it."[43]

Senator David I. Walsh (Democrat, Massachusetts) served as chairman of the Naval Affairs Committee. He recognized that there was now "no choice but to take speedy and decisive measures to defend our country.... It is too late now to ponder whether a different international policy would have averted war."[44] Whatever policy differences there might have been, it was no longer a matter of who was right or who was wrong. Events had made such matters irrelevant.

Republican senator and anti-interventionist Robert A. Taft of Ohio stressed that he had been a pessimist about the Far East. He had "long foreseen the possibility of war with Japan [and] I have prayed the tragedy of such a war would be averted." In light of the attack, "Undivided and unlimited prosecution of that war must show that no one can safely attack the American people."[45]

Even in our new age of rapid and virtually insantaneous communications we find that many facts are hard to get straight. Many events still take hours or even days before the full story (or something reasonably approximating it) is finally available. In that era of much more limited rapid communication, suspicious minds would hesitate before committing themselves unduly in one direction or another upon first hearing such a seemingly outrageous report as that of the attack on Pearl Harbor. Hence one did not necessarily have to be locked strongly into either a pro- or anti-war policy to want to get more facts before committing oneself and the nation.

Democratic Sen. Edwin C. Johnson of Colorado hedged with such considerations in mind: "If the report is true, and there is no satisfactory explanation for this dastardly act, war is inevitable."[46] In a similarly cautious mood, Democratic Sen. Dennis Chavez of New Mexico noted that "if the facts are as announced, I would be in favor of a declaration of war against Japan."[47]

Only one other scenario besides atrocious misreporting of what had happened, offered a possible way out of war: if the Japanese military had acted independently and in defiance of its government. Even that would avert war only if that government vigorously repudiated the act and somehow decisively and quickly brought its military to heel—an utterly improbable development in light of earlier military actions in mainland China that the Japanese military launched without formal government approval.

Democratic Sen. Walter F. George of Georgia clearly preferred such an interpretation of unauthorized action, but his comments also indicate that he saw no credible way that could have been the case: "Assuming this attack is a deliberate attack by the Japanese government, and all of the evidence indicates that it is, then the United States must of course repel invasion of its territory, because Hawaii is an organized part of the United States.... This is the beginning of a long war, and no one can see when or where it will end."[48]

From the standpoint of military logistics George recognized that what was coming was going to be complicated due to the "vast distances in the Pacific." Hence one had to avoid over-optimism and recognize that "it may take two or three years to fight this war to the end."[49]

Some clearly hesitated out of a fear that later information would severely modify the tone, substance, and context of the initial reports about what had happened. Such reactions were certainly not a blind "see no evil" mentality: Previous aggressive "incidents" by German submarines against American war vessels in the Atlantic had later turned out to represent considerably less than the clear-cut aggression that the White House had initially claimed. If one had the least reason to be dubious about war, such precedents provided more than adequate justification to hesitate, at least temporarily, upon hearing word of Pearl Harbor.

Senator Robert R. Reynolds (Democrat, North Carolina) was head of the important Military Affairs Committee. He was one of those not immediately ready to accept what had apparently happened: "I am 100 percent against war. I want to know all about what has happened before I say anything about declaring war."[50] (Throughout the pre-war years anti-intervention sentiment had received only modest support in the South.)[51]

Reynolds was of the view that two different factors had led up to the current situation. First was the clear cut Japanese-German-alliance, making them obvious adversaries of the United States. Second was the yearning of the British to "get us to protect their $3,000,000,000 investments in China and to relieve forces that can be sent elsewhere to fight."[52] In other words, if the British could persuade the Americans to take up their Far East responsibilities, it would free troops to send to Europe, thereby strongly aiding the British even without overt American intervention in the European theater.

America First Accepts War—In the Pacific

When former General Robert Wood, head of the America First Committee, arrived in New York, he at first declined to comment on Pearl Harbor since he had not previously heard about the attack. An alert reporter handed him a newspaper—presumably one of the many extras printed that day throughout the nation. Having scanned through it he responded, "If Congress declares war I'll support the war." He believed that the entire committee would support war, and he intended to call its executive committee into session as quickly as possible to consider the matter.[53] Whether the committee would remain active, he left as an open question to be decided later.[54]

Some anti-war spokesmen suspected that Roosevelt had somehow accomplished indirectly what he had failed to do directly, setting the stage for what ultimately became a major post-war alternate interpretation of the events. Eleanor "Cissy" Patterson was the publisher of the *Washington Times Herald* and had locked her publication into editorial opposition to involvement in war. As the first of her reporters gathered in her office on December 7th to start to put together an extra edition, she rhetorically inquired of them, "Do you suppose he arranged this?"[55] Even most of those who impugned Roosevelt's motives in regard to European diplomacy and his wisdom in regard to Asian affairs were unwilling at the time to go beyond raising the matter as a rhetorical question, at least in public.

In private it was a different matter. Wood, of America First, was convinced that what had happened was simply an indirect way of getting the nation into the European War. When speaking on the phone with Charles A Lindbergh on the next day, his first words were, "Well, he got us in through the back door."[56]

Lindbergh had been the most prominent anti-war spokesman, and to those of the other side was the virtual embodiment of that viewpoint.[57] Indeed, he had been speaker at 15 major America First rallies.[58] Hence he was obviously on the short list of individuals whose comment would be sought. He had been residing on Martha's Vineyard since August in order to secure a privacy not available at his Long Island home.[59] Instead of comment, he initially opted for the approach of silence.[60] Indeed, he instructed the telegraph company to deliver no messages to him and the phone company not to put through any calls at all.[61]

On Monday the New York chapter of America First issued a statement lamenting that its previous anti-war advice had been ignored. On the other hand it was now irrelevant: there had been time for argument before war had erupted, but, once that happened, the moral obligation of the government was to vigorously wage that conflict and throw into it every available resource."[62]

Leaving New York for Chicago the same day, General Wood reminded a reporter that America First had opposed the war in good faith, but now that it had been started they would fully support it. "We were as patriotic as anyone else. No one but people here in New York thought otherwise."[63] (To back up his words, General Wood returned to active duty and served in Chicago with the Army Ordnance department.)[64]

A similar agreement came from Charles Lindbergh—now willing to speak for the public record—since further confirmation of the details of the attack had become available. Again, it was not a change in his own convictions that made the difference: whether the foreign policy of the Roosevelt administration was as wise or prudent as it could or should have been no longer mattered to him. Lindbergh believed that, faced by foreign attack, the U.S. had not option but ot vigorously repel, and overcome the enemy; this required American industry to provide the military with the best resources ingenuity and planning could produce."[65]

He viewed war as a practical necessity, given what Japan had done. In private, he was skeptical of the negotiations that had preceded it. "We have been prodding them [the Japanese] for weeks," he insisted.[66] On the other hand, as he noted in his private journal, if he had been a member of Congress there was no doubt that he "certainly would have voted for a declaration of war."[67] There was no alternative: Avoiding war was one thing; pretending it had not actually arrived something else entirely. (Lindbergh's offered to enter the armed services was rejected. He ultimately traveled as a civilian to the Pacific and tried out new aircraft under the rigors of actual usage in that combat region.)[68]

A few days later, on December 11th, the America First Committee held an executive meeting and decided that its existence no longer served any useful purpose. It announced that "The time for military action is here. Therefore the America First Committee has determined immediately to cease all functions and to dissolve as soon as that can be legally done."[69] Even while the closed meeting was being held, office personnel shared with reporters the fact that they were already beginning the procedures to close their national office.[70]

The decision represented a reversal of the sentiments that a majority of its leaders had held immediately after Pearl Harbor. Ultimately the feeling of a majority was that no matter what issues they addressed in the future, their record of opposing war in Europe would be used to divert attention from those concerns.[71] Furthermore, a number of the organization's units had already either closed down or suspended operations preparatory to taking that step, both types of action guaranteeing a significant reduction in the amount of support the organization could count on in the future.[72]

Thus, effectively, died the isolationist movement. As time went by many forgot just how strong it had been. The vote to remove the arms embargo went through the Senate by a two to one majority in 1939 (63 to 30) but passed the House by a narrow 243 to 172. In November 1941, key anti-intervention aspects of the Neutrality Act were repealed by a modest margin in the Senate (50 to 37) and a narrow one in the House (212 to 194). During the summer of that year, the draft was renewed by a mere one vote.[73]

Similarly, what the president said during this period was carefully hedged. He repeatedly stressed his opposition to war while engaging in actions that could provoke such as retaliation. He avoided asking for authority that he wanted, but that he suspected would never pass Congress. For example, he wanted authority to send draftees beyond American boundaries in spring, 1941, but did not overtly seek it. In the same period he wished that Congress would pass legislation approving of the U.S. convoying ships with war supplies for Britain. Again he decided not to push for a confrontation he could easily lose.[74]

With the advantage of hindsight, postwar opinion looked upon the isolationist movement as horrendously misguided; at the time a very large minority bordering sometimes on a majority thought far differently. In addition, most who subscribed to the movement were willing either passively or actively to support increases in national defense spending and preparedness—not because they intended to permit any involvement in Europe, but as elemental national preparedness for this hemisphere, and in case something happened that made a different course essential.[75]

To complicate the picture further, much of the anti-war sentiment of the '30s was produced by a backlash against the First World War—the huge Western casualty figures, the feeling that the British had "conned" the U.S. into the war, and resentment at the harsh peace treaty that set the stage for another war two decades later. In a similar manner, the bitter controversies over Vietnam affected all consideration of war for decades even in regard to countries and situations where the issues, environment, and dangers were dramatically different. In a psychological and political sense, in both cases the preceding war was refought by those who had lived through the first conflict and by the children who were brought up with the biases and preconceptions of their parents and educators.

Bombing Before Negotiations Had Stopped: Japan Gains the Stigma of Duplicity

Whether one was an isolationist or simply opposed to deepening Pacific commitments as an obstacle to the main danger coming from Europe, there was a common feeling after December 7th that America had been duped. One columnist interviewed a half dozen officials (bureaucratic and elected) who had felt dubious about the assertiveness of the Roosevelt administration in the Far East. He found their common sentiments summed up in the words of one unidentified aggressively pro-compromise advocate: "Clearly the Japanese war party never wanted peace and was awaiting the first opportunity to end discussion of it by a military attack when and where we didn't expect it. The envoys and diplomats are puppets, whether willing and aware of their reprehensible status, remains to be seen."[76] In other words, they were doing the dirty work of their superiors whether or not they were let in on what was about to happen.

The *Washington [D.C.] News* had pressed for a buildup of American power in the Pacific and pointed to the attack as vindicating its stand. Even so, it also sensed that the nation had been duped:

> They have played us for suckers. So we have seemed to them—for did we not supply them the steel, oil, and other war materials to fight us? Yes, we paid that price for peace. And we lost. But in the losing, we gained something which Japan lacks—something essential to give a peaceful and democratic people the will to fight and the will to win. That essential is clear proof to Americans that their Nation is not the aggressor but the defender.[77]

Nor was it the broad course of preceding events that angered Americans the most; it was the chronology of December 7th itself. What angered Americans as deeply—probably more deeply—than the attack itself was the fact that it occurred while normal diplomatic relations were still intact between the two nations. Nothing could have symbolized in a more infuriating way the insult and infamy of Pearl Harbor than the fact that the Japanese diplomats delivered their final message not only after the attack had begun, but even after word of it had been received in Washington.

In their original instructions, the Japanese diplomats were was supposed to delivered the message just before the attack. Due to difficulties in preparing the diplomatic note for delivery, it had been unexpectedly delayed. The time margin was so thin that even if the original plans had been carried out, the fury would have been little abated, especially when the note merely ended negotiations rather than declared war.

1. Congress, Bureaucrats, Press and Public Opinion

The diplomats themselves were unaware of what had happened, though the wording of the text have impressed them as to the dire state of the relationship of the two world powers. Indeed, they weren't even sure what their next steps would be diplomatically or in public relations. As the two Japanese diplomats left the State Department, reporters—equally unaware of what had just happened in Hawaii—plied them with questions. "Is this your last conference?" This brought a response of silence. Even, "Will the embassy issue a statement later?" could not produce a direct answer. Though it was an obvious public relations response, the query received a non-committal, "I don't know."[78]

They might not have known what to do next, but the political leadership of the U.S. knew full well what it thought. Senator Connally summarized the universal outrage inside the United States as he received from his clerk the text of America's declaration of war in 1917: he described Japan, claiming to desire peace and friendship with the United States, as a robed assassin hiding a dagger with which to assault her fellow negotiator, with whom she was in a legal state of peace. "We shall repay this dastardly treachery with multiplied bombs from the air and heaviest and accurate shells from the sea."[79]

Secretary of State Cordell Hull was more restrained but equally blunt when he released a statement to accompany the text of the November 26th diplomatic exchanges between the two countries: "Before the Japanese Ambassador delivered this final statement from his government, the treacherous attack upon the United States had taken place.... It is now apparent to the whole world that Japan in its recent professions of a desire for peace has been infamously false and fraudulent."[80] In private Hull was even more vehement: After the two Japanese diplomats left his office, his aides noted that the secretary erupted in "a towering rage" and denounced the Japanese representatives as "scoundrels and pissants."[81]

As already stressed, it must be remembered that the final note only broke off negotiations. In fact no declaration of war was delivered at all in Washington—even that kind of document the secretary of state would likely have received at least marginally better and more calmly as being direct and to the point.

Indeed, it was a member of the American ambassadorial staff in Tokyo who—several hours after receiving a copy of this same text as Hull—was visited by a Foreign Office representative at the American Embassy. "I am instructed to hand to you, as representing the Embassy, the following document which I shall first read to you." The document openly declared what even the Japanese representatives in Washington had not been told: "I have the honor to inform Your Excellency that there has arisen a state of war between Your Excellency's country and Japan beginning today. I avail myself of this opportunity to renew to Your Excellency the assurances of my highest consideration."[82]

Even in Japan, the American Embassy had first heard news of the attack from a Japanese news report rather than from the government.[83] This and a governmental oversight at least temporarily permitted the embassy to obtain some limited information on what was happening after the assault. A staff member later described the first effort to cut off their communication with the outside world:[84]

> In the courtyard of the Embassy, employees were busy burning our codes and important documents in metal barrels. I went to my office and was told to help burn papers. After a few hours, the police came. We thought they were after the codes, but to our surprise they never tried to stop the burning. They looked only for radios, which they suspected might be used to signal aircraft. They missed one radio, in a car, which we used, most unsuccessfully, to pick up English-language broadcasts while we were interned.
>
> In the excitement, the Japanese forgot to jam the radiotelephone across the Pacific. We were able to communicate with the Department of State at least twelve hours after Pearl Harbor and were thus able to get an inkling of the extent of the damage from the raid.

Like Hull, editorialists were appalled at the idea of war being launched without warning and while there was no official hint that anything else than peace existed. The *New York Herald Tribune* observed that Americans had received "a dismaying shock. Because Americans could not themselves take such action, it is difficult for them to conceive of the mind which instinctively acts without thought of law or honor."[85]

The *Baltimore Sun* noted that, "It was begun by Japan on the day after the United States Government, through President Roosevelt, made a friendly and respectful appeal to the Japanese Emperor for a peaceful settlement of the issues in dispute. News of it came at the very moment when Secretary Hull was receiving Japan's two envoys, pretending still that they were representing a friendly power."[86]

The Rationality of the Attack: The American Perplexity

If the ethics of the Japanese attack seemed reprehensible to the public and to opinion leaders of society, the sanity of the action was viewed as equally challengeable. After all, the fundamental fact was that the United States possessed massive, untapped resources to throw into the fray. Why provoke such a force? In line with these sentiments, the fiercely isolationist *Chicago Tribune* editorialized that the "war has been forced on America by an insane clique of Japanese militarists...."[87] On the West Coast, the *Los Angeles Times* spoke of how "it was the act of a mad dog, a gangster's parody of every principle of international honor."

The *Philadelphia Inquirer* wondered, "Do the war-mad officials of the Japanese Government honestly believe they can get away with a crime like this? Or are they intent upon committing national hara-kiri?"[88] The *Atlanta Constitution* did not even pose it as a question, but simply stressed that, regardless of what was consciously in the minds of the attackers, the assault constituted "the act of hara-kiri, national suicide."[89]

Members of Congress were also appalled at the lack of prudence that seemed to be manifested in the attack. Senator Elbert D. Thomas (Democrat, Utah) had the distinction of not only being regarded as one of the closest congressional students of the Asian Pacific nations; he also knew Japanese well enough to have published a work in that language. So far as he was concerned the attack was "an act of desperate men and will result, as such acts generally do, in their own destruction. The Japanese government has plainly gone mad."[90]

The Unifying Effect of the Attack

There was a widely recognized positive side to the attack: It secured a national unity that no amount of argument, propaganda, or agitation had made possible. Previously it had been a bitterly debated question of whether war was avoidable. That question had been answered in a way that both pro and anti-interventionists would never have imagined. The *San Francisco Chronicle* was but one of many referring to this fact: "If war had to come, it is perhaps well that it came this way, wanton, unwarned, in fraud and bad faith, virtually under a flag of truce."[91] Or as the *Chicago Daily News* put it, "Thanks now to Japan, the deep division of opinion that has rent and paralyzed our country will be swiftly healed."[92]

The *Richmond (Virginia) Times Dispatch* noted that "America has been shocked into unity in a single Sunday afternoon. The bombs which came hurtling down yesterday without warning from Japanese warplanes upon our Pacific bases have closed the debate over the country's course."[93] The other major paper in that city, the *Richmond News Leader*, spoke in even more vivid terms: "A miracle was required to unify America for the performance of her duty in a war to save four-fifths of mankind from slavery. Nothing less than a miracle quickly could unsnarl division and unify the nation. By one of those mysterious processes that baffle intelligence, Japan has become the agent for the performance of that miracle."[94]

The Pivotal Question of Germany's Role: Was Japan Germany's Puppet?

The national mood was one of unity for war with Japan. At first opinion was unclear as to how much further into the maelstrom of war the event was to force the nation. To assure that the war momentum moved the nation toward intervention in Europe as well became the immediate priority of those who had been promoting that course for the last several years.

The attempt by interventionists to blame Hitler for Pearl Harbor was both widespread and the natural step to ride the tide of volatile American opinion. Its propaganda value represented not only guilt by association (since Japan and Germany were allies) but reasonable guilt by association: Both had manifested similar international aggressiveness and both claimed to be bringing a new world order into existence, to the harm if not destruction of the Western powers. Since Americans prevalently underappreciated the fighting power and intelligence of the Japanese, it fitted this image to see Hitler as pulling the strings for what Japan had done.

In this light the Fight for Freedom group had an ad in the *New York Times* insisting that "Japan's war on the United States is a last desperate effort of Hitler to turn American attention from the center of war against our world. That center is Berlin.... This treachery was masterminded by the thugs and gangsters of Berlin."[95] This and similar ads were placed at the direct request of Bob Sherwood, acting on behalf of the president: The president was concerned, he told the leaders of the group, that Americans would be so shocked by the Pearl Harbor attack that they would lose sight of the greater danger.[96]

Another major pro-involvement group was the Committee to Defend America. Either it did not have the finances available for a major ad campaign or it failed to grasp how what had happened could be most effectively exploited by such an approach. It simply issued a formal statement through its national chairman, Clark M. Eichelberger, making the same kind of tie-in between the Axis powers: "Obviously Hitler's grand strategy was back of the Japanese move.... We are engaged in total war against an Axis combination and we should wage total war in full cooperation with our Allies. Therefore, it seems to us that we have no choice but to recognize a state of war immediately with Italy and Germany."[97]

The motive was sometimes different, but the analysis the same even when it came from sources far less concerned with the politics of the situation. "The scope and planning of Tokyo's widespread offensive" caused unidentified "U.S. military experts" to see "clearly the expert hand of the German General Staff," reported *Newsweek* magazine. The presence of German military advisers in Japan was also pointed to as evidence consistent with that deduction.[98]

The *Louisville (Kentucky) Courier Journal* pictured the problem as a shared worldview that ultimately had to be eliminated if the United States was to survive: "Japan's attack on the U.S. is part of the world treachery, the world revolution which the Nazis have created. Japan's attack on the U.S. is the final effort of Berlin to distract us from the meaning of modern history, from the simple fact that men who honor no promises are tearing to bits the civilization of our twentieth century." Japan's destruction had to be followed by that of the German regime to eliminate the danger to civilization.[99]

The *Chicago Sun* viewed the Japanese-German alliance as creating a kind of united political animal and believed, therefore, that war with one part of that animal required war with the entire monster.

> It is war, now, grim and to the death. War to the death of Japanese and German militarism, or to the death of the United States of America.... Let no American think this is a one-ocean war, a one-handed war, or a war with one nation only. We have been struck by the Weltschlange—the world serpent—its head in Germany and its tail in Japan. Japan has plunged us into war to the hilt, not only with herself, but with Germany.[100]

The *New York Times* editorially viewed as irrelevant Germany's direct influence upon the initiation of the war. It was inclined to believe that it would have been counter-productive for Hitler to intentionally drag the U.S. into a war that inevitably would involve him as well. Whether, the Japanese military adventurers had invented the ultimately self-destructive policy on their own or whether they had fulfilled his wish for Japanese intervention (expressed through a prolonged campaign encouraging them to attack) would be unknown to Americans until later, indicated the report; the only important fact was that a massive attack had been launched upon the United States and it needed to be forcibly and decisively dealt with.[101]

There was also another method of linking pro-interventionism in Europe and the Pacific War—utilizing Pearl Harbor as evidence that the conceptual foundation of those opposed to involvement in the European conflict was thoroughly misguided. The *Cleveland Plain Dealer* took this tack:

> The tragic events which have drawn this nation into war are a terrible lesson to two kinds of people—the isolationists and the appeasers. The point should not be missed by those who still claim that the oceans are a barrier, that in order to attack Pearl Harbor the Japanese sent their ships and planes across an expanse of water that is several hundred miles wider than the Atlantic is at the broadest. What the Japanese have done to Pearl Harbor on a small scale the Germans could and would do to

Boston, New York, Philadelphia and Cleveland on a large scale should they once become masters of Europe and the British Isles.[102]

Arrest of Japanese and Other Axis Citizens

Early on December 8th, Attorney General Francis Biddle informed the press that a limited number of resident Japanese "are being rounded up in view of the situation."[103] This was done on the basis of a newly issued executive order by President Roosevelt.[104] A month previously Biddle had announced that mass arrests had been ruled out in case war erupted, as it now had.[105] This moderate position had been reaffirmed just the previous week by Eleanor Roosevelt, who stated that her remarks had been approved by the Justice Department.[106]

Stateside, the numbers would be limited, Biddle stressed. In contrast, in both Hawaii and the Panama Canal Zone a significantly different policy was likely: "temporary mass arrests were likely there."[107]

In continental America safeguards were promised to protect against accidental abuses. "Procedures," a Justice Department statement stressed, "are being established to provide a fair hearing for all persons apprehended. It is estimated that less than 1,000 Japanese nationals will be affected."[108] Later in the day, Biddle told the press that on the day of the attack 391 Japanese nationals had been arrested in Hawaii and another 345 in the continental United States.[109] Assuming that the estimate of a thousand detentions held good,[110] this implied that the bulk of anticipated arrests had already been made.

To set these numbers in context, the estimated combined number of ethnic Japanese (nationals plus naturalized citizens) was estimated to be about 150,000.[111] About 75,000 lived in Los Angeles (100,000 in California as a whole) and approximately 2–3,000 in New York City.[112] More than a third of the Japanese in America (over 60,000) were subject to potential arrest because they had not registered under existing obligatory alien registration measures.[113] That registration had involved providing both personal information as well as being fingerprinted.[114] Hence how many would be arrested and detained and for how long was a matter over which the federal government had maximum leeway, since so many had committed technical violations of American law on the subject.

In regard to the more limited category of Japanese citizens resident in the United States, their number was actually far below that of the other major Axis powers: Italy led the list with 694,971 unnaturalized individuals, Germany came in second with 315,004, and Japan third with 90,853, of whom about 40,000 number lived in Hawaii. Pro-Axis Austria and Hungary (for some reason combined, perhaps as a legacy of their

World War One era status as one nation) had 402,827 citizens residing in the United States.[115]

The danger of excess zeal on the part of state or local officials had the federal authorities extremely concerned. The assistant attorney general, Wendell Berge, sent a telegram to federal attorneys throughout the country telling them to stress to the local authorities that only the F.B.I. had jurisdiction in these matters. The government had "deep concern," Berge said, over published and broadcast reports indicating "State and local authorities in many parts of the country have apprehended Japanese aliens last night and this morning" solely on their own authority and without consultation with the F.B.I. This abuse had to be immediately stopped. "If necessary to secure compliance with this procedure [of federal action alone], you are authorized to appeal to the Governor of your State for his cooperation."[116]

To counteract the danger of wartime paranoia getting the best of common sense and fairness, the attorney general went on the public record stressing that "There are in the United States many persons of Japanese extraction whose loyalty to this country, even in the present emergency is unquestioned. It would therefore be a serious mistake to take any action against these people."[117] He re-emphasized this the following day: "We have good reason to believe that most aliens in our country are peaceful and law-abiding. We will apprehend the alien trouble-makers, but we will protect the others against prosecution and discrimination."[118] In other words: people should not take the law into their own hands on a local basis, and be liable to commit an injustice. Leave it to those who know what they are doing.

The legal basis of the various federal arrests varied from case to case and day to day: The earliest were taken on the basis of perceived immediate or potential threat with the exact legal niceties to be worried about later. These apprehensions fell into three broad categories: those the government felt convinced were definitely dangerous, those concerning people about whom they had doubt, and those who needed to be interviewed to determine their status.[119]

On the 9th the president issued a proclamation interpreting all resident non-citizen Germans and Italians and Japanese as de facto enemy aliens and subject to severe restrictions and, when deemed prudent, outright arrest.[120] The inclusion of the Japanese owed to the assault at Pearl Harbor, of course. The rationales for the inclusion of the other two nationalities seem difficult to take seriously except as hypothetical (rather than realistic) possibilities: "An invasion or predatory incursion is threatened upon the territory of the United States by Germany" and "[a]n invasion or predatory incursion is threatened upon the territory of the United States by Italy."[121] If one seeks a grain of humor in this, note that immediately below the *New York Herald Tribune* article reporting the presidential proclamation authorizing such arrests, the following article was headlined, "Monday to Be Observed as Bill of Rights Day."[122]

In both San Francisco[123] and Connecticut[124] the arrest of German and Italian nationals began the day after the attack. In Connecticut alone some 50 individuals were detained for questioning on that day alone.[125] Alien arrests involved not just major cities such as New York and Los Angeles; in New York State, a number of individuals living in Buffalo, Rochester, and Niagara Falls were apprehended.[126] Arrests also occurred in such diverse cities as Boston, Chicago, and Miami as well.[127]

By Tuesday night of the 9th, 2,303 foreign nationals had been arrested by U.S. officials.[128] By Thursday night, December 12th, this figure had risen to 2,541 foreign nationals. Of this number 169 were Italians, 1,002 were Germans, and 1,370 were Japanese.[129] Attorney General Francis Biddle issued a statement at the Justice Department that "Arrests were limited to persons whose activities have been under investigation by the FBI for some time."[130] The detentions were expected to be temporary except for those cases where there was "strong reason to fear for the internal security of the United States."[131]

(The numbers reported in this section are the contemporary ones. Erroneous estimates were inevitable in the tensions of the time. In addition, the temporary detention of some individuals by local authorities acting on their own initiative would produce a further discrepancy in the numbers. At the least, however, these figures provide a crude indication of what Americans thought was going on, which, in turn, shaped their perception of the events.)

Easily overlooked is the fact that a significant number of European Axis state nationals (as distinct from American citizens) had already been culled from the general population even before the December 7th attack in Hawaii. The *New York Herald Tribune* reported on December 8th: "Already in camps in this country are about 1,000 Germans and Italians. The Italians are being kept at Fort Missoula, Montana, and the Germans at Fort Lincoln, North Dakota, although for a time some additional Germans, mostly the crew of the scuttled German liner *Columbus*, also were detained at Fort Stanton, New Mexico."[132] The primary justification for the internment of these various individuals had been their refusal to register with the U.S. government, indicating their foreign nationality status.[133]

Even less publicized at this stage than the arrests of foreign nationals who were visiting or resident in the U.S. were the arrests of individuals who possessed American citizenship. On the 12th, the attorney general announced that 43 such arrests had occurred in Hawaii: Two involved those of Italian ancestry, 19 of German, and 22 of Japanese.

The Justice Department stressed that all had "been engaged in pro–Japanese activities in the islands."[134]

Conditions at the Japanese Embassy and Consulates in America

Japanese staff members were instructed to move into their embassy rather than remain in their normal homes and apartments. This sent the residents from approximately a dozen to three times that figure. Food began to run out on the 8th and a request was placed with a local market for a large food delivery of $200 worth of goods. When the grocer's delivery man reached the embassy he was offered a check and demanded cash instead. "Your funds have been impounded and your check's no good," he reminded them. After leaving and sharing the story of their discomfort with others, he chuckled, "Serves the little yellow bastards right."[135] This was grim humor on a grim day. If Americans were feeling miserable, most would not go out of their way to make things comfortable for the representatives of those who had caused their misery. (Today the delivery man probably would have left the racial part out—but at a time when war is only a day old extraneous insults are hardly unknown even in our presumably enlightened age.)

Faced with such intransigence, the embassy staff was able to scrape together $16, which enabled them to lay in a modest supply "of lamb, a crate of eggs, forty loaves of bread and 500 pounds of rice."[136] A similar cash-upon-receipt was required of all the varied stores the Japanese Embassy contacted to obtain food, beverage, and medication.[137]

This was on Monday, the day after the attack. By Wednesday the U.S. government had recognized that freezing all Japanese funds had made it impossible for the diplomats to obtain the necessities of life. Hence it decided that "on a strictly reciprocal basis" the Japanese Embassy would be permitted necessary access to its funds so long as the American diplomats in Japan were treated similarly.[138]

During the 7th, a crowd up to three hundred strong gathered outside the embassy. Generally young—mainly of school age—and perturbed, they both understood but were simultaneously annoyed by the strong police presence designed to avoid any damage being done to the embassy or its residents. A typical cynical remark was, "That's democracy for you! They kill us and we protect them."[139] The crowds virtually disappeared at night, though one of the infrequent passersby could be heard to make a similar remark as the large size of the American casualty count became better known.[140]

Recognizing that they were hardly likely to have friendly visitors, the embassy staff stopped answering the front door. Anyone who wanted admission had to go down the alley and use the entrance that fronted on it. After a police official and several others had to discover this procedure on their own, at least token information was provided by a diplomat who attached a penciled note to the front entrance: "If you have business here, please use the side entrance."[141] Of course the fact that it was in Japanese did not help those who could not read that language. On the other hand, desired or authorized visitors were rarely likely to be Americans or need an English language version.[142] If they did, they could always consult the police who were on constant guard.

At both the Washington embassy and various Japanese consulates, efforts were made to burn the remaining diplomatic materials—until the police intervened.[143] In San Francisco, the consulate avoided a public burning (tempting police intervention) by attempting to dispose of its papers in a fireplace. Forcing so many documents into it at one time, however, resulted in the creation of such intense heat that the wall caught fire and the police department had to send a unit to keep the building from going up in flames.[144]

In Chicago, the consulate began burning its papers on the basis of press reports it had received that war had erupted, rather than await formal instructions to do so. Kiagachiro Ohmori, acting consul, explained to an enquiring reporter that the burning of documents was a traditional action in such an uncertain situation. "That is customary even when there is only one chance in a hundred or a thousand that it is necessary [because war may have broken out]."[145]

Limitations on Japanese and Other Axis Correspondents

Japanese newsmen were an immediate target of limitations. The Osaka *Ashai* and the Tokyo publication of the same name both had offices in the *New York Times* building. Acting at the request of the U.S. government, the *Times'* manager issued a letter to the papers noting that "your use of any New York *Times* material or transmission facilities" was cancelled effectively immediately.[146]

German correspondents were sucked into the maelstrom on a more gradual basis. The night of the seventh Japanese newspapermen had their press credentials cancelled.[147] Hearing of this, Kurt G. Sell, representative of the D.N.B. German news service (who had been covering the United States for 15 years),[148] called the Secret Service on Monday

1. Congress, Bureaucrats, Press and Public Opinion

and enquired, "I understand you have taken up the press cards of the Japanese. Do you want mine?"[149] The Service responded in the affirmative and sent one of their men to pick up the documentation. At this point the removal simply cancelled Sell's privilege of attending government press conferences; otherwise he retained the right to report on what was happening (subject to censorship on all outgoing dispatches).[150]

Such was the perception of the German press men who thought the temporary prohibition of all outbound dispatches for D.N.B. on the 7th was merely a temporary inconvenience, until formal censorship procedures were in place.[151] This was not an illogical conclusion, since Germany had neither declared war nor been directly involved in the attack. (Though the American rumor mill soon got it in its head that a substantial number of German pilots had been serving with the attacking Japanese aviators—a tale that roared around Capitol Hill the following day.)[152] For comparison's sake, though American reports from Japan had already been terminated, regular stories were continuing to flow in from both Germany and Italy from American correspondents assigned to those countries.[153]

On the 8th, Radio Corporation of America, which handled most European-bound communications, announced that it had received orders not to permit the transmission of any reports to Germany, Italy, or Finland, even if a report had passed censors' approval.[154] At least for the time being Germany continued its non-censorship policy of foreign dispatches going to the U.S.[155] Although censorship was perceived (and often was) a heavy burden, since reporters' work was subject to the caprice of individual and inconsistent editing, at least what was sent had the more-or-less official endorsement as noninjurious to the nation that was permitting the dispatch. In the no censorship situation of Germany, however, reporters who sent the wrong or allegedly misleading information were subject to whatever restrictions and retaliations (including expulsion) that the government desired. Hence both official and self-imposed censorship created problems for the reporter seeking to cover the story in an enemy land.

The remaining freedom of movement for the German press soon ended when all such correspondents were detained "for investigation," in the words of the U.S. State Department. Some were placed under house arrest and others were housed in various hotels. At least one of the detained was permitted a visit by a German Embassy staff member.[156] The detention of some was announced by the New York Police Department; that of others by the German Embassy in Washington.[157] Representatives of the Italian press were similarly reined in.[158]

Paul Schmidt, the press spokesman for the German Foreign Office, dealt with the matter in his next daily noon meeting with foreign correspondents: "According to an official communication just received, seventeen German newspaper correspondents in the United States have been arrested. This, according to our information, was done without notice or statement of motive. To the American Government, therefore goes the responsibility of breaking with all recognized international customs."[159]

When the State Department heard protests from Berlin of these "arrests," its representatives unofficially emphasized that this was not that extreme an action—so far none of the detentions had risen to the level of a formal arrest.[160] This was a legally correct distinction, but one of little use to individuals whose freedom of movement had been effectively terminated.

In retaliation for the detentions, 15 American correspondents in Germany (one for radio and the remainder newspaper reporters) were told that their press credentials had been revoked and were ordered to remain in their places of residence.[161] Retaliatory arrests for what the Americans had done soon began.[162] not merely in Berlin but in German occupied Paris as well.[163]

The Italian government quickly followed the German lead and revoked the credentials of the 10 American correspondents residing in their country.[164] The Italians were slower, however, to detain formally the correspondents than their German compatriots.[165] It was generally assumed in the press that when the Axis and the Americans exchanged diplomats, their respective reporters would be returning home with them.[166]

Japanese, German, and Italian Efforts to Defuse Hostility

Japanese Americans attempted to defend themselves against the backlash caused by anger at their ancestral homeland—and the violence that could easily erupt at the hands of misguided zealots—by an ad hoc two-pronged strategy. The first was to stress their Americanness. Katsuma Mukaeda, of the Los Angeles Japanese Cultural Society conceded that "This is an unprecedented crisis for us, but we shall acquit ourselves proudly. America is our home, our permanent residence."[167]

The second prong of their approach was to vehemently denounce what had happened. They shared in the abhorrence of other Americans at the attack and were equally outraged at the government that controlled the land of their ancestors. The Japanese American Citizens' League consisted of 25,000 members scattered in 55 organizations over 11 states. Based in Los Angeles, the night of the attack it issued a formal statement condemning the assault and emphasized the full determination of its membership to be strictly loyal to the United States.[168]

Togo Tanaka was editor of the Los Angeles Japanese language newspaper *Rafu Shimpo* and stressed that the people of his community had been closely cooperating for a number of years with the F.B.I. and other agencies in regard to possible spying and other dangers.[169] Tanuka said of the attack itself, "We think the Japanese Government is stupid and has embarked on a campaign it has absolutely no chance of winning.... This may well be the end of Japan as a power."[170]

Those of German ancestry also attempted to defuse a potential domestic reaction against them in the following days, especially after Germany formally entered the war. As with the Japanese-Americans, they stressed their patriotism either by implication or by direct statement. Bernard Hofmann, president of the Wisconsin Federation of German-American Societies, for example, emphasized that "We will do everything in our power to help our government and sacrifice to the utmost to win this war for the United States, our country."[171] The New York German language *Staats Zeitung und Herald* ran a front page editorial stressing that "we will fight until this danger to our way of life is eliminated."[172]

Similar embrace of the war came from the Italian-American community as well.[173] Perhaps one of the most effective statements came from the lieutenant governor of New York, Charles Poletti, who was himself of that heritage. He stressed that his community had proved its loyalty not just by word but by volunteering by the "thousands and thousands" to serve in the American military. By doing so, "They stand ready to die for victory of the democratic way of life as against the ruthless methods of the dictators."[174]

It was not very convincing, however, when the pro–Nazi German-American Bund's newspaper editorially embraced the war. The accompanying headline, consciously or not, hedged that support: "Our country, right or wrong, *when invaded*" (emphasis added).[175]

Japanese and German Arrests of American Citizens

In Japan, the arrest of foreign nationals began the day of the attack. Although the exact number of Americans remaining in the country was unknown, most had left the country earlier as tensions had heightened during the preceding months.[176] The largest identifiable group consisted of the 45 individuals attached to the U.S. Embassy.[177]

A Japanese broadcast reported that some hundred foreigners had been arrested the first day, although it did not provide a breakdown of the nationalities.[178] As of December 12th (the 11th in the U.S.), the number of British and U.S. citizens arrested "as a precaution and for their protection and well-being" had risen to 120.[179] This group included a few unidentified Western reporters.[180] An earlier Japanese broadcast, however, had set the total number of detainees as 1,270—a figure which included Americans, Australians, British, and Canadians.[181]

Tomokazu Hori, a spokesman for the Japanese Cabinet, asserted that specific decisions on internment would vary according to the occupation, age, and sex of the individual.[182] They would be affected by how citizens of their own country were treated abroad. On the other hand he stressed that this was a war between nations and not individual citizens, so government felt obligated to secure the welfare of every American and British national living in their country.[183]

The actual policy gave every indication of being far more strict and quickly implemented than any official pronouncement was likely to lead one to believe. As a staff member of the American embassy in Tokyo later recalled, "I was also assigned the job of checking the status of American businessmen and others in Tokyo. I could not leave the compound and therefore had to rely on the telephone. *Most of the calls went unanswered.* As we later learned from the Swiss, many American businessmen, correspondents, and tourists had been imprisoned by the Japanese."[184]

In Washington the Japanese diplomatic community had been ordered to move into their embassy. In Tokyo, the Americans undertook a similar move voluntarily.[185] All shortwave radios were confiscated and contact with those outside the grounds cut off—though for at least the first day some other diplomats found ways around the restriction to come, visit, and give their best wishes for the future.[186]

When Germany entered the war she also began a series of arrests of American nationals. The initial public formulation of the policy was pure tit-for-tat: For every German arrested, one American would be detained.[187]

2

The Presidential Address and Senatorial Action: Declaring War on Japan

The Psychological Atmosphere: A Nation Still in Shock

In that pre-television era, radio provided rapid mass communication. On December 7th, millions listened to the limited data being revealed about the attack and the responses of prominent Americans. On the morning of the 8th, the nation's newspapers had benefited from at least a few hours to digest the details and share them with their readers. Rather than lessen the alarm, those details, if anything, increased it and further inflamed the nation's collective and political anger.

F. R. Kent, Jr., was likely the only correspondent in attendance at Congress that day who had also been present in the House of Commons when it had declared war two years earlier. In a personal commentary on the two events, he wrote that the Commons was dominated by a sense of quiet confidence. It was a distinctive upbeat mood because the uncertainties of the past had now been definitively removed.[1]

Not so in the American Congress:

> Today in the House of Representatives the atmosphere was not that of relief from tension. Rather it was a heightening. The entire body was aroused and angry. More than that, it wanted action, not high-flown verbiage.

Republicans and Democrats alike were imbued with the desire to do something—do it quickly and effectively and with unity of purpose. For the first time in many months, Congressmen neither wanted to talk nor to hear their colleagues talk.[2]

What they could do was precious little in the short term. They could speak briefly and vent their rage at the enemy. They could promptly pass the declaration of war and express their anger at any who tried to stay its passage. But beyond that the decisions of policy and action had to be made on the presidential and military level, and could take days, weeks, or even months to emerge fully. Yet even knowing that so much lay beyond their reach, what they *could* accomplish they were determined to complete quickly and promptly.

The President's Speech

Since the Senate proceedings were far shorter than those of the House, we will examine those first and, in that context, the president's speech urging a declaration of war.

By House Resolution 61, adopted by the Senate in an abbreviated morning session, the two branches of Congress agreed to meet in the House chamber at 12:30 P.M. to hear the chief executive. Twenty minutes before the agreed upon time, the Senate was led en masse by the vice president and president pro tempore to the House side of the Capitol building.[3]

Before 11 A.M. Marines (complete with bayonets) guarded both the White House perimeter and Capitol Hill.[4] The streets between the two were sealed off from traffic to maximize the president's safety.[5] At the Capitol, new barricades had been installed at the entrances and everyone was being required to show his pass.[6] Indeed, the passes had to be checked three times before a person was permitted to enter the chamber where the speech was to be made.[7]

Security was so tight that even traditional ambassadorial courtesies were sometimes ignored. Dr. Hu Shih, ambassador from China, for example, was prevented from entering. Only the intervention of Senator Thomas D. Connally (Democrat, Texas), finally got him through the checkpoints and into the diplomats' gallery.[8] Also taking a seat there was the British Ambassador, Lord Halifax, whose government had an obvious and intense interest in the decisions to be made that day.[9]

With perhaps greater self-assurance under the circumstances than wisdom, Representative Clare E. Hoffman (Republican, Michigan) calmly insisted to the policeman at the initial checkpoint that he had no identification card because he was a member of Congress. Furthermore,

2. The Presidential Address and Senatorial Action 37

"I don't need any," he insisted, and pushed through the doors. One of the guards rushed in pursuit and grabbed him around the arm.[10] Several other guards quickly converged but were able to confirm Hoffman's identify for him.[11] The unharmed but quite angry congressman stomped off to hear the speech.[12]

When it came time for the president to make the trip to the Hill, two carloads of Secret Service men were the escort. Each vehicle had riot guns attached to the sides.[13] The presidential cavalcade itself consisted of six limousines, and Roosevelt was escorted by his wife Eleanor, son (Captain James Roosevelt, U.S. Marine Corps), and key advisers and staff members.[14] The predominantly female crowds[15] who watched the unusually well-guarded president cheered as he made his way through the streets.[16] When he returned, they stood quietly as he drove by,[17] the immediate outbursts of support having perhaps yielded to the solemnity of entering into a massive new war. However fervent the cheers, reporters noted the underlying sense of seriousness that gripped both politicians and city residents in general.[18]

After arriving at Capitol Hill, the President was escorted through one of the less used entrances to the House Speaker's office, where he remained for the short time until the speech.[19]

The Speaker of the House, seeing that the time had come for the presidential address, appointed three senators and three congressmen to formally escort the chief executive into the joint session.[20] When the president entered the chamber, he was holding onto the arm of his son James for support,[21] an action only those aware of the president's serious physical disability would have fully understood. There was momentary silence and then the loudest ovation of applause that reporters could remember Roosevelt ever having received as president.[22]

The president's wife and the wife of his son James had already joined the watchers in the galleries.[23] The balconies were full of well-placed individuals of socio-political importance and anyone else who was of that limited number who could wrangle an admission ticket for what all recognized as an event that would go down in history. There were influential women of the current administration present: the wife of the Vice President and the wife of the Secretary of State, in particular.[24] Symbolically important, Mrs. Woodrow Wilson was attending,[25] inevitably forcing memories back to the earlier world war. In addition the President's adviser Harry Hopkins was there along with Robert Sherwood, the prominent author.[26]

The youthful daughter of a future president later wrote of how she managed to attend in spite of ill-health and limited seating:

> I soon followed [my father to the Capitol] thanks to a neat trick I pulled on my mother. I was still running a fever, but I fooled Mother into think-

ing it was gone by holding my mouth open after she inserted the thermometer. I was not going to let a cold keep me away from seeing history made. Mother gave me her entrance ticket and I zoomed to the special session of Congress.

By the time I got there the only seat left was in the photographers' gallery. This gave me the same view that the rest of the nation later saw in the movie theaters, as President Roosevelt announced the day of infamy and called for war. I then followed the senators back to the Senate, where I heard my father vote for a declaration of war.[27]

To the president's left were the judicially robed members of the Supreme Court. To his right, in front, were members of the Cabinet. Behind them were the members of Congress.[28] Also on the floor were the heads of the three branches of the American military: Army General George C. Marshall, Navy Admiral Harold R. Stark, and Marines Major General Thomas Holcomb.[29]

On the House floor were also a number of thoroughly unauthorized children—unauthorized by age and because they were not members of the legislature or otherwise officially approved to be present. Noticed by the Speaker of the House, all such unofficial visitors were ordered out and several went. A reporter noted that the congressional fathers of five of the children then sat them on their laps, thereby allowing them technically to occupy the seat of someone who was supposed to be present. No one took time to challenge this behavior further.[30]

Five retired senators invoked their traditional privilege of attending sessions after their retirement. One of these was former Republican senator from Iowa Smith W. Brookhart. As he explained to reporters, he had a deep personal interest in what was happening: One of his sons was currently in the (locked) American consulate in Shanghai while another was serving in the Army Air Corps and faced potential duty in the Far East.[31]

The speech was covered by all three major U.S. radio networks—Columbia, Mutual, and the National Broadcasting Systems.[32] Estimates ranged from 75 to 100 million listeners to the speech.[33] Courts adjourned so that they and their workers could hear it. Some judges played the speech on radios in their courts. At Times Square in New York City, it was broadcast live over loudspeakers, where even the police present for crowd control seemed more interested in hearing the message than in their current assignment. At some companies, the workers took time off to hear the address.[34] At National Airport in New York City, Mayor Fiorello H. LaGuardia stood in the crowd waiting for their flights—thoroughly unnoticed and unrecognized—as they all listened to the president's speech.[35]

It was one of those unique addresses that were of obvious personal importance to every citizen, one of those rare occasions when one had

2. The Presidential Address and Senatorial Action

to be totally oblivious to world events to avoid feeling that one was standing at, for better or worse, a pivotal turning point in the life of the nation.

The president began by stressing that the United States had been attacked in such a manner that there could be no doubt that it was both intentional and long in preparation:

> Yesterday, December 7, 1941—a date which will live in infamy—the United States of America was suddenly and deliberately attacked by naval and air forces of the Empire of Japan.
> The United States was at peace with that nation and, at the solicitation of Japan, was still in conversation with its Government and its Emperor looking toward the maintenance of peace in the Pacific. Indeed, one hour after Japanese air squadrons had commenced bombing in Oahu, the Japanese Ambassador to the United States and his colleague delivered to the Secretary of State a formal reply to a recent American message. While this reply stated that it seemed useless to continue the existing diplomatic negotiations, it contained no threat or hint of war or armed attack.
> It will be recorded that the distance of Hawaii from Japan makes it obvious that the attack was deliberately planned many days or even weeks ago. During the intervening time the Japanese Government has deliberately sought to deceive the Untied States by false statements and expressions of hope for continued peace.[36]

The chief executive minced no words that the casualties had been large but gave no estimate of their number: "The attack yesterday on the Hawaiian Islands has caused severe damage to American naval and military forces. Very many American lives have been lost. In addition American ships have been reported torpedoed on the high seas between San Francisco and Honolulu."

Certainly this could not be dismissed as an isolated incident. In a steady drumbeat of short but pungent sentences, Roosevelt pictured the emerging portrait of a fast moving enemy striking out in many directions simultaneously,

> Yesterday the Japanese Government also launched an attack against Malaya.
> Last night Japanese forces attacked Hong Kong.
> Last night Japanese forces attacked Guam.
> Last night Japanese forces attacked the Philippine Islands.
> Last night the Japanese attacked Wake Island.
> This morning the Japanese attacked Midway Island.[37]

(The references to Hong, King, Wake Island, and Midway Island had been added in longhand to the final draft, as additional data came in preceding the speech.)

This widespread intervention put its interpretation beyond doubt and it did not require the president to explain its significance: "Japan has therefore undertaken a surprise offensive extending throughout the Pacific area. The facts of yesterday speak for themselves. The people of the United States have already formed their opinions and well understand the implications to the very life and safety of our Nation."

The president himself had already taken the first steps that his position required. It was now time for the people to brace themselves for a long and bloody war—one that must be fought, regardless of its cost, to the utter defeat of the attacking nation

> As Commander in Chief of the Army and Navy I have directed that all measures be taken for our defense.
>
> Always will we remember the character of the onslaught against us.
>
> No matter how long it may take us to overcome this premeditated invasion, the American people in their righteous might will win through to absolute victory.
>
> I believe I interpret the will of the Congress and of the people when I assert that we will not only defend ourselves to the uttermost but will make very certain that this form of treachery shall never endanger us again.
>
> Hostilities exist. There is no blinking at the fact that our people, our territory, and our interests are in grave danger.
>
> With confidence in our armed forces—with the unbounded determination of our people—we will gain the inevitable triumph, so help us God.
>
> I ask that the Congress declare that, since the unprovoked and dastardly attack by Japan on Sunday, December 7, a state of war has existed between the Untied States and the Japanese Empire.

Never again in the twentieth century would an American president stand before Congress and ask for a declaration of war. Not in Korea. Not in Vietnam. Not in the varied short term military actions that were wars in everything but law.

Roosevelt made no plea for understanding the foe. No time for what some in a later generation would call conflict resolution. The time for understanding and reconciliation had passed. With an open assault on an American territory in general (i.e., Hawaii) and its military bases in particular, those noble options now had to be replaced by the drawn sword, one Roosevelt fully intended to see it capably used. A self-centered and usually peaceful sleeping America had been roused from its slumber. Although bloodied and bleeding, the nation would soon be a pursuing attacker.

The speech was tumultuously received. The British Ambassador, Lord Halifax, was among those important and fortunate enough to be able to obtain a seat to hear the speech. He telegraphed home about the impact of the president's words: "He was received with prolonged applause on entry, spoke with quiet force and so far as could be seen there was com-

2. The Presidential Address and Senatorial Action   41

plete unanimity among crowded House and galleries. Particularly significant demonstration was when all present rose and applauded his statement that however long it might take [the] United States would ensure that this kind of treachery should not be possible again."[38]

Proposed Modifications for Roosevelt's Speech

The speech that Roosevelt gave was far different from that which advisers had recommended. Secretary of State Hull had wanted a detailed summary of the diplomatic activities prior to the conflict.[39] He wanted a lengthy 20 to 30 page summary of that context.[40] Sumner Welles wrote this summary; Hull argued for it with the president on Sunday and got absolutely nowhere.[41]

Lowell Mellet also wanted a major change: He urged an itemization of the nation's goals so that a postwar Senate could not do to Roosevelt what had been done to Wilson (i.e., the scrapping of the League of Nations proposal). Such approaches Roosevelt rejected and opted for a simple, direct, and short speech.[42]

He was amenable only to Harry Hopkins's addition of the penultimate sentence, "With confidence in our armed forces—with the unbounded determination of our people—we will gain the inevitable triumph, so help us God."[43] This rhetoric with its overtones of both prayer and a judicial oath appealed to the president as appropriate to the seriousness and grimness of the occasion.

The Silence About Casualties and Losses

In the context of the moment, perhaps the most fascinating aspect of the speech (and perhaps what gave it much of its power) was Roosevelt's careful avoidance of any hint of criticism of those who had stood against military intervention in Europe. Though it would have been a politically advantageous moment to rub salt in their wounds, the president stuck strictly to what had happened rather than attempt to take political advantage of the occasion.[44]

Just behind this omission in terms of interest is Roosevelt's avoidance of giving any details about the attack. It had happened. It was American territory. That was sufficient.

This brevity may have been partly tactical. Giving the enemy confirmation of the ship toll would only encourage further hostile attacks at Hawaii or at other places that it conceivably might hesitate to move against if the data were kept obscure.

It was also a simple reality that anything approaching a definitive estimate of casualties was simply not available. More importantly, the attack was too close, immediate, and mind-numbing; even to the minds of professional military men those details that were known were unnerving in their grim picture. This was a time for rallying the forces of indignation produced by the attack and not casting the nation even further into depression at what had happened.

Yet it did not take a vivid imagination to suspect the worst. After all, the waters around Hawaii were recognized as part of an America sea. The military complexes located there were among the strongest in the world. Such was general public knowledge. For a large Japanese fleet to have successfully penetrated undetected as far as Hawaii and inflicted major damage on the installations there—that fact by itself argued the worst.

The interventionist leader Bishop Henry Hobson had passionately crusaded for war but was thoroughly shocked at the reports coming out of Hawaii—his full confidence in the power of the American fleet to crush any foe had proved an illusion.[45] Another interventionist leader, Francis Miller, recalled, "It was a moment when you were shaken to your very roots and wondered about the future of your country."[46]

Those with a military background reasoned similarly even before details were available to them. Admiral William D. Leahy, who was then serving as U.S. Ambassador to Vichy (unoccupied) France, later recalled, "We still were without much detail on the damage suffered at Pearl Harbor, but I knew if the Japanese had managed to get in without warning, we had suffered a serious setback at a time when we needed that fleet. There were always too many ships in Pearl Harbor to take an air attack."[47]

The details confirmed the evaluation that a successful surprise attack had to be, by its very nature, a devastating one. As the president's secretary Grace Tully recalled of that day, "Within the first hour it was evident that the Navy was dangerously crippled, that the Army and Air Force were not fully prepared to guarantee safety from further shattering setbacks in the Pacific. It was easy to speculate that a Jap invasion force might be following their air strike at Hawaii—or that the West Coast itself might be marked for similar assault."[48]

As information began to drift out, even the partial data frightened those who had access to it. Archibald MacLeish, who served as head over the Office of Facts and Figures, remembered that day vividly: "I have never been as frightened for the Republic as I was by midnight that night."[49]

Breckinridge Long, a major subordinate official at the State Department wrote in his diary entry of December 8th, "Sick at heart. I am so damned mad at the Navy for being asleep at the switch at Honolulu. It

2. The Presidential Address and Senatorial Action

is the worst day in American history. They spent their lives in preparation for a supreme moment—and then were asleep when it came. At the Defense Communications Board this morning I learned of the extent of our losses—and it is staggering."[50]

Cabinet member Harold L. Ickes first heard of the attack from press reports relayed by a friend. "He did not have the report that I was to get later that evening, but it was bad enough to show that the situation in Hawaii was serious and critical."[51] At that night's White House meeting the president reported the figure as four battleships sunk and two more badly damaged, not counting other craft that were in harbor.[52]

And, of course, anything a major bureaucrat, congressman, or senator knows will quickly be shared with key friends and associates. Hence Ruth Sarles wrote to Robert E. Wood of America First the information passing through their Washington office on December 10th:

> It is difficult the profound sense of shock experienced by the men on the Hill at the enormity of the catastrophe that has literally overwhelmed us in the Pacific. Yesterday Secretary Knox and Admiral [Harold R.] Stark [Chief of Naval Operations] appeared before a secret session of the Senate Naval Affairs Committee. One of the Senators, as he left the meeting, remarked that we would be lucky if we kept Hawaii.
>
> These men told the Senators that one half our effectives are wiped out, that three capital ships have been destroyed and four or five (I think the latter figure is correct) have been put out of commission indefinitely....
>
> The powers that be will sit on the lid as long as possible but it is doubtful the facts can be concealed for long. Tonight, all 96 Senators must know the story and some House members. It won't take long to travel.
>
> We had 17 battleships altogether; according to the best estimate, 4 in the Atlantic and 13 in the Pacific. Take out the 8 destroyed and damaged, and we have 5 left in the Pacific, as against Japan's 15. We would not have parity even in our own waters.[53]

Such data had to put something of a damper on the enthusiasm of more fervent interventionists for a two-front war, and provided anti-interventionists yet more reason to oppose entering the European conflict with such horrendous chaos in the Pacific. Yet the suppression of the specifics of the Pearl Harbor disaster carried with it an unintended bonus for those favoring the expansion of the conflict: Anti-interventionists could not publicly cite specific numbers (which would buttress their case), while pro-interventionists knew that what had happened had created an automatic momentum toward war as rage against one of the Axis partners rubbed off on the others as well. Time, guilt-by-association, and overt German actions could well make a two-theater war essential however ill-advised the current battle losses made it appear.

War Goes Before the Senate

When the Senate reconvened at 12:47 P.M. and a roll call certified that 82 senators were present, Senator Tom T. Connally (Democrat, Texas) introduced Senate Joint Resolution 116 to make the fact of war a reality in law as well as on the battlefield:

> Whereas the Imperial Government of Japan has committed unprovoked acts of war against the Government and the people of the United States of America: Therefore be it
> *Resolved, etc.,* That the state of war between the United States and the Imperial Government of Japan which has thus been thrust upon the United States is hereby formally declared; and the President is hereby authorized and directed to employ the entire naval and military forces of the United States and the resources of the Government to carry on war against the Imperial Government of Japan; and to bring the conflict to a successful termination, all of the resources of the country are hereby pledged by the Congress of the United States.[54]

Normal procedure required that this resolution be referred to the appropriate committee for its recommendation and later returned to the Senate for a vote by the entire body. The seriousness of the occasion was demonstrated by the willingness to waive this custom in order to complete quickly action on the measure.[55]

Roosevelt's astute request for a declaration of war against Japan—conspicuously not mentioning any other nation—assured that a divisive fight over intervention against Germany did not cloud the issue. Theoretically, there was absolutely no reason one could not continue to oppose the latter option while supporting the Pacific War, especially since another nation had initiated the overt military moves. In the real world, however, opposition to one war could be used as a rhetorical club for foes to use in the coming months. Hence some anti-interventionists felt the understandable need to put themselves on record in such a manner as to uphold their prior course while fully embracing the new conflict.

Therefore when Senator Tom T. Connally called for an immediate vote on the text, Senator Arthur H. Vandenberg (Republican of Michigan) said that he wished to speak on the matter. Connally responded that "those of us on this side of the Chamber are withholding remarks. I was hoping that there would be no comment."[56] Vandenburg insisted upon his prerogative of speaking and assured his opposite numbers that there would be no significant delay.

2. The Presidential Address and Senatorial Action

An Anti-Interventionist Defends the New War

Arther H. Vandenberg (1884–1951) was one of the most pivotal figures in the Republican Party, and both courtesy and political common sense required that his request be granted. Vandenberg had served as editor of the Grand Rapids, Michigan, *Herald* for more than two decades after completing his legal education. Upon the death of one of the state's senators in 1928, he was appointed to serve as his replacement and continued to be re-elected until he ultimately vacated his post by his own death.

Originally he became most well known for his determined opposition to the expansion of the federal government's role in providing job and other emergency relief programs during the Great Depression. He opposed the growth of what he called "the tyranny of a nationalized and planned economy."[57] Of what value was it, he demanded, to help raise the economic well being of the lower third of the population if it had to be done at the price of dragging down the other two-thirds?[58] Becoming minority leader of the Senate he was staunchly aligned with the wing of the Republican Party advocating non=intervention as the best means to preserve the nation from the danger of war.[59]

Within this context of his long established views, he now spoke. He began by heavily stressing the infamy of what had happened and his confidence that America would unite and strike down the new foe:

> I should not want to proceed further without making the record clear.
> Mr. President, out of peaceful Sunday skies, without a word of warning—yes; and even screened by the infamous treachery of pretended amity in pacific negotiations at Washington—like an ambushed murderer, Japan has violated our soil, killed our citizens, struck at our possessions, assailed our sovereignty, and disclosed to us the pattern of a purpose which reeks with dishonor and with bloody aspiration.
> There can be no shadow of a doubt about America's united and indomitable answer to the cruel and ruthless challenge of this tragic hour—the answer not only of the Congress but also of our people at their threatened hearthstones.
> To the enemy we answer—you have unsheathed the sword, and by it you shall die.
> To the President of the United States we answer—for the defense of all that is America we salute the colors and we forward march.[60]

Having put himself emphatically on record concerning his support of the war, Senator Vaudenberg then turned to the potentially embarrassing matter of his own earlier opposition to involvement in Europe:

> Mr. President, I am constrained to make this brief statement on my own account, lest there be any lingering misapprehension in any furtive

mind that previous internal disagreements regarding the wisdom of our policies may encourage the despicable hope that we may weaken from within.

I have fought every trend which I thought would lead to needless war; but when war comes to us—and particularly when it comes like a thug in the night—I stand with my Commander in Chief for the swiftest and most invincible reply of which our total strength may be capable. It is too late to argue why we face this hazard. The record stands. The historians can settle that conundrum upon another day, when we have finished with this task.

For now, it is enough that the attack has come. For now, nothing else will be enough except an answer from 130,000,000 united people that will tell this whole round earth that though America still hates war, America fights when she is violated. And fights until victory is conclusive.

God helping her, she can do no other.[61]

In private Vandenberg was marginally more cynical. In his diary entry of December 8, he noted that he still "believe[d] that a wiser foreign policy could have been followed—although now no one will ever be able to prove it.... Without condoning for an instant the *way* in which Japan precipitated hostilities, we may have *driven* her *needlessly* into hostilities through our dogmatic diplomatic attitudes."[62] As he implied on the Senate floor, such conjecture would have to be faced on a different day, but only after victory had been gained.[63] But the thought was already, quite clearly, firmly in his mind. As he wrote to a constituent, the "final ultimatum to Japan two weeks ahead of Pearl Harbor (*culminating these policies*) made a Japanese attack inevitable."[64]

This mindset continued throughout the war. In October 28, 1944, Vaudenberg he still spoke of the "secret diplomacy which pointed straight toward war for many months preceding Pearl Harbor."[65] A good part of this resulted from what a later generation would have described as cutting the Congress out of the loop of discussion and interaction in foreign policy making: The president had " 'isolated' the Congress and the country from any conscious knowledge about the inevitable war which he knew was on the way."[66]

In short, Roosevelt saw foreign policy as too important to let the Congress get in the way or interfere with what best served the nation's interests—as defined by Roosevelt, of course. This isolation of Congress continued, to Vandenberg's thorough aggravation, even after the nation was irrevocably in the war. In February of 1942 he growled in private to his wife that it was made worse by Roosevelt's determination to build upon the New Deal's changes in the socio-economic structure of America: "Come what may, I'm going to 'speak my piece' one of these days. Roosevelt ... hasn't demobilized a single one of his old 'social revolution' units.... The country is getting ugly—and I don't blame 'em. So

2. The Presidential Address and Senatorial Action

am I. Even we in the Senate can't find out what is going on. This is Roosevelt's private war! He sends out troops where he pleases—all over the map."[67]

Only in the early months of 1945 did the breach partially heal, as the two leaders sought out a mutually acceptable policy for the peace after the war's end.[68] The war years convinced Vandenberg that an overt and open, ongoing involvement in foreign affairs would be essential to avoiding future wars after the current one ended.[69]

It is intriguing that the postwar consensus on foreign policy evolved from groups beginning with very different initial premises. The former interventionists adopted the belief that a forward policy of active involvement abroad was the best means to continue to protect the national interests. The isolationists (an oversimplification of the views of many of them) embraced such internationalism as the best option for keeping America out of needless wars and of avoiding being manipulated by other nations with their own foreign policy goals. By this new accommodation, the two groups bridged the gap that had so divided the nation only five or six years previously.

Senator Connally's Background and Role

Vandenberg's words represented the majority of the senatorial words devoted to a discussion of the war vote. Indeed, so short was the entire war debate (it is hardly worthy of that term since there was no dissent) that it occupied almost exactly one page of the *Congressional Record* and nothing more.[70]

The only other words spoken on the Senate floor concerning the decision were those of Senator Connally, who argued that the words of Roosevelt had more than adequately summed up the views of his fellow Senators. It is hard not to see a touch of irony when he immediately adds, "We are, of course, glad to have the agreement of the Senator from Michigan."[71]

Connally (1877–1963) was a lawyer and had served as a major during the Spanish-American War and captain during World War I. After serving five terms in the House, he entered the Senate in 1928. He became chairman of the Committee on Foreign Relations in 1941 and as leader of that group steered such legislation as this through the House.[72]

He was the key leader of the move to repeal the Cash and Carry Act of 1939, which had effectively worked as an arms export limitation measure, though falling short of banning all such exports. In a similar manner, he played a pivotal role in pushing through the explicitly pro–British Lend Lease Act (1941).[73] After the war was over he and Senator Vandenberg shared major responsibility in crafting a bipartisan foreign policy that created a general consensus in favor of the U.N. and a strong overt American presence abroad.[74]

Senatorial Opinions Off the Floor

Although only these two Senators took a role in the proceedings on the Senate floor, a number of others had made their opinions known the previous day. In addition to those already quoted in the previous chapter, the comments of a few others would be useful to help gain a better grasp of the profound anger that pervaded the Senate.

Senator Joseph C. O'Mahoney (Democrat, Wyoming) thought the Japanese decision as self-destructive as a national policy ever could be: "It seems that the Japanese have called the play, and now they'll have to take it. The decision is out of our hands. The Japanese are committing hari-kari."[75]

Senator Henry Cabot Lodge, Jr., (Republican, Massachusetts) emphasized that there was no longer any room for discussion. "The time for united action has come. The time for words has passed." It was an "intolerable act of aggression" that must and would be dealt with.[76]

Senator Frederick Van Nuys (Democrat, Indiana) was clearly as much concerned with American over-reaction to the attack as to any possible danger. Though he conceded that the current situation was both "distressing and crucial" he stressed that, "Now is the time to keep our heads."[77]

Senator Millard E. Tydings (Democrat Maryland) hoped that the attack would shake the nation out of its lackadaisical approach to national defense, one in which it was taken seriously but not seriously enough: "That it was deliberate and plotted by the military crowd and apparently with the connivance of high Japanese officials is self-evident. It means that immediately we must discard our spring-fever attitude toward national defense and settle down to preparing for a terrific struggle in which each of us in our own respective place must do his part."[78]

Politically, the situation clearly called for minimizing partisanship. Senator Warren R. Austin (Republican, Vermont) summed up well the minority party's sentiment as he went into the presidential-congressional meeting the previous night: "I think we're going to have a vacation now from politics. Congress should be unanimous."[79]

From the House side, Representative Joseph W. Martin, Jr. (Republican, Massachusetts) was even more significant due to his dual roles as chairman of the Republican National Committee and Republican Minority Leader in the House: "This is a serious moment and we don't

2. The Presidential Address and Senatorial Action

talk about politics. There is no politics here. There will be none. There is only one party when it comes to the integrity and honor of the country."[80] Of course, in real life the politics remained present—subdued, usually kept under a tight rein, but always present as the two parties quietly attempted to stake out clear-cut positions that would favor the nation as a whole as well as their more narrow political interests.

The Vote

At this point a final reading of the text was made and the formal vote was taken: 82 to 0. Four Senators remained in office from those who had voted on the April 4, 1917, declaration of war against Germany. Three of them voted in the affirmative in both cases.[81] Only Senator George W. Norris (Independent, Nebraska) had demurred from the previous conflict; in this case, though, even he also came on board.[82] As he explained to a reporter on the 7th, "If we don't fight now we might as well sink our navy, dissolve our army, haul down the American flag and hail Hitler."[83] Of course he would vote for war: "I couldn't do anything else, the situation is entirely different from 1917," he stressed.[84]

As he explained in his war-time autobiography,

> In 1917 there was no immediate threat of war reaching American soil. In 1941 an act of war was committed by Japan against the United States at Pearl Harbor under the most treacherous and despicable circumstances, and the following day Germany and Italy issued declarations of war against the American people.
> In the present struggle, the Axis plan of aggression and conquest in my eyes constituted a direct threat to the safety and security of the United States.[85]

Although he far preferred peace to war and viewed war as inherently abominable, he was under no delusion that it could always be avoided. War did settle at least some questions.[86] Furthermore, national political, economic, and moral self-interest could not be completely ignored in making such determinations in regard to a specific conflict.[87]

Such considerations had moved him to publish an article in the *Sunday Oregonian* of September 14, 1941 under the heading, "U.S. Must Save Britain Even If It Means War." In it he emphasized the dramatically different circumstances between 1941 and 1917,

> We were, in my opinion, not justified in entering the last war, but conditions which confronted us then have no similarity to the conditions which confront us now. At that time there was still honor among nations and men, even though they were enemies upon the battlefield. The enslavement of peoples was not then at stake. There was no likelihood

that the life of our nation, as well as that of every other democracy in the world, would be endangered, no matter what the outcome of that war might be. There was no claim or belief in the mind of anyone that, if Germany won the war, it would be followed by a war in this hemisphere. However, in this war, we are confronted with an enemy whose ambitions are known to the world and that means destruction of every democracy in the world.[88]

Senator Robert M. La Follette Jr. (Progressive, Wisconsin) had not been involved in the earlier vote but his father had been, and he had voted against the German war. His son felt that what had happened at Pearl Harbor left "no alternative" but warfare and "its prosecution with the whole-hearted support of the people and their representatives in Congress."[89]

He had vigorously opposed many of Roosevelt's interventionist steps on the Senate floor,[90] but had left the public crusading to other Senators.[91] Although his brother was an active member of America First, the organization was only able to convince the Senator to make one radio address on the subject (in September, 1940),[92] perhaps because he felt uncomfortable with an organization which had so many economically conservative members and leaders.[93] (Nor was it unlikely that he wished to avoid some of the backlash his father had endured for his own earlier anti-war stance.[94] To be faithful to one's principles was one thing; to court public criticism needlessly was something else.)

Even so, as late as October 25, 1941, La Follette had written in the *Progressive* of the eerie similarity of events that seemed to be leading inexorably to a repetition of the mistake of two decades before: "I have never advanced the claim, and I do not now, that this present war in the Old World is like World War Number One. I do venture the prophecy that future unbiased historians, if such there may be, ... will recite the deadly parallel between the steps whereby we entered World War Number One and those by which apparently we are entering the present conflict."[95]

As with the rest of the anti-war contingent, LaFollette now fully embraced the new war. Yet he differed from many of them in that he never blamed the conflict on the negotiating inadequacies of the administration nor took refuge in the suspicion that it had all been intentional provocation.[96] Nor did he go out of his way to stress that his own anti-war stance would have made the war avoidable if it had been followed—again differing significantly from many of those who shared the same sentiments.[97] Perhaps it was partly temperamental. Or, perhaps, he reasoned that even if either assertion were true, what practical value would be served by dwelling on such matters when a highly dangerous war stretched for an indeterminate time into the future?

2. The Presidential Address and Senatorial Action 51

In addition to these individuals, five pro-war House members of 1917 had moved on to the Senate and all five repeated their affirmative votes in 1941.[98]

Senator Nye's Suspicions

As already alluded to, voting "yes" on war did not, however, mean that critics had been converted. Serious skepticism of the interventionist position remained: That war had been thrust upon the nation did not automatically prove that the pro-war demands in regard to Europe had necessarily been vindicated by what had happened in the Pacific. Senator Gerald P. Nye (Republican, North Dakota), for example, had gone on the record the previous day as smelling a rat.

He received initial word of the attack as he prepared to address an America First rally.[99] Knowing that previous alleged Axis aggressions had turned out to be either exaggerated or significantly misrepresented in initial reports, he saw no need to give the matter any further immediate thought.[100] During his speech a newsman slid him a note saying that the Japanese had confirmed the attack. He shared the report with the audience but remained skeptical of what was really happening.[101]

After the rally was completed, he cynically suggested to the press that this was "just what Britain had planned for us.... Britain has been getting this ready since 1938."[102] "It sounds terribly fishy to me," he insisted.[103] On the other hand if true, "If Japan attacked, there is nothing left for Congress to do but declare war."[104]

In a separate response the same day he saw the malevolent hand of American bureaucratic interventionists responsible as well. The United States had been "doing its utmost to provoke a quarrel with Japan. If we were bluffing, our hand has been called."[105] Even though the U.S. had no choice but to enter the Pacific War if the reports of an assault on Hawaii were verified, that did not significantly change his views about staying out of the European conflict.[106]

When he voted for war on the 8th, his sentiments remained essentially the same—war in the Pacific was now thrust upon the nation and it must unite behind the commander in chief. On the other hand, the America First policy of national defense without involvement in entangling alliances in Europe had still been the better policy.[107] Nye was convinced that only Japan's ultimately fatal decision to go to war with America had kept that policy from triumphing over Rooseveltian interventionism: Except for that "extreme folly of the Japanese on December 7th, this effort would have accomplished that thing for which we were fighting, namely, freedom from involvement in these wars by the United States."[108]

Those Absent

In a sense the term "unanimous vote" for what was done that day is a little misleading. In actual fact there were 13 not voting. This was in the age before rapid transportation, and a number of legislators were simply too far away to arrive in time. Senators Rufus C. Holman (Republican, Oregon) and Monrad C. Wallgren (Democrat, Washington) did not arrive in the capital until after the vote.[109] Holman was "flying to Washington" at the time it occurred[110] as was Senator Wallgren of Washington.[111]

Republican Senator Arthur Capper of Kansas was also in transit and was expected to arrive later on Dec. 8 or the following day at the latest.[112] The prediction was slightly off; it did, indeed, take him until the next day to arrive. At that point he told the Senate that "when the news of Japan's attack was flashed to our people I was in Kansas. I started for Washington as quickly as possible, but regret I could not reach here in time to cast my vote for approval of the President's stand."[113]

In contrast, fellow Republican Ralph O. Brewster of Maine had to travel from Puerto Rico and would definitely not arrive until a later day.[114] At the moment, he was somewhere in the air—literally.[115]

The Democratic Senators Theodore G. Bilbo of Mississipi, Mrs. Hattie W. Caraway of Arkansas, George L. Spencer (also of Arkansas), Carl Hayden (of Arizona), and Patrick A. McCarran of Nevada were described by one of the senators present as unavailable because they were "detained on official business."[116] Bilbo was later described as "en route,"[117] as was Caraway.[118] McCarran was "in Arizona on official business, attending a hearing of a subcommittee" and was currently traveling back to the capital.[119]

Illness and death kept three senators away. Senator John Thomas (Republican, Idaho) was at home due to a family death.[120] Senator H. H. Schwartz of Wyoming (a Democrat) had been appointed as part of the official delegation to attend the funeral of ex–Senator Adams of Colorado. As a result he was also unable to make it back to the District of Columbia in time.[121]

In a not quite as devastating vein, Democratic Senator Homer T. Bone of Washington was unavailable "because of illness."[122] He was "under the care of a physician," it was later reported in the session.[123]

The isolationist Democrat Burton K. Wheeler is described at the beginning of the day's session as "necessarily absent,"[124] a remark later amplified by the remark that he was "en route to Washington. If present, he would vote 'yea.' "[125]

Thirteen senators were absent, but this was one of those rare votes that no senator wanted to miss. Both patriotic and pragmatic reasons

2. The Presidential Address and Senatorial Action

were involved: Senators were as hard to defeat in those days as in the twenty-first century, but none likes to have a potentially embarrassing absence that might be exploited by a future challenger. Those present did their best to cover these absences.

When the names of the absent were called, various other senators announced that if that individual had been present there was no doubt that they would have voted in the affirmative.[126] Indeed, by the close of the day, all of them had passed word through fellow senators or through their spokesmen that such would have been their action.[127] The roll call would omit their names from the "yea" column, but their affirmations that they were just as pro-war as those actually present were now on the official and unofficial records of the day.

3

The House of Representatives Responds to War with Japan

The Presidential Speech and War Proposal

At Noon the House was called to order after an introductory prayer by its chaplain. After the reading of the last day's minutes was dispensed with, Congressman John D. McCormack (Democrat, Massachusetts) introduced a joint resolution calling for the Senate to join members of the House at a 12:30 P.M. session in the House to "receive such communications as the President of the United States shall be pleased to make to them."[1] McCormack's initiative grew naturally out of his role as majority leader—a role he had served in during the previous Congress and in which he would function for some 20 years. After the motion was passed unanimously and concurred in by the Senate, the president addressed the two houses with his "day of infamy speech" analyzed in the previous chapter.

After a short intermission for the president and the attendees at the joint session to leave, the House was called back into session. House Joint Resolution 254, which was then introduced, differs significantly from that of the Senate only in the preceding introductory text to the formal declaration and in adding an entire sentence to it as well:

> Declaring that a state of war exists between the Imperial Government of Japan and the Government and the people of the United States and making provisions to prosecute the same.
> Whereas the Imperial Government of Japan has committed repeated acts of war against the Government and the people of the United States of America: Therefore be it
> *Resolved etc.,* That the state of war between the United States and the

Imperial Government of Japan which has thus been thrust upon the United States is hereby formally declared [and the remainder of the text remaining the same.²

The Senate introduction had spoken of the "unprovoked acts of war," while the House speaks of "repeated acts of war." The first stresses the ethical innocence of the United States ("unprovoked acts") while the second emphasizes that this was part of a pattern ("repeated acts"), whose significance could not be ignored.

The Speaker inquired of the House, "Is a second demanded?" Jeannette Rankin of Montana, a Republican and unrepentant anti-war activist, promptly threw a small monkey wrench into the proceedings: "I object," she insisted. The Speaker reminded her of what would likely have been obvious under less stressful conditions, that "This is no unanimous-consent request. No objection is in order."³

As Rankin later explained, she was trying to get the matter referred to a committee for consideration, thereby delaying the vote.⁴ Such a referral would have been normal procedure for any resolution or piece of proposed legislation.⁵ Unlike World War I, when there was a large body of opinion unwilling to go to war,⁶ this time there was simply no base of congressional sentiment on which for anyone like her to build and the Speaker both could—and did—firmly brush her aside.⁷ From one Democratic⁸ Congressmen came the shouted demand, "Sit down, sister!"⁹)

The Speaker again raised the question of whether a second was to be required by the House. One member so demanded and the Speaker responded that he considered that the record should note that "a second is considered as ordered," i.e., there was so much support for the measure that it would be accepted that a second had been given. This position passed without objection.¹⁰

The Discussion Begins

Congressman McCormack of Massachusetts kicked off the discussion with extreme brevity. After referring to the fact that the president had just addressed Congress he felt that little more needed to be said. He contented himself with noting that, "A dastardly attack has been made upon us. This is the time for action."¹¹

Next came Congressman Joseph W. Martin, Jr., also of Massachusetts though of the Republican Party. Just as McCormack was a major player in Democratic Party affairs on the national level, so was Martin in Republican business. Just as McCormack was majority leader in 10 Congresses, Martin served the opposite role of minority leader in eight.

Martin spoke at considerably more length than his Massachusetts compatriot. He stressed that the nation "is being challenged by a ruthless, unscrupulous arrogant foe" who had carried out "a treacherous attack under cover of darkness."[12] (Actually it was very early morning).

So far as his own preferences, he was opposed to war, period: "No one hates war more than I. Every night I have uttered a silent prayer that America might be spared active involvement in a frightful war. I know the horrors which come with war—the loss of lives, the sacrifices which must be made by all, the sadness and desolation it always brings."[13]

Such concerns were no longer adequate. "America is challenged. That challenge comes in a ruthless way which leaves but one answer for a liberty-loving, self-respecting people. We are compelled by this treacherous attack to go to war. From now on there can be no hesitation.... When the historic roll is called I hope there will not be a single dissenting vote."[14] His hope was almost, but not quite, answered.

A Veteran Opponent of FDR Endorses War but Later Is Convinced He Was Misled

Congressman Hamilton Fish (Republican, New York) was even more emphatic in conceding that it was time for his own non-interventionism to be set aside. He was a key member of America First and, ironically, the congressman from the district in which the president himself resided[15]—not to mention that he was considered the most vigorous and vehement opponent of the president's interventionist policies in the House.[16] Hence it is not surprising that the two men deeply loathed each other.[17]

Yet the attack was so provocative that he immediately reversed all of his years of vigorous anti-war effort since the changed circumstances demanded it: The Japanese had not only started a war but they had done so in the most unethical and insulting manner imaginable: "I have consistently opposed our entrance into wars in Europe and Asia for the past three years, but this unwarranted, vicious, brazen, and dastardly attack by the Japanese Navy and air force while peace negotiations were pending at Washington and in defiance of the President's eleventh-hour personal appeal to the Emperor, makes war inevitable and necessary."[18]

It was time to put aside past accusations toward each other and substitute the unity needed in wartime. "Interventionists and noninterventionists must cease criminations and recriminations, charges and countercharges against each other, and present a united front behind the President and the Government in the conduct of the war."[19]

Fish was especially astounded by the apparent irrationality of the Japanese act. "Whom the gods would destroy they first make mad. The

Japanese have gone stark raving mad, and have by their unprovoked attack committed military, naval, and national suicide."[20]

He was prepared to put his own life in peril as well. "I shall at the proper time volunteer my services as an officer in a combat division, as I did in the last war, preferably with colored troops."[21] (He had served as a captain over the black Company K of the Fifteenth New York National Guard during that conflict.)

He concluded his remarks with a plea to those who had shared his anti-war stance: "I appeal to all American citizens, particularly to the members of my own party, and to noninterventionists, to put aside personal views and partisanship, and unite behind the President, our Commander in Chief, in assuring the victory to the armed forces of the United States."[22]

The president deserved a clean bill of health. So it appeared to him at the moment. As new data began to surface during the war, he felt horrified as he discovered what he regarded as confirmation of the worst interpretation of the facts that was possible—that FDR not only conspired to provoke a war-producing confrontation with the Germans (already a given in his reading of the data), but that the Pearl Harbor disaster itself was also the result of a similar policy of provoking an international conflict. As Fish summarized a few key points in a postwar book,

> FDR was evidently thinking of getting into war with Japan as far back as October 8, 1940, when he told Admiral Richardson, then in charge of the fleet at the Hawaiian base, that sooner or later the Japanese would make a mistake and we would enter the war. That was a year and two months before Pearl Harbor and shows that Roosevelt was already considering a war with Japan as a means of getting into World War II.
>
> At the Atlantic Conference, August 1941, President Roosevelt conferred with Prime Minister Churchill regarding an agreement to protect the British interests in the Far East ... Churchill's statement to Parliament on January 27, 1942, verified this agreement: "The probability since the Atlantic Conference at which I discussed these matters with President Roosevelt, that the United States *even if not attacked would come into the war in the Far East* and thus make victory sure, seemed to allay some of the anxieties."[23]

He conceded that this was a course of desperation, produced by FDR's failure to embroil the U.S. in war with Germany. The *Greer* attack incident in the Atlantic had been presented as premeditated aggression by the Germans. Actually the *Greer* had been shadowing the submarine for hours and providing data on its location to the British. After a British aircraft failed to sink it, then and only then did the Germans launch torpedoes against the Americans. Similarly the reported attack on the *Kearny* was represented as aggression when the facts were materially different.

Yet it was such incidents that Roosevelt used to justify his shoot on sight order in regard to the German submarine force.[24]

When such incidents failed to provoke the sought-for German attack that would be clear-cut and undeniable by all, the president fell back upon Japan and made demands that in no way possible would or could be met.[25] Yet it was clearly the efforts to encourage a German attack that Fish remembered with the greatest anger:

> The intense pro–Roosevelt apologists may try to defend his un–American, undemocratic and unconstitutional methods of provoking war. They will probably say that the end justifies the means and he knew best what was in the interests of the nation. That doctrine is a total repudiation of our democratic institutions and representative and constitutional form of government. It violates Lincoln's "government of the people, by the people and for the people." It turned to ashes the principles and policies of neutrality...."[26]

Few men are angrier than those like Congressman Fish: convinced at the time that the president was intentionally provoking a needless war against one power, embracing a war against another only after an unprovoked assault, then to discover to his horror that *both* seemed to be the result of deliberate and unneeded provocation by his own government. Yet that was for him to discover in the future. At the time it could only have been, at most, a worried suspicion.

Democratic Congressman Sol Bloom of New York came next in the discussion of December 8th. Having served since 1923, he was now chairman of the Committee on Foreign Affairs and, because of that position, a voice to be reckoned with in discussions of international affairs. He politely lambasted the tendency already made manifest that more than a few Congress members seemed more interested in talking than in acting. His plea was simple: "Mr. Speaker, speedy action, not words, should be the order of the day."[27] He followed his own entreaty by sitting down and shutting up. He did not, however, have an impact on how many spoke or how long they took—except, probably, to cause them to put most of their comment in the additions they contributed to the permanent *Record* of the session rather than saying it all at the moment.

Texan Democratic Congressman Luther A. Johnson (another long termer with over 18 years of congressional service behind him) was appalled at both the "unprovoked attack" and the fact that the foe had struck "without notice, while peace negotiations were still in progress...." This type of two-faced behavior "is characteristic of those totalitarian outlaws who talk peace while they have already drawn the dagger with which to strike. We have but two choices today, either to fight or to surrender, and America, thank God has never surrendered and never will surrender."[28]

Women Members Speak Out for War

Congresswoman Edith N. Rogers of Massachusetts (a Republican) also stressed indignation at an attack occurring at the same time negotiations were proceeding: "The Japanese envoys were engaged in diplomatic sham and committed one of the most dishonest acts in the world's history." It was such a shameful act that she could not imagine anyone who had moved here from any part of the world condoning what had happened. "Those of every national strain, proud of their American heritage and citizenship will stand up to the challenge made by Japan of their freedom."[29]

In that age before gender issues became a subject of public controversy, it was still accepted that women might well react differently to matters of war and peace than males. Indeed, the stereotype of women as ruled by emotion and therefore "weak" was one that could easily be a matter of concern. Probably recognizing this stereotype, the congresswoman argued that the exact opposite was the case, at least in the current hour of crisis. "Mr. Speaker, we know American men are brave, American women, too, are brave; together a united courage such as ours is certain of victory. We are willing today to make every sacrifice to achieve our goal."[30]

Rogers had been elected in June of 1925 to complete the term that her husband had originally been elected to serve. After taking his place she proceeded to set a still existing record of unbroken service (18 total electoral victories), a record only ended by her death in 1960.[31]

In the late 1930s she was a cautious supporter of steps that could lead to American intervention in Europe. In 1937 she opposed the Neutrality Act and in 1940 she supported imposing a peace-time draft.[32] In three elections Democrats could not be found to run against her, and within her own party her lengthening service resulted in a corresponding unwillingness of potential opponents from attempting to replace her. Looking at all of her elections cumulatively, she averaged 60 percent of the vote during her lengthy career.[33]

Next to speak was the very different Congresswoman Katharine E. Byron, a Democrat from Maryland. Like her compatriot, she also had taken her dead husband's place—though only in May of 1941. After completing that one term, she was content to permanently retire from politics.

Ms. Byron candidly confessed that this war was going to strike into the depth of her home, but said that she was willing to pay the price even so:

> Mr. Speaker, my late husband, Bill Byron, was in the last war. One of my sons is near military age. Should this conflict last long enough, I am willing to give my sons to their country's defense. I am 100 percent in

favor of avenging the wrong done our country and maintaining our country's honor. We must go into this thing to beat the Japanese aggressor. I shall do everything by voice, by vote, everything within my power to bring about this end.[34]

The Pro-War Chariot Rolls On

In his fourth and final term, Congressman Joseph E. Casey, (Republican, Massachusetts), couldn't resist the temptation to toss a verbal dagger into the isolationist camp while conceding that this was now a matter of past history: "Mr. Speaker, prior to yesterday we were a divided Nation with respect to our foreign policy. This division of sentiment has interfered with the efficient marshalling of our energies and our resources. America has been a sleeping giant. This attack by the Japanese has awakened us. We are no longer divided."[35]

Then came another Republican congressman, Charles A. Eaton of New Jersey. With two decades of congressional service behind him, he spoke of how "yesterday against the roar of Japanese cannon in Hawaii our American people heard a trumpet call; a call to unity; a call to courage...." In Churchillian phrases he spoke of "a long battle of blood, of tears, of sweat, and sacrifice." This would enable America to "stand in the forefront to help create a world civilization of freemen everywhere, just as Americans today are free on American soil and propose at any cost to remain so."[36]

Republican congressman Earl C. Michener of Michigan was another deeply ensconced member. Since 1919 he had been out of Congress for only a single two-year period. He stressed that this was not some kind of "idealistic war"; rather, it was a war to save ourselves. The "one honorable and realistic answer" to the Japanese attack was to declare war.[37]

He made no apology for his past opposition to war:

> As is well known in the House, and to the constituents whom I have the honor to represent here, I have been definitely opposed to involving our country in any foreign war except in case of defense. My voice and my votes in the Congress have been directed to that end. I believe thoroughly in America and in our way of life and doubt the wisdom of attempting to compel the world, by force, to adhere to the principles of government which we enjoy and which by choice we will defend to the end.[38]

Now, however, the situation had irrevocably changed. The United States was under direct attack: "Japan has cast the die. It is either surrender or fight."[39]

California Republican Congressman Bertrand W. Gearhart came next. Like so many others in the House, he had a background in law.

Unlike many, however, he had served active combat duty in the 609th Aero Squadron during the First World War. He insisted that the nature of Japan's surprise attack at Pearl Harbor "will find no counterpart in the bloody annals of man's rascality." Japan was now self-condemned as an "outlaw nation" whose "murderous assault will be avenged."[40]

To do so, however, would require everyone's active participation in one form or another: "Let there be unity, in our every thought, in our every deed. Let every man, woman, and child lend the strength of his or her individual might. With the Nation united, no force in this world can prevail against our brave soldiers, sailors, and marines."[41]

Charles A. Wolverton (Republican, New Jersey), who had served since 1927, used similar language in describing the enormity of the attack:

> Never in the recorded history of civilized nations has there been a parallel of the treachery and deceit evidenced by Japan in its unprovoked attack upon our outposts in the Pacific. It took advantage of the white flag of truce under which its emissaries were conferring with our own representatives, ostensibly to determine a treaty of peace, and struck a dagger into our back. The reprehensible and diabolical character of this act does not admit of adequate description and condemnation.[42]

Wolverton calculated that it took "at least two weeks preceding the bombing" to prepare the assault. Yet during the whole time, Japan was acting out the pretense of negotiations.[43] In these on-going outbursts of indignation and predictions of ultimate victory, Congressman Wolverton demanded realism as well.

> Do not let us make the mistake that our task will be an easy one. That is the way to fail.
> Our adversary has worked and labored for ten years looking forward to the day it would challenge America. Unfortunately, we have helped them in their preparation for war against us. For many years Japan has received steel, copper, oil, and other manufactured products from us. We must now assume that they have been turned into weapons to be used against us.
> Furthermore, to prosecute a successful war we will be called upon to wage it thousands of miles from our home base. This will have a tendency to delay and hinder a quick conclusion. We must be ready to bear early reverses like those suffered on Sunday morning, when hostilities were directed at several of our Pacific island possessions. It is natural that some early successes would result from the fact that our enemy struck suddenly and without warning. But we may rest assured that early success does not mean final victory.[44]

Frank C. Osmers of New Jersey was another past Republican foe of FDR's attitude toward the European war: "I have been a consistent opponent of this administration's foreign policy. For that opposition I make no apology. But the time for political differences is passed."[45] He planned to put himself in the line of danger. "It is my intention to offer my services to the armed forces for the duration of the war."[46] He enlisted as a private, successfully completed Fort Benning Infantry School, and was placed on the inactive list by presidential order in July 1942, since Roosevelt considered it bad policy to have congressmen actively serving in the military. Osmers solved this difficulty by not standing for re-election, returning to active duty, and pulling assignments in the Pacific Theater of the war for the duration of the conflict.

Osmers reminded the listeners in the House and the nation that the foe had unleashed forces with consequences it could not guess: "Mr. Speaker, this is a tragic hour for the American people. History will record it as a more tragic one for the peoples of the Japanese Empire."[47] Hence in spite of the catastrophe that had occurred, Osmers clearly viewed it as bearing the seeds for horrendous though deserved retribution.

Osmers was not the only congressman to choose active duty—either temporarily or for the duration. Albert Vreeland (also of New Jersey), for example, took the same course. He entered military intelligence and later transferred to the infantry. He was also returned to Congress involuntarily by presidential order and solved his problem in the same manner as Osmers—declining to stand for re-election. After that he served in Australia and New Guinea.[48]

The most famous congressman to go on active duty—though his fame lay far in the future as majority leader, vice president and president—was Lyndon B. Johnson of Texas. Hoping to move on from the House to the Senate, he campaigned in 1941 on the pledge, "If the day ever comes when my vote must be cast to send your boy to the trenches, that day Lyndon Johnson will leave his Senate seat and go with him."[49] It was a powerful, direct, and effective pledge that Johnson echoed in the bulk of his speeches and writing. The positive reaction was overwhelming.[50]

Hence though he was still in the House when war erupted, Johnson saw no choice but to carry out his pledge. Whatever edge of political expediency may have been involved, it was also the kind of action that Texans and most Americans expected of someone who had so firmly and repeatedly given his word as to how he would act. Some pledges politicians can conveniently forget and their constituency will forgive them, but the circumstances surrounding Pearl Harbor put this one in a distinctly different category.

Republican Congressman Roy O. Woodruff of Michigan spoke next. Although several of the members of the House, due to the length of their remarks in the *Congressional Record*, give every indication of having expanded their statements for the published version of the debate, Woodruff's text is of such extent that it manifests an abandonment of the relative restraint exercised by most others.[51] He pointedly refers to how he had written his remarks, how the war resolution had passed with only one dissenter, and how his comments were being composed the night of the vote.[52] Indeed, it might well be called a post-vote meditation upon what had happened to the nation.

The most significant part of Woodruff's remarks concerns how that, though the time was not immediate, sooner or later a convincing explanation had to be given of why it had been possible for the attack to succeed. Since he had served as an officer in both the Spanish-American War and the First World War, he was well acquainted with the concept of command responsibility and was naturally concerned with how it applied in the current situation:

> America tonight is stunned by Hawaii. It is amazed by Pearl Harbor. It is utterly without any explanation for what, on its face, appears to be an utterly inexplicable event. It is impossible at this time to find any explanation for what apparently happened, for it is impossible to know the extent and the effects of the shattering blow delivered so suddenly by the Japanese.
>
> America had considered Pearl Harbor impregnable. Pearl Harbor was the pride of the armed forces of the United States. Pearl Harbor was the alert outpost standing strong as a Gibraltar between the Untied States mainland and the threat of the Japanese. So America had been told again and again and again. That was what America had been led to believe. It was what America had a right to believe....
>
> There must be some explanation for the stunning events at Pearl Harbor. There will have to be an explanation—sooner or later—and it had better be good.[53]

If the anti-interventionists would have to deal with the reproach of having opposed war—even though the center of their opposition was a very different war at the opposite side of the world—the Roosevelt administration would have its own reproach to bear that was potentially even more explosive: How in the world had it "permitted" the tragedy to occur? Although Congressman Woodruff was not willing to make it an issue at the moment, this haunting question would quietly (and sometimes not so quietly) ferment within many congressional minds throughout the war itself.

Even the scapegoating of the Hawaiian commanders only quieted the tempest rather than eliminating it. The concern persisted that the catastrophe was so vast that responsibility, at least in part, must have been borne by those far higher up the chain of command.

The next congressman to speak was Republican George H. Bender of Ohio. After four unsuccessful campaigns for the position, he had finally been elected in 1938. He echoed the sentiment of earlier speakers that the attack was a "totally unprovoked aggression of the Japanese Empire," made at the very time we were doing "everything within our power" to arrange for a general peace in the Far East. The tense of his remarks also indicate post-vote revision: "The Japanese military clique must take the full responsibility for the war we have just declared in response to the action of Tokyo."[54] Without consciously realizing it, such comments laid the rhetorical foundation for ultimately permitting Hirohito to remain as emperor: It was the Japanese *military* that had to take "full responsibility for the war."[55]

Republican Congressman Everett M. Dirksen of Illinois viewed the Japanese action as violating the norms of conduct one would expect even from an enemy: "We face the task of overwhelming a nation which has displayed a complete disregard for the virtues of fairness, decency, and sportsmanship. The President and Secretary of State have exercised gentleness, patience, and restraint in preserving peace in the Pacific. Their gentleness has been flouted, their patience mocked, their efforts trampled under heel."[56]

Dirksen had seen war in the previous world conflict, first as a private and then as a second lieutenant. He did not minimize the danger. The challenge was serious and not to be under-estimated. "It will be a grim, serious, and undramatic business. Let us discharge it grimly, seriously, undramatically. Let us not underestimate the size or duration of the task."[57]

Congressman Edward A. Kelly of Chicago, Illinois, a Democrat, reviled the attack with an animal analogy: Like "a slimy creature crawling in the dark, it struck without warning and struck while negotiations were in progress for a hoped for peace in the Pacific." He was both angry and sad: angry because he had served in the field artillery during the earlier conflict and had seen the pain of war first hand, and sad because he had hoped for a peaceful solution to the ongoing tensions: "Having served in the last war, little did I think I would ever see this day come again in America; I had hoped for a peace, but you cannot deal in terms of peace with such people."[58]

Democratic Congressman Martin L. Sweeney of Ohio was another who had vigorously opposed any action that might land the United States in the European War locking Germany and Britain in a bloody embrace. Unknown to himself, he was in the last of his several terms of congressional service.

> Mr. Speaker, forty-eight hours ago if someone would have said to me, "You will soon vote for a declaration of war against a foreign power," I would have considered that individual non compos mentis.

> Since the outbreak of World War Number Two I have consistently and conscientiously opposed and voted against every step which I considered was in the direction of our involvement in foreign war. I have proclaimed from the floor of this House, and from many platforms throughout the Nation, and over the radio to the American people that I would never vote to plunge this country into a war of aggression, and that only in the event of attack upon our sovereignty would I vote and support a resolution that would put us into a defensive war.[59]

That situation of direct attack by a foreign power had now occurred. Sweeney made clear that this was not a war to protect British colonialism: "Our war with Japan must not be construed as a war to protect the material interest of any other nation in the Orient."[60] Nor did the waging of an Asian war require engagement elsewhere. As Sweeney reminded the congressmen, "This is the only war in which we are now officially engaged."[61]

He expressed serious concern that when peace came it might do so with the same fundamental mistake being made that occurred at the end of the previous world war. He believed that the United States had refused to apply the Christian principles it was founded upon at the peace conference. Therefore it was vital that the next time America "speak for the poor and distressed people of the earth. It is a well-known fact the doors of the peace council at Versailles were closed to the God of infinite justice and mercy, with the result that practically all the civilized nations of the earth are once more engaged in the holocaust of war."[62]

Congressman John E. Rankin of Mississippi—a Democrat, as were all Deep South congressmen in that decade—was particularly outraged at the pagan vs. Christian aspect of the attack and that it involved the needless death of many American civilians. He could find nothing in all history equal to this "attack made by pagan, godless Japan on the United States and the Christian people of the island of Hawaii on yesterday. It was not only cruel and unprovoked warfare against a nation that had befriended Japan for almost a hundred years but it was malicious mass murder of innocent men, women, and children, who were blown to pieces on the streets of Honolulu."[63] Not only did Rankin blatantly exaggerate civilian casualties (out of panic? misinformation?), but spoke he not a word of comment on the horrendously large military casualties.

Charles F. McLaughlin (Democrat, Nebraska), shared the conviction that this had been "an unprecedented act of perfidy." It was not only their "solemn duty" but also the "one course open to the Congress" to formalize "the existence of a state of war with Japan" that now so clearly existed.[64]

When Congressman Charles A. Plumley's turn came (another long-serving Republican, this time of Vermont) he was happy to begin his remarks by stirring in a hefty dose of overt racism, arguing that it was fully justified by what had just happened: "Mr. Speaker, the diabolically infamous treachery of the Japanese brands the race as never to have been and not now entitled to be trusted or treated as civilized. It confirms the judgment and wisdom of our forebears, who would and did exclude them from citizenship."[65]

As to the attack itself, a state of war clearly existed. "Can anyone doubt it with at least fifteen hundred Americans dead at the hands of the Japanese...? They cannot. It is an incontrovertible fact." Hence, though there was no choice but to recognize the reality, he cautioned against over-optimism: "We will not win this war as speedily nor as easily as we could wish or, as some believe, but we will win," nonetheless. Because there was no alternative. This was not merely war but a war against "the enemies of civilization and Christianity" itself.[66]

"This is a fateful day which we have all sought to avoid," began Republican Frederick V. Bradley of Michigan. He stressed that he had voted for increased defense appropriations while simultaneously opposing intervention abroad. Not only his own but the nation's best efforts to maintain the peace in the Far East had failed. "During the very hour in which so-called peace negotiations were being conducted in Washington, Japan launched upon our Pacific possessions and upon our nation a most cowardly, treacherous, and dastardly stab-in the-back attack." As to his own course, he had that day "volunteered my own services" to the U.S. Navy.[67]

Congressman Frank E. Hook (Democrat, Michigan), who was in his fourth term, now arose and stressed how "this came without warning, unprovoked, and without just cause."[68] This attack was an incredibility unifying action—the very opposite of what the foe desired. "People of all nationalities" had come to America and they would join in the retaliation for the damage done to their adopted homeland.[69]

The support would know no gender or occupational schisms: "Men and women from all walks of life will rally to the standard of liberty. Those who don the uniform of the field of battle or on the high seas may rest assured that full and supreme sacrifice of those at home, in the fields, in the factories, the mills, the mines, the forests, the offices, from town, county, and city, will be given as fully and completely as possible."[70]

Why Were They So Foolish as to Go to War?

Throughout the day's debate, the inability to comprehend how the Japanese could rationalize their act runs quite deep. Wars occur and usually both sides can grasp the "why." Even sneak attacks occur, but usually both sides readily understand what went astray in their relationships. On the 8th the congressmen couldn't find it.

One sees throughout the discussions preceding the vote a sense of perplexity at the apparent irrationality of what had happened. Congressman Lewis D. Thill (Republican, Wisconsin), now arose and went into this aspect with more than the passing mention that was typical of the day.

> The radio news flashes of war in the Pacific burst like bombshells in the homes of our people on Sunday afternoon. It was scarcely believable, hardly conceivable that Japan should wage war against our country. There was no threat of armed attack, no hint of violence, no break of diplomatic relations prior to Japan's sudden attack upon Hawaii and American possessions.
>
> Without warning Japan has loosed tons of explosives upon our property and our people. This has caused terrific damage to our Navy and our Military Establishments, and it has resulted in much loss of life. If only the military leadership of Japan had used reason instead of emotion. If only Japanese leadership had followed the will of their people for peace. If sanity instead of madness had been the watchword of the governors of Japan—there would have been no outbreak of hostilities between our two nations."[71]

When long-serving (since 1919) Republican Congressman Daniel A. Reed of New York stood up to speak, he made only passing mention to "the infamous act of treachery committed by Japan against our Nation." The remainder of his brief remarks were classical July 4th flag waving, perhaps best summed up in the one sentence, "Our American boys can handle anything genius can invent."[72] In the context of that grim December day, the language seems somehow inappropriate to the challenge and danger that his colleagues so readily conceded.

It was to be a battle "between the governments of the peace-loving people of the United States and the subjects of the treacherous, military despots of Japan," argued Charles R. Clason (Republican, Massachusetts). "We, the men and women of America, in the factories, on the farms, in every walk of life, pledge our every effort to our Army and our Navy that they shall bring victory to our cause."[73]

The apparent hypocrisy and gall of the foe was a theme that we have already seen and will see touched upon time and again by the various speakers. That a major power had to prepare for war at the same time it negotiated for a way out of one did not seem to dawn upon the congressmen. (Today we take "dual track" foreign policy as elementary prudence—negotiate for the best compromise but militarily prepare for the worst result.) Even if it had, it would certainly have been regarded as irrelevant in this particular case: the traditional diplomatic courtesies expected prior to conflict—a break of relations if not overt declaration of war—had been blatantly ignored by Japan, which continued diplomatic negotiations up to the time of the attack itself. If the congress men and women had known that the final Japanese message was supposed to have been delivered barely prior to the attack, the legalistic nit-picking would have outraged rather than calmed them.

Another who stressed the incredible ethical breach in Japanese behavior was Congressman Leslie C. Arends (Republican, Illinois). He spoke of how,

> At the very moment our Government was bending every effort to maintain the peace between the Imperial Government of Japan and our country through negotiation, and when promises and more promises were being made by their representatives that they desired peace, at that very moment, like a thief in the night, our American soil was attacked, leaving both death and destruction as a reminder that our enemy had started on its program of war against the United States.
>
> As we now, with as much calmness as possible, view this "knife in the back" action, and realizing the careful premeditated planning necessary to carry out this assault on our bases in the Pacific, we face the fact that the challenge thrown down to us will and must be met.[74]

The United States was partially prepared. "Huge appropriations" had been made in the past two years. Now yet much more would have to be done to make victory possible.[75]

Republican B. Carroll Reece of Tennessee—a decorated veteran of the First World War, with honors from both the American and French governments—summed up in a few sentences the longer comments of others. It all boiled down to one thing: The United States did not want this war, but having been forced into it had no choice but to win it.[76]

Using the War Resolution to Gain Support for a European War and Social Improvements at Home

If isolationists wanted to keep the focus on the war that all agreed had to be fought with Japan, some interventionists were not above using the opportunity to link what had happened with Japan's Axis partner, Germany. This carried with it the clear implication that sooner or later Congress would have to deal with this other foe as well. Congressman Arthur W. Mitchell (Democrat, Illinois) raised this specter when he stressed, "This attack is a combined effort to wipe out the possibility of democratic government and to establish in its stead abject slavery. The bloody struggle engaged in by Germany, Italy, and now Japan is a challenge to civilization itself."[77]

Mitchell, a black congressman who had graduated from the Tuskegee Institute, had been a teacher, and then learned law, used the opportunity to stress the need for full respect and rights for the black citizenry of the nation. In a post-session addition to the *Record*, he argued,

> I fully concur in the resolution which we have just adopted in compliance with the President's request and pledge the unbroken and continued loyalty not only of the First Congressional District, which I represent, but that of the 15,000,000 Negroes in America. This seems to be a struggle to the death, and will determine for years to come, and perhaps for all time, the form of government that we are to have in this country, and perhaps in the world.
>
> I wish to suggest that in this struggle, as in all previous struggles, the Negro proposes to give and will give all he has, including his life, for the success of our effort to withstand Hitlerism. In view of the sacrifices which my group has always made and in view of the sacrifices which we are bound to make in this struggle, let me remind the Congress and the Government that the Negro expects the same treatment under our so-called democratic form of government that is accorded all other citizens. He would be unworthy of citizenship in this country if he contended for less.
>
> It is my hope that the contribution which we have always made and shall continue to make will cause those in power and authority and will cause this country to recognize the Negro as a full-fledged citizen. If he is good enough to die for his country, he should be given the largest and fullest opportunity to live for his country without any type of racial discrimination. We are loyal Americans, and you can depend on us to the last man.[78]

To use the hour of crisis as a pivot to gain for black Americans the rights white Americans took for granted was quite understandable. White racism was just as profound in the North as in the South, though there was more leeway for self-advancement economically and socially in the North. Yet the regional *degree* of difference should not be unduly magnified, either. The right to vote was certainly there. Better job opportunities also—due to greater industrialization. But most neighborhoods were closed by convention, restrictive real-estate covenants, or the threat of violence. Likewise those of African descent were looked down upon as *collectively* inferior and, with that, the assumption of *individual* inferiority was a common misdeduction encouraged by the white view of the black community as a whole.

The war provided an utilitarian opportunity to urge whites to embrace in practice what white political rhetoric would have already granted if the white race had been the subject. During this his final term in the House, Congressman Mitchell repeatedly used the war as a tool to aid the moral case for the equitable and just treatment of all citizens regardless of their skin color.[79]

The coming of war did not surprise Congressman L. Mendel Rivers (Democrat, South Carolina); its timing did. This first-term member (he proceeded to serve just days under thirty years overall) conceded that, "A majority of the Members of Congress last week predicted war with Japan, but none of us felt or could conceive that it would come as it did."[80]

The Japanese, incredibly, had sunk to a level beneath that of even the most dangerous creatures in nature: "The vilest snake, the lowest animal, and the most ravenous bird of prey gives its intended victim some warning before it strikes. The Japanese failed even to exercise the impulse common to all other living creatures. The only warning they gave our peaceful and slumbering people was a burst of shrapnel and the howl of dive bombers."[81] Since the only choices now were to surrender or fight, war—a victorious war—was the only alternative.[82]

When Democratic Congressman Joe Starnes of Alabama rose, he repeated the now common litany: "This attack was made under cover of darkness. It came without warning. It came while our President was still seeking a peaceful solution to the problems of the Pacific."[83]

He linked the war mentality of Japan with that controlling Germany and Italy: "This attack along a wide-flung battle line clearly reveals that Japan, like the other Axis members, is bent upon world conquest and nothing will stop her short of superior force."[84] A long-time member of the Alabama National Guard and veteran of the First World War, Starnes was defeated in a bid for renomination in 1944. He then went on active duty, served as an infantry officer in Europe, and then pulled occupation duty in Japan.

Delegate Samuel W. King, a Republican, was the non-voting representative of the territory of Hawaii. Although he could not cast a vote in the formal tally, he wanted it known that both he and the people of his territory fully concurred that the war was "unjustifiably forced upon us." He conceded that the attack had given "temporary advantages" to the foe but that "this indefensible conduct will result in the destruction of Japan as a military power."[85]

King represented a region as much on the front line as imaginable. In his fourth term at the time of attack, he withdrew from the race the following year even though he had been renominated for another term. After a year in the Naval Reserve, he served on active duty in the Pacific through February, 1946.

A Congressman Recalls the 1917 War Vote

Perhaps those most profoundly moved by the Pearl Harbor assault was that small minority of Congress who had either seen combat or who had voted on the 1917 war resolution. Promised the "war to end wars" if the nation only entered the conflict, both groups had seen the resulting peace turn out to be only illusionary. Allen T. Treadway (Republican, Massachusetts) spoke of this when it was his turn to endorse the pro-war vote:[86]

> The occasion here today reminds me of a similar one nearly twenty-five years ago when President Wilson, addressing the Congress in an extraordinary night session, solemnly asked for a declaration of war against Germany. There are fifteen Members of the present House who were Members of the World War Congress. I know the other fourteen Members have wished as I have, that we would never be called upon to vote for another war declaration. I have many times said that I would never do so as regards our participation in any foreign war.
> Today, however, we have had war brought to our own doorstep. The United States itself has become the victim of aggression.

Republican congressman of Pennsylvania J. William Ditter barely mentioned the attack itself. Instead he spent the bulk of his words on the need to have the nation embrace an on-going commitment to encourage peace between nations. But that was for the future; something else was necessary in the short-term. "Fervent as have been our hopes for peace, they now give way to a grim determination. War has been forced upon us."[87]

Congressman Joseph A. Gavagan (Democrat, New York) criticized what had happened as "one of the foulest attacks in the history of this Nation," but one that had also united her.[88] He took the opportunity to rub salt in the hide of the anti-interventionists for the rhetoric he and other pro-war advocates had endured for years:

> This Nation closes ranks; no longer shall we hear the voice of the isolationists lulling us with the oft-repeated lullaby, "They can't attack us—the two oceans are our protector." Yea, we close ranks and in battle array go forth to meet this foul challenge; we shall not be deterred, please God, until this act of aggression has been avenged; we shall show the world we are not too proud to fight; that we are worthy scions of our sires who fought, bled, and died that we might live in peace and freedom.[89]

Congressman Jared Y. Sanders, Jr., part of the all–Democrat delegation from Louisiana, stressed two themes that one hears over and over again on that day of discussion: Peace negotiations had been going on at the very time the attack occurred; and "this Government has done everything in its power to avoid war with the Japanese Empire."[90] However, he also cast the attack in its broader setting, emphasizing that its vast scope argued clear premeditation: "These attacks, not only upon our naval base at Pearl Harbor but on numerous other islands under our flag, and synchronized so as to occur simultaneously with other attacks over a wide range of thousands of miles in the Pacific, together with the sinking and capture of our merchant vessels, show that these attacks were deliberately planned."[91]

In other words it wasn't one of those horrible accidents or miscalculations that may have been such, or which, out of prudence, might be officially interpreted as such by both sides to avoid a major war.

Rooseveltian Negligence as a Contributing Cause to War?

If some interventionists were willing to, in passing, put a forensic fork in the hide of their foes (and also, if one so chose to do so, interpret their remarks to imply that their opposition to war had helped create the current crisis), some anti-interventionists were also willing to hint at something at least equally significant, if true—that negligence of the Roosevelt administration may have lain behind the hostilities instead. Congressman Robert F. Rich (Republican, Pennsylvania) spoke of how he would vote for war but was concerned that the president had not adequately involved the Congress in the search for peace:

> I have been opposed to the United States interference in the political and economic life of nations in Europe, in Asia, and in Africa. I have maintained that America should stay in the Western Hemisphere to assert our authority and then only when the conference table was no longer of use to nations.
> I wanted to use our good offices in America by the President, by the Secretary of State, and by the Congress to arbitrate differences for the Eastern Hemisphere. To the end that the conference table be used I have been zealous in extending our aid. Perhaps the President and the Secretary of State should have consulted the Congress during the deliberations in the past three weeks with the Government of Japan, but they were not disposed to do so, and now we find ourselves at war with the Imperial Government of Japan because she fired the shot against the Government of the United States in Hawaii Sunday, December 7, heard the world around.[92]

Rich was in his sixth term at this point. The following year he decided not to seek renomination. Coming back in the following election he served three more terms in his old seat.

Anti-war sentiments were also echoed by the next speaker, another Republican, Thomas A. Jenkins of Ohio. He argued that—unlike some—he had opposed intervention while noting that he had refused to paint himself into an ideological corner by claiming that there never would be a situation where he voted for war:

3. The House of Representatives Responds to War ...

> Most of us are opposed to war. During the present emergency I have voted constantly against every action that I felt would lead us into war. My philosophy has been that we should stay as far away from war as possible. I felt, however, that should the time come that we would be compelled to go to war, either because of our unwise statements or conduct, or because of the aggression of some other country, I would so conduct myself as that I could in fairness and in good conscience give my unqualified support to my country.
>
> I have never felt it the part of wisdom to have made any statement or any promise to the effect that I would not under any circumstances vote for war. On the contrary I have felt that since war had from the beginning of time been the accepted method of settling disputes between nations it would probably continue to be until the spiritual inclination of the peoples of the world had taken a loftier plane than that which they hold at this time. The action of Japan yesterday impels the most peaceful individual to the conclusion that it is not safe for any country to adopt a policy of complete pacifism.[93]

Assuming that he could, indeed, present the statements and record of votes to back his claim, Jenkins had astutely positioned himself for the next election to tackle any opponent who might claim he had helped create the situation that made the attack possible.

The next speaker suggested what was obvious to many: There was actually nothing to debate, argued Republican Richard M. Simpson of Pennsylvania. "The fact is clear. Any invasion of the United States, its possessions or its interests, is war."[94]

A similar sentiment was expressed by Democrat Louis Ludlow of Indiana. "By the resolution before us we are not putting our country into war with Japan. We are already in war, and no one knows how soon or from what quarter the next attack will come."[95]

But this did not let the Roosevelt administration off the hook. Its policy had been founded on erroneous premises and had promoted warlike and war-involving measures. These Ludlow still repudiated, and he hoped that after this conflict was over, the nation would not make the same mistake again:

> Mr. Speaker, I think that our entire foreign policy in recent years has been fundamentally wrong, in that it has utterly disregarded the wise advice of Washington, Jefferson, and other founding fathers against foreign entanglements. I want the record to show, as it does show, that I have not, by any acts of mine contributed in any way or at any time or in any degree to what I believe to be this erroneous policy of world involvement.
>
> I have opposed, and whenever Congress was allowed a vote, I have voted against every one of these deviations from correct principles because I wanted America to remain free, strong, and independent, and at peace with the world. By no act of mine have I contributed to the deplorable situation that now confronts us.
>
> I shall be glad, indeed, if in my capacity as a Representative of the peo-

ple who have to suffer and die in war I may be helpful in accomplishing, at the proper time, a reexamination and revision of our foreign policy that will bring us back to sounder and safer ground.[96]

The anti-interventionists were open to the accusation that their opposition to defense measures had encouraged Japanese aggression. Ludlow's argument could easily be the basis of reversing the argument: If the United States had not followed misguided efforts to be involved in the world's affairs, this war would not have occurred and the question of the amount of defense expenditures would have been irrelevant.

The generation that came to age in the 1960s and 1970s saw this basic issue presented as whether America would be "the world's policeman" or not. One side viewed active military involvement abroad as the surest way to assure the long-term safety of the nation; the other side saw it as the surest way for involvement in conflicts where the national interest was either non-existent or marginal. It was different rhetoric but the same basic either/or thinking that existed in the pre–Pearl Harbor years as well.

This "stab in the back under the cover of night," argued Connecticut Democrat DeRoy D. Downs, was but the prelude to "the dark days ahead." It cast tremendous pressure and responsibility upon the president, but he felt certain that he would successfully lead "us through this struggle to victory. He will live up to the occasion."[97]

Bolivar Pagan, the non-voting representative of Puerto Rico in the House, played up the military importance of the island in its role as "watchdog at the entrance of the Panama Canal." Furthermore, "as the representative of the only Latin-American territory under the American flag," he felt he was in an especially appropriate position to express that "hope that all Latin-American republics will back the United States of America in this great hour, when at stake is the security, the liberty, and the destiny of the whole Western Hemisphere."[98]

Maryland's Thomas D'Alesandro, Jr. (Democrat) spoke next and briefly. After describing what had happened as "an unwarranted, unprovoked and treacherous attack by Japan," he suggested that it was time for all to restrain their natural tendency as politicians to want to speak at length. "This is not the time for speeches, but we must meet the challenge with action.... I have always contended that President Roosevelt was right from the start, and I will continue to support him 100 percent."[99]

Next to rise was Democratic Congressman Stephen M. Young from Ohio. He was content with the mild criticism that "Isolationists have been proved wrong by the merciless logic of events over which they have no control." But, he said, it was not a time to boast of such ideological triumphs. The simple fact was that "uncertain hours, desperate days, grave dangers, a long and bitter struggle confront us" in the coming years. Whether we sought it or not, in the conflict with Japan and Hitler, "We have a rendezvous with destiny. Let us dedicate ourselves with heavy hearts and firm resolve to see this thing through."[100]

Young's suggested military strategy was one of concentration of forces for homeland defense and then a quick retaliatory slash: "Although we were caught off guard, and only partially prepared for an offensive campaign against Japan, wisdom now dictates that this Nation devote all its energies to making this continent impregnable. We cannot do this, yet at one and the same time divide our armaments and scatter our forces. Every gun and every ship will count from here on."[101]

Yet just two sentences later he insisted, "We have been attacked. We must now strike back, and quickly."[102] How he proposed to execute the policies of centralization and rapid counterattack simultaneously he did not explain.

When Young lost in the next election, he entered the United States Army. Having World War I experience, he received a major's commission and saw combat duty in both North Africa and Italy.

Pennsylvania's Hugh D. Scott (Republican) cited his own press release to the Philadelphia papers of the previous day, vowing to support any action requested by the president. He now reaffirmed that pledge, stressing that "the American people are united in a determination to put an end to international gangsterism."[103]

Next Congressman Aime Forand (Democrat, Rhode Island), spoke of how he shared in the shock of so many others that the attack could have occurred at the very time negotiations were still proceeding. To him it was conclusive proof that the recent negotiations had been nothing more than a pretense to mask the last moves of the Japanese forces into place: "Naval experts say that from at least ten days to two weeks were required for Nipponese submarines and other war vessels to get to the positions in which they were when they launched their attack. This is definite proof that the presentations being made by Nomura and Kurusu were not sincere."[104] (Actually Admiral Yamamoto, who planned the operation, had put his subordinates under the strictest orders to cancel the attack if the diplomats somehow delivered a last-minute breakthrough.)

Indiana's Robert A. Gillie (Republican) stressed that America's distaste "for war should not be construed as weakness, for once aroused, once an enemy threatens our homes, our institutions, or our way of life, no people are more to be feared." As the result of the attack the American people were both "aroused and united in a demand for vengeance against our common enemy."[105]

Congressman Raymond S. Springer (Republican) from Indiana, a veteran of the previous world conflict, held the foe in contempt. Unlike the older and longer-established nations of Europe, the United States had followed a policy of hands-off tolerance toward the Far Eastern nations,[106] giving it a claim to moral superiority over nations that attempted to control the world, and even though the war could no longer be avoided, American ethical integrity would unquestionably be retained:

> We are a patient and peace-loving people. Our national ambitions have long been far above the avaricious tendencies of the Old World. We have sought by every decent means to stay out of a world conflict from which no good can possibly be derived. We will not even now suffer a loss of our high ideals, but act to further strengthen them by dealing as only we can deal with international bandits, highwaymen, and thugs, who violate all decency and out of the dark assault us.[107]

In terms of logical reasoning—even granting a superior political morality of the U.S. in comparison with the European nation states—this war had *not* sprung from that continent. Instead it had come from the Pacific regional power of Japan. Perhaps in the back of Congressman Springer's mind (and this can only be conjecture) was the suspicion that in some shape or form European encouragement to aggression was the ultimate deciding factor for Japan.

The Japanese had acted "like murderous imps from hell [and] are clutching at our throats," argued Republican Homer D. Angell Oregon.[108] Indeed, "the stench of hell [was] upon his garments [for] extending the olive branch with one hand, while with the other hurling death-dealing bombs upon innocent unsuspecting people. God, in His infinite wisdom, will visit the just retribution of the damned upon the perpetrators of this vile perfidy."[109] After what had happened, "No one will halt or hesitate until these brown devils from over the seas have been crushed to earth and civilization saved from the ravages concocted by the diseased minds in control of this treacherous nation."[110]

It does not seem unjust to suggest that this supercharged rhetoric grew not only from anger but also from Angell's personal humiliation for having vigorously pushed the anti-intervention position. As he noted in the middle of his condemnation of the foe,

> Many of us gave a solemn pledge to our people that we would not vote to send our soldiers beyond the Americas to fight in foreign wars unless we were attacked. I made this pledge. I have maintained my pledge. We have now been attacked in the Western Hemisphere. We are fighting a war of self-defense. Japan has not only cruelly attacked us behind our backs while professing to plead for peace but she has actually declared war upon us.

I have done everything within my power, as God has given me the vision to see the way, to maintain our country at peace. Our efforts have been impotent to ward off the evil day. War has now been thrust upon us. It is not ours any more to decide. All that remains now is to defend ourselves.[111]

Perhaps the oddest remarks of any present were those of South Carolina's Democrat Joseph R. Bryson. Instead of making any remarks at all—or amplifying upon them before the *Record* went to press—he simply inserted the text of two letters he had written. The text of the two is identical and in them he lobbied the president and secretary of war for a declaration of war against all three Axis partners:

> It is my opinion that a declaration of war should be declared against, not only Japan, but Germany and Italy as well. My reason for believing that war should be declared against Germany and Italy while declaring it against Japan is that these states are all members of an unholy alliance, seeking world domination by brutal force; and there should be no further waiting in declaring our intention to crush that aggression in all its parts.[112]

Having failed to persuade the president to take such a course, Bryson simply entered his position into the *Record* and left it at that.

The Impact of the Attack on the American Psyche

One of the most astute analyses of the day was given by Congressman H. Jerry Voorhis, (Democrat, California), in his expanded version of his remarks that appeared in the *Record*. First he analyzed why the Pearl Harbor attack had so rattled the foundations of the collective American psyche:

> Millions of Americans had not believed such a thing would happen. They had believed the choice of war or peace was still theirs. But when the decision passed from their hands they were ready to meet it with all the determination and devotion of a united and intensely patriotic people
>
> A hundred million people throughout the Untied States spent the afternoon and evening of Sunday, December 7, 1941, with their ears very close to their radios. And as they listened they began to realize that their world of that morning was gone and that they would be confronted on the next day with beginning the long and sacrificial task of building a new world on the wreckage of the ambitions of nations like Japan whose leaders place no limitations on the expansion of their power except the limit of military conquest which they could effect.[113]

Looking with amazing equilibrium beyond the immediate shock of the hour, he argued that the stress of war should not result in Americans forsaking either core religiopolitical or sociopolitical values:

> From that point [of war erupting] on the manifold task of the American people will include the following:
> First. To gather together the full strength of the Nation in order to bring the conflict, already joined, to as speedy and successful a conclusion as possible.
> Second. To distribute the burdens as equitably and evenly among all our people as humanly possible—requiring of each a sacrifice commensurate with his ability to make sacrifice.
> Third. To understand the causes of these wars, to see clearly they have come upon the people of the world because of the control of certain nations by groups which put their whole reliance in an arrogant and unconfined use of force.
> Fourth. To cling to the fundamental values and ideals which have been the basis of civilization through all the ages and to begin even now the work of trying to bring the world back to them.
> Out of the suffering and destruction through which the world must pass in the months and probably years that lie immediately ahead there must come certain forces of regeneration. They will be essentially religious and spiritual forces. For only that kind can survive [the] time into which we are heading. The sooner they begin to appear the better, for without them there will be hopelessness and despair. And hope is the one thing mankind cannot live without.[114]

Voorhis was even able to look at the demands of postwar rebuilding. If the nation and the West permitted their core religio-ethical values to grow to their logical conclusions, then action would have to be taken against the central ideological and social causes of international conflict.

> Two principal evils have brought this world-wide conflict upon mankind. The first of these is the ambition of selfish and arrogant men and the belief of certain peoples that they are superior to other men. The regenerative forces I have spoken of will strike down pride wherever they find it; they will level it to the ground; they will exalt the simple people of the earth on whom the full weight of this stark tragedy will fall.
> The second evil that has brought this tragedy to the world is the failure of the leaders of the nations to provide the means of distributing an abundance of goods among all the people. For this lies at the root of the drive for living room, and of raw materials. The answer to this problem is the answer to war and even the secure foundation for peace. Even as we seek to defeat the forces of wrong which have made war on the peace of the world we must address ourselves to this problem. Upon its solution depends the whole fate of future generations.[115]

California Democrat John M. Costello's remarks were placed in the *Record* next, even though he had not been present until after the vote.

He also vigorously supported the decision he had not been present to personally advocate.[116]

The solemnity of the occasion was emphasized by Congressman Michael J. Kennedy (Democrat, New York): The presence of president, Senate, House, cabinet, and Supreme Court could not help but impress those who were there. It was not merely a matter of defeating Japan, but of preserving fundamental freedoms including not living in terror of what enemies might do: "Our freedom of speech and expression, our freedom of worship, our freedom from want, and our freedom from fear must and will be preserved, so help us God."[117]

A Front Line Veteran Meditates on the New War

William F. Cole, Jr. (Democrat, Maryland) began by speaking of what had to be the minds of a number of those present: what they themselves had been through on the field of battle and how close to their own homes the new conflict was striking:

> Mr. Speaker, twenty-three years ago today I was in France after two battles rejoicing with the men of my command and all others in uniform over the fact that we had just won the greatest of all wars—to end war. I returned a few months later to see for the first time my son, then six weeks old, who today, twenty-three years of age, wears the uniform of his country as part of the great and splendid army we have been training to meet any eventuality.
>
> I never thought in those days I would be called on to vote for a declaration of war as I intend to do in a few moments, but such is to be the unanimous decision of a Congress, which has done its best to prepare the Untied States to defend itself and at the same time has prayed and hoped its desire for peace would be absorbed by others throughout the world, thereby avoiding hostilities.[118]

Cole also raised a matter that earlier speakers had skirted: How was the war to be brought to an end? Through unconditional surrender by the foe. "I shall strive hereafter not alone to bring victory to our cause but, more important, to demand that no armistice shall be permitted to stop our onward march to a clean-cut victory, but surrender, and that alone, shall end this war."[119] Furthermore, if negotiations of any type were to precede surrender, they could not involve those tainted by responsibility for the attack on the U.S. "Our dealings in the future with those who seek peace at our hands must be by those whose hands are clean and above the table."[120]

Having seen service in the 79th Division during World War I, Cole did not attempt to enter active duty again—perhaps in part because he was entering his early fifties. Instead, when he resigned office in 1942, he did so to move to the United States Customs Court, where he served six years as judge.

Should War Have Begun in 1937?

Democratic Congressman Guy L. Moser of Pennsylvania was the only congressman to argue in his extended remarks that the war should have been declared years before, when Japan was involved in its expansive maneuvers in mainland China and had bombed the *U.S.S. Panay*. He scalded the Roosevelt administration for its prolonged negligence in appeasing Japan:

> The action I will take today, and the vote I will cast in favor of the resolution, might the better have been cast during the first session of the Seventy-fifth Congress after Japan had launched her undeclared war on China and had bombed the U.S.S. *Panay*. "Sorry, sir! Excus, plees!" [sic] is as inadequate then and treacherous as the example brought home to us today.
>
> The President of the United States with Neutrality Act of 1935 operative, mandating him to impose an embargo when a state of war was found to exist between states, to my dissatisfaction, obviously could not recognize the then state of war existing but divested himself of his "quarantine speech" in Chicago, while under commercial treaty we continued to do "business with Japan as usual." Steel, scrap iron, oil, and gasoline continued to be exported—"business as usual."
>
> Throughout the early autumn of this year, we were confronted with the situation of an alleged gasoline shortage to American citizens as represented by Secretary Ickes, while Secretary Hull was still supplying shipments of the American product to Japan. I recall and preserved the cartoon of Secretary Ickes operating an American gasoline station, turning down the American customer, and Secretary Hull operating the pumps at a competing station "business as usual" to Japan.[121]

At this point, Moser was in his third term in office and was then serving as chairman of the Committee on Census. When the time came in 1942 to nominate candidates for the session beginning the following year, he failed to gain renomination. Three later efforts to return to Congress also met in failure.

Louis J. Capozzoli, a freshman Democrat, from New York, noted that the declaration of war "does nothing more than recognize the existence of a situation thrust upon us and which we know exists, much as we would like it to be otherwise."[122] In an inadvertent way, the attacker had unwittingly done the nation a favor: "These outrages were committed by a country which, at the very time of their perpetration, was falsely representing itself as desirous of continuing peaceful negotiations. It is my firm opinion that nothing else that might have happened could have been more effective in convincing America of the dangers confronting it in the world today and of the necessity for complete national unity."[123]

Democrat Thomas E. Scanlon, Congressman from Pennsylvania, was another who recognized that a direct attack on the United States could have no response but war. Yet he also had seen the horrors of the battlefield and knew all too well what was coming even for members of his own family:

> Once before in my lifetime the very foundations upon which the freedom of this Nation is established were threatened with destruction. I am proud to say that in that grave hour I was able to serve my country and my flag. I was able to see at first-hand the ugly side of war. I am not unmindful of that ugly side of this war, neither am I unmindful to the sacrifice which those behind the lines will be called upon to make, but our freedom would be worth nothing to us unless we have the courage to make those sacrifices.
>
> Casting a vote in favor of a declaration of war against the Japanese Empire is something I am doing with firm conviction, but with a heavy heart. I have an only son who today is the same age as I was in 1917 [i.e., when he himself had served in World War I].[124]

A Congressman with First-Hand Experience of the Military at Pearl Harbor

To Pennsylvania Republican congressman James E. Van Zandt, it was not only a matter of a sneak attack, it was a matter of human blood crying out for justice. "Already the flesh and blood of hundreds of American fathers and mothers have been sacrificed through the treachery of a nation who violated all civilized law in attacking this Republic while here in the Nation's Capital spokesmen for both Governments were attempting as peaceful nations to arrive at a mutual understanding of the differences involved."[125]

All else was superfluous. "This is no time to quibble. Our Nation has been attacked. What are we waiting for?"[126]

(On a visit to Japan with the Veterans of Foreign Wars in 1936, Van Zandt had received a special decoration as a symbol of international amity. The inscription read, "In token of our friendship and hands across the sea to endure to the end of the world."[127] Apparently the more he thought about this, the more it annoyed him, so a few days after Pearl Harbor he returned the decoration—presumably to the Japanese embassy.[128])

Members of Congress were handling gingerly the question of

responsibility for the success of the attack. For example, some interventionists got in verbal digs at isolationists, and others faulted Roosevelt's pre-war diplomacy as inadequate. But by the following day the search for a scapegoat (legitimate or otherwise) was in full swing. It would be much easier for the strong congressional faction favoring intervention in Europe as well as the president—who bore ultimate political responsibility—if the failure could be passed down the chain of command to those in charge at Pearl Harbor.

This approach also had in its favor that these individuals were sufficiently high ranking military officers that it was inherently credible that they *should* have been able either to keep the attack from happening or to keep it from turning into the disaster it became. This interpretation became even more viable in light of the lack of public knowledge of the vast amount of data Washington had prior to the attack and the still-debated question of whether civilian and military officials in the capital had adequately interpreted and analyzed its significance.

It would be several years later before it become generally known that for months before the attack, even decrypted communications directly discussing Pearl Harbor—covertly intercepted and translated from the Japanese communications—had not been shared with Hawaii. Hence the desire to protect the president from political damage, and the lack of public knowledge of inadequate data sharing, made it highly advantageous and credible to place the responsibility on the lower level of the Pearl Harbor commanders.

Van Zandt was in the unique position of having personal, first-hand knowledge of conditions at Pearl Harbor due to a recent active duty stint in Hawaii. Based upon this experience, he vigorously went on record on the 9th against the shifting of responsibility downward—a sentiment that grew stronger and more popular as data later became available as to the lapses at the Washington end of the decision-making chain.[129]

The Debate Continues

Van Zandt's additional remarks about Pearl Harbor came the next day. On December 8th the immediate question was the war vote itself. Ohio Republican Congressman John M. Vorys defended his earlier course by arguing that he had been following a two-track policy in opposing the European War. "I have opposed the steps our country has taken toward war: I have supported the steps our country has taken to prepare and protect itself if war should come to us."[130]

He conceded that "the first news is shocking and discouraging...." On the other hand, he called for a commitment to a higher purpose than mere revenge: "Our united loyalty is pledged not to a hatred, not to a man, but to an ideal—to bring peace for earth for men of good will, and to fight for that ideal."[131]

In the expanded version of his remarks, Vorys attempted to dilute any possible criticism of his earlier anti-war efforts by stressing that he had been on the record as to concerns about the Far East at a time when his colleagues were obsessed with the European tensions and war:

> On June 29, 1939, before the war in Europe had started, but while the China-Japanese struggle was in progress, I said on this floor: "I think we are making a great mistake in trying to determine our possible conduct in a future war in Europe before we determine our present conduct in a present struggle in the Orient. We have let our excitement about what *may* happen to our remote interests in Europe blind us to what *is* happening to our immediate interests in the Orient, where our treaty rights are being violated daily. We should stop arming Japan instead of planning to arm Europe [emphasis added].[132]

So far as he was concerned, "the present world-wide reign of terror and lawlessness began when the Japanese entered Manchuria in 1931 and the democracies of that day failed in their obligations to each other and to the world." If a more active (diplomatically speaking) interventionist foreign policy had been adopted, not only might the situation in the Far East have been resolved, but war in Europe discouraged as well. He conceded that "I knew that the negotiations between our country and Japan were difficult and that there was a possibility of failure," but he had never dreamed of the possibility of such "black perfidy" as had happened at Pearl Harbor.[133]

Karl E. Mundt, one of South Dakota's two Republican House members (and most remembered due to his later lengthier service in the U.S. Senate), was in no mood for any effort to attribute the moral responsibility for the attack to failures in American foreign policy. Yes, such failures may well have been present, but there was no way to draw a meaningful correlation between them and what had happened at Pearl Harbor. "While there may be some reason to wish that our administration had pursued a less provocative foreign policy while we were perfecting our own defenses, there is nothing which can remotely justify the jackal attack of the Japanese which was made at the very time their official representatives were presenting protestations of peace to our State Department."[134]

Mundt was shocked not only by the attack being launched without any of the traditional preliminaries to war, but also by the sacrilegious aspect of its timing. "Let the Congress and the country, therefore, join today in a mighty and unceasing drive to defeat these forces of evil and to help reshape the world so that once again God's Sabbath can become a day of worship rather than a day of launching crusades of wanton and wicked destruction."[135]

Louisiana Democratic Congressman Overton Brooks had served as an enlisted man in the Army field artillery during the previous war. He stressed that the nature of the surprise attack was of such a provocative nature that even a coward would not dare back down. "I have prayed God that this day might not come and that this Nation might be spared the blight of war. In this matter we had no alternative, even had we sought to avoid war at the expense of our own honor and decency. The gage of battle has been thrown to us, and we fight for our very existence and that of our homes and our families."[136] The war was now not one of foreign entanglements or of ideology but of national survival. The ground rules for the very conception of the nature of the war had been fundamentally changed.

Edouard V. M. Izac Democrat, California, spoke of his support for the president during the preceding five years. He praised FDR's foreign policy as one of remarkable astuteness and restraint in a rapidly changing world: "Foreign relations have no mathematical rigidity. Directing a nation through the maze of conditions and situations that are constantly in flux requires a master hand at the helm of government. This we have had. And if the exercise of patience and discretion had received its just reward, we would not now be faced with a state of war."[137]

Unfortunately it had not worked out that way. The attack on December 7th grimly manifested that far more was at stake than usual in international conflicts. The nature of the attack had exhibited "a pagan philosophy, championed by the greatest war machine of all time...." The issue had become whether "to rise in defense of our civilization or to permit our Christian philosophy to succumb before the onward march of tyranny...." There was only one choice that the American people would accept, and Izac ended with a quotation from an earlier generation: "Liberty is not only a heritage but a fresh conquest for each generation."[138]

Laying aside the blatant extremism of the Hitler regime, Izac had no reason to feel predisposed to any expansionist German regime in the first place. He had suffered serious injuries while a prisoner of war of the Germans, wounds so severe that he later had to retire from active military duty. Rarely could a congressman claim, as he could, to have received the Congressional Medal of Honor for wartime service.

Congressman John Jennings, Jr. (Republican, Tennessee) was the only speaker of that day who recognized the military-economic implications of Japan's strategy and how it held the potential for even greater disaster further down the road if she were successfully permitted to expand and consolidate her seizures:

If she is permitted to seize the natural resources of Asia—oil, tin, copper, iron, rubber, and other strategic war materials in which that great continent and the islands of the Pacific are rich—and if she becomes the master of the manpower of that vast region, she would control limitless war making materials and be in command of one-half of the population of the globe. Thus armed and equipped for conquest, the Japanese could and would force a black-out of civilization and Christianity throughout the world. If she is permitted to succeed in her godless, overleaping, and limitless ambition, mankind would, for centuries, bow beneath her ruthless might.[139]

Anti-Interventionists Vigorously Assailed

Congressman Adolph J. Sabath (Democrat, Illinois) was especially disappointed because it was the second time in his political career he had voted for war: "I am the only Member still serving in Congress who, as a member of the Committee on Foreign Affairs in 1917, voted for the resolution declaring war against Germany."[140]

He attributed the new tragedy to the failure of the United States to enter the League of Nations. Had it done so, "we would today find a world free of war. It is so evident now that if the League of Nations had been a potent body the long series of aggressions that have culminated in this war would have never occurred."[141]

This utopian interpretation is, of course, subject to the strong challenge that even with American participation the international body would have had extreme difficulty in summoning the political will to adopt sufficiently strong measures to counter the newly emerging dictatorships. With the blood bath of World War I a fresh and bitter memory—even in the minds of the victors—no one was likely to embrace a policy that would—for mere abstract principle, as distinct from clear national interest—run the probability of war. The weakened ability of the Western militaries to enforce such a policy if it had been adopted also demands consideration.

Sabath was convinced that "due to our tremendous moral and economic power, it would have been possible to prevent war by economic sanctions."[142] He was clearly unaware that the very success of the American and Western total embargo on Japan that began in the summer of 1941 had forced the Japanese to make a war decision that had hitherto been delayed and which otherwise would have been delayed still longer.[143]

Taking full advantage of his right to expand his remarks, Sabath engaged in repeated slurs against the Japanese, while blaming the isolationists for their obstruction of the interventionist policies of the Roosevelt administration. On both points he exceeded the venom of any other speaker that day.[144] Sabath called not only for victory but a vindictive and extremely punitive peace to follow to assure that it was utterly impossible for Germany ever to start another war.[145]

From Kansas, Republican Ulysses S. Guyer spoke next. He candidly conceded that, "I have opposed what has been called the president's foreign policy because I was convinced it would lead to war. That is water over the dam." The United States had been directly attacked so war was inescapable.[146]

Yet if Congressman Sabath was unwilling to forget prewar opposition, neither was Guyer, but that controversy was for a future day. War "is here and the only course is to forget our differences for the present. There will be time for argument after we have finished this job with the Japanese and their allies."[147]

The Final Speakers

James A. Shanley (Democrat, Connecticut) was content to state that what must be done now was summed up by the Guilford, Connecticut, poet Fitz-Greene Halleck:

> Strike—till the last armed foe expires;
> Strike—for your altars and your fires;
> Strike—for the green graves of your sires;
> God—and your native land.[148]

Shanley was in his fourth term in office. He was defeated in the next election in his attempt to make it five terms.

From Kentucky's delegation, Democratic Congressman Virgil M. Chapman took the opportunity to speak next. He expanded his on-the-floor remarks in the printed form of the day's proceedings. First he described at length how the idealistic streak within human civilization in general and Christianity in particularly had longed for peace on earth, only to be repeatedly plagued by the curse of war. Then he waxed eloquent—and the words are effective—describing the horrible assault on civilization launched by Adolf Hitler's aggression and Mussolini's complicity in it.[149]

Then he verbally pasted together the European aggressors with the nation against which the U.S. was making the transition from de facto to de jure war:

> Not only are our institutions menaced by this military coalition of ruthlessness and murder, but at dawn yesterday, on the holy Sabbath, while our wise and peace-loving Secretary of State was striving to preserve peaceful relations with Japan, while their diplomatic representatives were

still holding out delusions of hope that peace might be preserved, the Navy and air force of Japan made an unprovoked, premeditated, treacherous, destructive attack on the land and the armed forces of our country.[150]

In the remaining half of his remarks, Chapman appealed for interparty unity during the conflict and quoted both poetry and history to support his demand for full harmony. He demanded a no retreat and a no compromise policy in the conduct of the war.[151]

Virginia Democrat John W. Flannagan, Jr., rose to speak next. His remarks centered on two themes. One was that the traditional front line no longer existed. In the past it was the soldier upon whom the burden fell but Pearl Harbor had proved that, potentially at least, no place was totally safe. "The battlefield now covers not only those places where the roar of the cannon and the zooming of the plane may be heard, but every mill, factory, store, mine, field, office, and home in this Republic. Every man, whether he uses a pen or pick, hammer or plow, is now in the service."[152]

He was confident that, with the nation united, victory would ultimately come. He was equally concerned with the peace that would accompany it. It would be an uncomprising one that dug out the roots that had produced such irresponsible behavior.

> There is something wrong with a civilization that can produce leaders who, while yet professing peace and a disposition to adjust grievances, commit inhuman, stealthy, dastardly, cowardly acts, such as the Government of Japan visited upon our country on December 7, 1941. That civilization must perish. There can be no lasting peace so long as such a civilization occupies even a small part of the world.[153]

Hence "we will write into that [peace] treaty terms that will live on down through the ages to curb such a people from ever again committing stealthy, vicious, dastardly acts against a peace-loving nation."[154]

The ethical aspects of the attack (striking while still negotiating) and doing so on a day of religious observance as well, deeply stirred John S. Gibson of the all–Democrat Georgia delegation, as it had several others. This first-termer reminded his listeners of the ancient adage, "He that will live by the sword must die by the sword, and I say to the American people on this crucial day when sorrow envelops our emotional existence, that Japan and her people will pay in blood one-hundredfold for the innocent blood they stole on yesterday."[155]

Republican Earl Wilson of the Indiana delegation stressed that all the second guessing one might do was irrelevant. As the result of the attack the nation needed to heed the words of Stephen Decatur: "Our country! In her intercourse with foreign nations, may she always be in the right; but our country, right or wrong."[156]

The ultimate war goal was simple but the price might be high: "the complete destruction of her war machine. Let us hope and pray that a minimum of lives will be lost."[157]

The final speaker was Republican Chauncey W. Reed of Illinois, who stressed that by their "insidious, dishonorable, and cowardly blow directed against our fleet, our territory, and our citizens," Japan had unleashed depths of fury that would be its undoing. "Japan will rue the day that the fury of peaceful, liberty-loving people was unleashed."[158]

The Vote

At this point Congressman McCormack called for an immediate yea/nay vote on the resolution. The one open opponent of the resolution intervened:

> Miss Rankin of Montana. Mr. Speaker—
> The Speaker. The gentleman from Massachusetts demands the yeas and nays. Those who favor taking this vote by the yeas and nays will rise and remain standing until counted.
> The yeas and nays were ordered.
> Miss Rankin of Montana. Mr. Speaker, I would like to be heard.
> The Speaker. The yeas and nays have been ordered. The question is, Will the House suspend the rules and pass the resolution?
> Miss Rankin of Montana. Mr. Speaker, a point of order.
> The Speaker. A roll call may not be interrupted.[159]

The Speaker had not permitted her to delay proceedings before and was not going to now. In one sense it was an exercise of his raw power as Speaker; on the other hand viable opposition must have a core minimum of strength to resist a heavily running tide, and Rankin was standing alone.

Her isolation was reinforced by Speaker Sam Rayburn's (Democrat, Texas) whole-hearted conviction that no other choice than war was tolerable. As presiding officer and in the interest of keeping the discussion as brief as he could, there was no way he could get his own sentiments on the record that day. Speaking back in his congressional district later that month, he made those convictions clear:

> We tried to stay out of the conflict. We were loath to engage in this carnage and make of it a world war, but now we are in it because we could not, despite our best efforts, stay out of it. Therefore, there is one task which now is supreme above all others.... We must win this war in the quickest, most decisive way.
> We must do it for our own sakes. We must do it for the sake of all other peoples. We must do it for the sake of future human progress. We must

do it for the sake of unborn generations whose destiny we now are called upon to decide. On the outcome of this conflict will depend whether those unborn generations shall be born into slavery, ignorance, superstition and life-long suffering, or whether they shall be born into a world where human values, spiritual progress, cultural advancement and material comforts such as we of this generation have known may be their portion also. The destiny of humanity rests upon our efforts.[160]

With that frame of mind—and it was the overwhelming one of the day—opposition to war was now not just bad politics or bad judgment; it also represented a base betrayal of the current generation's obligations to those who would come afterwards. In other words, it was a fundamental moral issue and not only a geo-political or even geo-military one.

With Rankin's repeated efforts to delay the proceedings frustrated, the vote was now promptly taken: 388 voted in favor of immediate action on the resolution and in favor of its adoption, 41 did not vote, and one (Rankin) voted against. Miss Rankin was loudly booed for doing so.[161] Speaker Rayburn had pounded his gavel and demanded order so the vote could be completed.[162]

After permission was granted for those present to expand their on-the-floor remarks and those not present to insert their views,[163] unanimous consent was sought to introduce and adopt the Senate version of the war resolution. (Established parliamentary procedures required that the text of the resolution match in the two houses.)[164] Congressman Martin of Massachusetts inquired whether "this is the same declaration that we just passed?" He was assured it was. The measure was read the required three times and passed unanimously.[165]

At this point McCormack asked "unanimous consent that the proceedings by which the House passed House Joint Resolution 254 be vacated and that the resolution be laid on the table." This was accepted without objection.[166] By this piece of legislative legerdemain, the war resolution was adopted unanimously—that feat being obtained by the unanimous acceptance of the pro-war resolution of the Senate in place of the House's own version, with its one dissenter.

It had taken only a few minutes for the president to give his speech and 33 minutes to complete the discussion and vote in the two branches of Congress.[167] At 1:00 P.M. came the Senate adoption; that of the House, meeting independently, came 10 minutes later. At 3:15 Speaker of the House Sam Rayburn signed the measure and eight minutes later the vice president did so for the Senate, as presiding officer of that body.[168] The formal paperwork was completed and ready for the president's signature at 4:10 P.M. the same evening.[169] In contrast, in 1917 the process had taken four days between proposal and presidential signature.[170]

Presenting one of those little ironies that occur in history, the staff member of the Senate who delivered the material to the White House was the same individual who had typed the declaration of war that brought the nation into the preceding war.[171] In an informal gathering at the White House, the president quickly signed the document in the presence of key congressional leaders and a large contingent of press and photographers.[172]

The United States now legally recognized what had actually been the situation since the preceding morning—it was at war with the empire of Japan. But lawyers being lawyers even in 1941, there naturally had to be the question of when the U.S. had officially entered war: when the House approved the measure at 1:10 P.M., or when the president signed it at 4:10? "Most," the *New York Times* reported, "inclined" to the latter.[173]

Those Who Missed the Vote

As with the Senate, it was not physically possible for all to be present on short notice. Congressman John M. Costello explained his own difficulties in reaching the capital and how the journey eastward brought him and two other members together in their frantic rush to be present for the debate and historic vote:

> The speed with which this resolution was voted on, prompted by the desire of the American people to move with all possible unity and dispatch, frustrated by a few moments my opportunity to cast my vote in favor of the resolution. Had I been able to obtain transportation to Washington which would have brought me to the Capitol but a few minutes earlier, I would have voted for the resolution declaring us to be at war with Japan.
> When the news of the treacherous Japanese attack on Hawaii reached me I was in Los Angeles and immediately made arrangements to obtain a place on the first available east-bound plane. This plane, a TWA stratoliner, left Los Angeles at 6 o'clock Sunday evening and carried me to Indianapolis this morning. I then proceeded via American Airlines to Washington, reaching the Capital Airport at 1:28 Monday afternoon, five minutes ahead of the plane's regularly scheduled arrival.
> With me on the plane were my colleagues the gentleman from Pennsylvania, Congressman McArdle, and the gentleman from Kentucky, Congressman Vincent, and through the splendid cooperation of the Metropolitan police of Washington we reached the Capitol with the greatest possible haste. Our arrival proved to be mere minutes after the voting was concluded.[174]

Beverly M. Vincent had rushed back from the bedside of his sick wife in Kentucky. He elaborated on the rush of the local police to cooperate in the three men's last-minute futile rush to reach Capitol Hill

3. The House of Representatives Responds to War ...

before the vote: "We reached the airport here at 1:15 P.M., which is about twenty minutes ahead of schedule. We were met there by two motorcycle policemen, and they cleared the road of traffic and led the way to the Capitol. I want to congratulate them on the fine work they did."[175]

Vincent of course, had intended to vote in favor of the war resolution. His own role in the affair would begin the next day. "The Naval Affairs Committee meets at 10 A.M. tomorrow, and we are putting the finishing touches to some matters that I think will make our armed forces more effective."[176]

The third member of the trio who had arrived together, Joseph A. McArdle, had been on vacation at the time of the attack. "Being assured by the leadership of the House that there was no important legislation coming up, I decided to take a few days' rest. I went to Florida. It was not until late Sunday that I learned of the unwarranted attack on our ships and shore stations by Japan. As quick as I could arrange transportation I left for Washington," though he arrived back immediately after the vote was taken. He also strongly favored the resolution.[177]

Costello had found a means to get back to the House on the vote day, though on Sunday he had been as far away as California. Some others did not make the effort due to the distance and difficulty in making the necessary connections in the limited time available. John R. Murdock (Democrat, Arizona) was in San Francisco and contented himself with a telegram supporting the war resolution while he remained on the West Coast for "public lands hearings with an official congressional committee."[178]

Congressman Clyde T. Ellis (Democrat, Arkansas) was unable to get back due to civilian aviation being curtailed in wake of the crisis, but was amazed at how fast Congress had moved:

> I missed the vote today against Japan. Yesterday afternoon I left Washington and drove straight through to Knoxville, Tennessee, arriving there at 2:30 this morning without knowing that the Speaker had requested that all Members return immediately. At 7:10 this morning I heard the announcement and began at once a frantic effort to find airplane transportation.
> After calling Speaker Rayburn twice from Knoxville I chartered a plane but could not get it off the ground because of Civil Aeronautics Authority orders to ground all civilian pilots. At 10:05 we got clearance, and although we made it in less than three hours the vote on the declaration of war against Japan was completed before I could get to the House Chamber. That is how fast democracy works once it is severely shaken.[179]

Others who arrived in time did so only with luck and good fortune and a little strong-arming of politically less well-placed individuals. Margaret Truman tells the story of how her father, Senator Harry S Truman (Democrat, Missouri) raced to make it back:

Out in the Pennant Hotel in Columbia, Missouri, Dad put on his clothes and raced across the road to a private airport, where he begged the owner to get him to St. Louis as fast as possible. They flew in a small plane, and he arrived just in time to catch a night flight to Washington. It was quite a trip. Every time the plane landed, another congressman or a senator got on. Ordinary citizens were ruthlessly ejected and pretty soon the plane was a congressional special. They arrived in Washington around dawn. With no sleep, Dad rushed to the Capital.[180]

At least one person who did make it in time to vote had fallen into a new trap created by wartime conditions: He had not taken into consideration the tight security cordon in the area when deciding when to leave for the day's session. Francis E. Walter (Democrat, Pennsylvania) apologized to the Speaker of the House for his delay: "due to the fact that a cordon of police and soldiers was thrown around the Capitol Grounds, thereby preventing the taxicab in which I was riding to come within several squares of the House."[181]

Whether the missing ever provided a formal explanation for their absence or not, sentiment was so passionately anti–Japan that their presence would simply have increased the size of the majority.[182] Indeed all of the absentees in both House and Senate issued statements—either directly or through their congressional associates—expressing that they would have joint in the affirmative in voting on behalf of war.[183]

If some had been unable to be present, others came in at the cost of great personal physical discomfort. Mary Norton (Democrat, New Jersey) had been laid low with a bronchial infection for weeks. Over on the Senate side, Clyde M. Reed (Republican, Kansas) had been out for months but managed to make it in for the vote. Senator Robert F. Wagner (Democrat, New York) had been out for almost a year, but he also attended.[184]

The Lone Dissenter

As the one vote against war, Jeannette Rankin deserves special analysis.[185] A graduate of the University of Montana (1902), she did advanced studies in social work in New York City. After a brief career as social worker she became a forceful public advocate of women's suffrage, first in Washington State (1910), then California (1911), and then back in her home state of Montana as well. In February, 1910, she was extended the privilege of addressing Montana's House of Representatives on the issue. She was treated well and received flowers, but the members refused to move beyond acts of courtesy. Persistent lobbying finally paid off and the franchise was granted to women in 1914.

She cast her first vote two years later—for herself as a member of Congress—at a time when women did not yet have the Constitutionally granted right to vote on the national level. From one standpoint this was an extraordinary success for a first-time political candidate. From another, the timing would ultimately destroy her chance of becoming a successful long-term politician.

When election day 1916 rolled around, the issue of the European War was receiving increasing attention. But the growing pro-war movement had modest impact in Montana. Rankins stance as a Republican progressive struck a chord in the voting population. Voting rights for women, federally mandated child protection legislation, and prohibition were all aspects in that agenda. Ironically enough, later generations would tend to look upon national prohibition as an incredibly horrendous mistake; before its enactment, however, there was widespread support for it as a tool for general societal betterment.

There was no secret that Rankin was a dedicated pacifist. What no one could have predicted was that this minority view would become pivotal in her success or failure in the national legislature, for no sooner did the new session begin (March 4, 1917–March 3, 1919) than she found herself in the middle of the bitter dispute about whether to declare war on Germany.

She was the recipient of widespread pressure to join the pro-war movement. Most importantly this pressure came from friends and relatives. Her own brother—her most trusted political adviser—counseled a war vote. Many suffragists feared that the appearance of weakness on national defense would be used as a tool to prove that women were too emotionally irresponsible to be trusted with the franchise.

The sentiment in Congress was strongly pro-war when the issue came to a head, but the passions were intense and the anti-involvement members were determined to be heard. It took 14 hours of debate for everyone to have his or her say. Although she abstained from participation, Rankin succinctly summed up her feeling upon the roll-call: "I want to stand by my country, but I cannot vote for war. I vote no."[186] She joined 49 male members in that stance. They formed a distinct minority but still a significant bloc. In the Senate the vote had been 82 to 6.[187]

The vote was a bitterly controversial. Many suffragists disowned Rankin: Several groups informed her that they were canceling their arrangements to have her come to speak.[188] The press considered her contemptible rather than courageous. The Helena Montana *Independent Record* rebuked her as "a dagger in the hands of the German propagandists, a dupe of the Kaiser, a member of the Hun army in the United States, and a crying schoolgirl."[189] If one rejects her pacifism one might better consider her a dupe of an absolutist ideological pacifism—for that is what her actions grew out of. German duplicity certainly played no role in it, and the crack about "a crying shoolgirl" would have been considered hitting beneath the belt if she had been a male.

Her feminist agenda payed a price as well as her popularity. Although Rankin helped steer a Constitutional amendment granting female suffrage through the House, the Senate voted it down.[190] Since such an amendment passed the Senate soon after she left Congress, in 1919, it would be hard not to suspect that a number of Senators had made the fatal mental correlation of women's suffrage with the anti-war sentiments of its only nationally elected spokeswoman.

She backed off running for re-election. Seemingly confident that her position had greater support than many suspected, she made a bid for the Republican nomination for senator in 1918, but was unable to obtain it. Failing to gain a senatorial nomination by conventional means, she ran as an independent but with equal lack of success.

Returning to private life, she bided her time and allowed the vigorous pro-war sentiments of the war years to calm down and be replaced by the equally strong anti-war sentiments that became commonplace afterwards: Had not the British deceived us into the war? What did we get out of it but thousands of casualties and a large national debt? When the Depression hit—and stayed and stayed—there was a widespread feeling that it was even a greater reason to concentrate on the national business of recovery than becoming involved in potentially lethal foreign affairs with foreign powers apparently ungrateful and deceitful.

In spite of this sea change in public sentiment, Rankin stayed out of elective politics until she ran for the 77th Congress, which took office in January 1941. Since two decades had passed, with Rankin living in Georgia in the interim, she decided to begin her campaign a year before the election so she could take her message far and wide throughout Montana. A literally new generation needed to become acquainted with her.[191]

Twenty some years before, her pacifism had been peripheral to her campaign. This time it became a central tenet. In the many schools she spoke before, she repeatedly urged the young boys and girls to urge their parents to oppose American intervention in the new European war between Germany and the British.[192] This strategy of appearing at every high school within her congressional district was her campaign until she received the Republican nomination.[193]

Rankin's anti-war sentiments were repeatedly manifested in office. Time and again she pushed for legislation and resolutions that would severely limit the president's power to unilaterally involve the United States in Europe. Legislation that would mandate explicit congressional endorsement for American troops being sent out of the Western Hemisphere was high on her priority list.[194]

In addition to her efforts to derail consideration of the war measure on December 8th, Rankin's only direct espousal of her sentiments came when her name was reached on the roll call. Perhaps because it was part of her response to the request for a yea/nay vote (and not a part of the formal debate), it was not entered into the Congressional Record: "As a woman, I can't go to war and I refuse to send anyone else."[195] (Alternatively, perhaps someone of importance thought the remark cast her into an even worse light than her opposition to the conflict and managed to have the remark suppressed for that reason.)

The locating of the words as during the session may well be a piece of pious myth, however, utilizing a genuine quote but misplacing the place of delivery. The next day's newspapers reported her as explaining her vote off the House floor later in the day: "The situation looks the same to me today as it did in 1917. As a woman I cannot go to war and I refuse to send anybody else. I voted my convictions."[196]

Once again foreign affairs doomed Rankin to be a one-termer. Her decision to oppose involvement in a war in which—profoundly unlike the First World War—American territory and American citizens had been consciously, knowingly, intentionally, and with clear premeditation struck down doomed her to that ghetto of marginalized peace-advocate purists. Faced with the reality of the situation, she did not seek re-election, but retired to private life while remaining involved in the peace and women's rights movements for the remainder of her life.

That day in Congress was one of intense emotion for one and all. In 1917 there was plenty on both sides of the issue. At the time of her earlier vote, there had been dozens who joined her in opposition. This time Rankin was standing stark naked—alone and with no one willing to express agreement. Psychologically and politically this would have intensified the pain in making what was the lone dissent against the majority consensus.

Arriving back in Washington by train before the vote, she drove around Washington—alone.[197] Being determined not to be influenced by others (nor to make them feel embarrassed by their failure to change her mind), she carefully avoided all contact with her supporters and friends that morning.[198] Presumably to make sure that her futile objections would be heard by the Speaker (see above), she sat on the front row of the Republican contingent as members of both House and Senate crammed into the space normally occupied only by the House.[199]

What she heard as she voted "no" did not help her state of mind: an abundant array of boos and hisses. Some came from the galleries where the public watched; others from fellow members of Congress.[200] Both during the preliminary discussions and while the vote was still being taken, Congressman Everett Dirksen and several others tried to persuade her to vote in favor of the action, and after the vote had been cast, to reverse her position while there was still time before the tally was complete. She wouldn't change for them either.[201]

One Congressman reminded her, "They really did bomb Pearl Harbor." Her response was, "That makes no difference; killing more people won't help matters."[202]

Representative Harold Knutson (Republican, Minnesota) was a long-time friend of hers and had joined her in an anti-war vote back in 1917. He came by her seat several times attempting to persuade her to vote in favor of war this time around. She refused his pleas.[203] Both Representative Henry C. Dworshak (Republican, Idaho) and James F. O'Connor (Democrat, from Rankin's own state of Montana) also intervened unsuccessfully.[204] Samuel W. King of Hawaii came by her desk and similarly unsuccessfully pled for her support for the war.[205]

Everett Dirksen pleaded, "Does it [the negative vote] have to be?" "Yes," she insisted.[206] Dirksen later wrote in his autobiography of how he had unofficially been appointed the representative of the other members to intervene with her:

> That one negative vote in the House carries with it its own little story. Fast and furious as the action was, the word got out almost immediately that there might be a vote against the resolution and it could possibly be Jeannette Rankin, who had been elected to the Congress from Montana. I knew her very well. She was a sweet, charming person and had deep and settled convictions on the subject of war.
> House leaders knew that Jeannette Rankin and I met and consulted very frequently on many legislative matters, and they therefore felt that perhaps I might be able to dissuade her from casting the lone negative vote. I sat with her in the chamber and told her how important it was to manifest to all the world that the Congress and the people were united and unanimous as never before in meeting the challenge which the Japanese assault had laid on our doorstep.
> After I had exhausted every argument which I thought might be persuasive, she said, "Everett, I cannot do it. I cannot vote for a declaration of war. For my whole lifetime I have been dedicated to the cause of peace. War can only mean death for many young men of this nation, and I cannot subject them to this horror. My heart, my conscience, my conviction, compel me to vote no. I am sorry."
> And so the roll was intoned and there was the one dissenting vote by Congresswoman Rankin of Montana.[207]

In light of heightened public passions, Rankin prudently sought—and received—a police escort from the premises.[208] With so much anger aimed her way, she quickly released a statement explaining her action. As William "Fishbait" Miller—long-term doorkeeper for the House—later recalled,

I couldn't believe my ears. It was that, first of all, the stories about what had gone on in Pearl Harbor were only radio stories as yet. And though they were probably true, one should still wait for "more authentic evidence" than radio reports. And second, that "sending our boys to the Orient will not protect this country." She said that sending our men there was not under the heading of "protecting our shores"—and protecting our own shores was the only reason for fighting.[209]

Just as in 1917, Rankin's vote against war in 1941 was equally vividly and vehemently impugned. During Roosevelt's war speech, she sat quietly in her seat and never stood nor gave any applause.[210] The picture of a congresswoman so passively, tranquilly, and (seemingly) without anger accepting the deaths of thousands of American fighting men and sailors was not one fitting the public perception of the horror of the events. Her negative vote made a firestorm of protest inevitable.

Fellow Republican Dan Whetstone, a member of the National Republican Committee, began to receive indignant protests from party members across the state. Echoing their resentment, he promptly telegraphed Rankin, "Messages from all parts of Montana indicate disappointment over your attitude in failing to support the war declaration. I urge and beseech you to redeem Montana's honor and loyalty and change your vote as early as possible."[211] Changing the vote was impossible since it had already become part of the permanent record; recanting the vote was impossible on a moral level, as well—at least so far as Rankin's perspective went.

Few Americans were willing to concede anything positive about her action. The editorialist for Virginia' *Richmond Times Dispatch* was one of that small minority. He rooted his generosity in the fact that her action was, essentially, irrelevant, "Miss Jeannette Rankin, a conscientious pacifist, is entitled to her convictions with respect to armed conflict, and is not properly subject to severe condemnation, despite what we believe to be her utter wrong-headedness, in voting 'no.' As hers was the only negative vote, the country's unanimity was hardly less than astounding."[212]

As the weeks passed after Pearl Harbor, Rankin became deeply suspicious of the events that lay behind the attack, and that suspicion evolved into an outrage at the president. Before long she was making it known that she believed that Roosevelt had intentionally set out to provoke the Pearl Harbor attack as a means of getting the United States into the war. It was a message she repeatedly conveyed to all who were willing to listen.[213] The evidence? First FDR's ignoring of the requirements of the Neutrality Act of 1936 in regard to Japan, and then his ultimately swinging to the opposite extreme of banning all exports to that country, a step that did tremendous damage to its civilian economy.[214]

In remarks a year later that were designed for the *Congressional Record* of December 8, 1942, Rankin discussed at length her explanation for what had happened. She said that American publications had noted the need for American assistance in maintaining Britain's Far Eastern Empire. She quoted from a British volume on propaganda written between the wars, which had spoken of the difficulty of embroiling the U.S. in any future conflict. It suggested that the best means of doing so would be through a war with Japan.

Acting on that assumption, Churchill persuaded Roosevelt at the August 1941 Atlantic Conference to adopt a maximally provocative anti–Japanese foreign policy. The powerful and stringent economic embargo was soon imposed. Roosevelt "changed his policy" of permitting large exports "and cut off not only war supplies but virtually everything required by the civilian population as well." All that remained was a military incident to justify formal intervention—and Pearl Harbor delivered that.[215]

Rankin concluded,

> A year ago, one of my congressional colleagues, having observed for months the adroitness with which President Roosevelt had brought us ever closer to the brink of war in the Atlantic only to be continually frustrated in the final step by a reluctant Congress, seeing fate present the President on December 7, 1941, with a *casus belli* beyond all criticism—exclaimed in despair: "What luck that man has!"[216]

The denunciation went totally unnoticed by fellow politicians, by the press, and by the public at large. It was all "just ignored," Rankin later lamented.[217] Soon, she too, would become ignored. Principled stand or foolhardy—wise or obsessed by a thoroughly misguided and unrealistic idealism—call it what one will, Rankin paid the price by becoming, once again, a one-term congresswoman.

4

Germany and Italy Join the War

By not seeking a declaration of war against Germany, President Roosevelt put the decision squarely in the hands of the Germans. This was both good politics (avoiding inflaming the isolationists) and avoided a controversy over the best military tactics (should the U.S. risk a two-front war after taking such a beating at Pearl Harbor?) Yet that did not preclude him and others from doing everything they could to encourage Americans to come to terms with the ultimate need for such an intervention.

Cultivating Public Opinion for a War with Germany

In addition to the numerous congressmen and senators and editorial opinion that viewed Germany as threat equal to or greater than Japan, the syndicated columnists of the day were generally of the same opinion, and their views inevitably shaped those of much of the reading public.

David Lawrence began his column for the day after the attack with the assertion, "Hitler—not just Japan—has attacked the United States. Using the militarists of Japan as his cat's-paw, he has thwarted the liberals, moderates and peace-loving elements of Japan. The war which for many years has been thought inevitable by many Americans, especially in the army and navy, is here at last."[1]

Westbrook Pegler spoke of how "Hitler made the war and Japanese struck our country a sneak punch on a quiet Sunday morning while the envoys of Japan were sucking wind and grinning peaceful remarks to our Secretary of State. This is going to be, as it has been up to now, an utterly ruthless, dirty war, thanks to Adolf Hitler, and the amenities of civilization are going to be waived."[2]

Those avoiding attributing a direct responsibility to Hitler for the Hawaiian assault generally still viewed him as a foe that had to be dealt with. Walter Lippmann, for example, stressed that unless Hitler was defeated as well as Japan it would be but a short term victory. Indeed, a Japan-only strategy "would be for us the certain road to defeat.... No victory we can win in the Pacific could give us security if we had then to turn around and face Hitler victorious in Europe and Africa and in the Atlantic."[3]

With those nay-saying the connection being few in any area of American government, press, or population, this consensus could easily lead to the deduction that war with Germany had to be a matter of "when" and no longer "whether."

Anti-interventionists were quite concerned with this perception and the fact that any Japanese war could extremely easily bring in their German allies as well. Senator Hiram Johnson (Republican, California) was senior minority party member of the Senate Foreign Relations Committee. In a show of both courtesy and good politics, he was invited to the meeting at the White House of key political leaders the night of the attack.[4] Johnson believed that the "worst part of this Japanese war" was this very fact that it could "very easily" propel Americans into the European conflict as well.[5]

Senator Robert R. Reynolds (Democrat, North Carolina), who was not friendly to such an involvement, was important because of his role as Senate Military Affairs Committee Chairman. Yet even he felt compelled to speak not of the desirability of a two-front war but, rather, of its apparent inescapability. "This probably means war in both oceans. If and when we begin active participation in a shooting war, of course, that is good news to the British."[6]

Some interventionists came out and directly advocated such a policy. Senator Claude Pepper (Democrat, Florida) had been a major figure in the pro–European war movement and told the press on the 7th that "not later than tomorrow" the U.S. should declare war "upon the whole Axis band of conspirators" and not on Japan alone.[7]

Over-all, anti-war senators were conspicuously noticeable for their silence on the matter, and were keeping all options open.[8]

Norman Thomas, the frequent Socialist candidate for president, was one of the few men of any ideological stripe to make a distinction explicitly and publicly between the two areas of conflict. In a Baltimore rally on the 9th he called for a minimalization of American participation. In this light he was "pleased" that the president had not called for a declaration against the Germans and Italians as well as the Japanese. "Insofar as it is possible to control, I believe that the smaller the area of American troops the better. I hope they are not to be involved in expeditionary forces in either Asia, Europe or Africa."[9]

Even so far as Japan itself, Thomas insisted that her actions had to be put in historical perspective. "The act of Japan in attacking us while her ministers were still negotiating peace in Washington was an act of premeditated treachery, but let us not be such complete Pharisees as to believe it has no antecedents. Japan, awakened from the sleep of centuries by the United States, acquired technology and imperialist aims from its teachers of the West."[10]

Hence "we must win the peace as well as the war."[11] For this reason Thomas proposed a negotiated peace that would include a rejection of imperialist goals in the Far East and intervention with the British and the Dutch to encourage them to follow the same course.[12] His was a rare voice indeed. Neither negotiation nor the ethics of imperialism was on the minds of most Americans. To them victory was the sole question, and the thought of negotiating anything short of total capitulation was guaranteed to inflame their sense of justice and the need for bloody revenge for what had happened.

Priorities in Case of a Two Ocean War

Even if a European war occurred, it did not guarantee *which* theater of conflict would have the priority. As early as January, 1941, secret discussions with the British had agreed that if the U.S.A. became involved, the priority would be defeating the Germans.[13] After the severity of the Pearl Harbor assault, the British were deeply concerned that this policy would be reversed, and it was with considerable relief that they discovered it would not be.[14]

On the other hand, former isolationists usually reversed these preferences: The Asian war was uniquely ours (we were thrust into it by direct enemy military action), but the European conflict was primarily a British concern into which we had been drawn by a combination of presidential predilection, British pressure and propaganda, and, ultimately Hitlerian miscalculation in declaring war.[15]

Even some interventionists—working on the assumption that the Pacific War could be completed relatively quickly—believed that priority had to be put upon Japan. William Randolph Heart editorialized on this theme in his traditional front page location in the *New York Journal-American*:

The worst thing about the war with Japan is that it will divide our efforts and prevent us from rendering the all-out aid to England that we were doing and planning further to do. But we will still manage to keep Britain going with our right hand while we poke Japan in the nose with our left.... The European war, to be frank and factual, is not going to be so easy [as the one with Japan, but we can win it and will. We will do our best to help England now, and after we have washed up Japan we can concentrate on Europe and straighten things out there.[16]

Roosevelt's Policy of Letting Germany Make the Choice for Him

In the short term, however, the question was still whether the U.S. would enter the European War. Whether those traditionally opposed to entering it would roll over and agree was far from certain. The America First headquarters issued a statement in the evening of the day of the attack specifying that the organization would give full and total support to the war against Japan. Conspicuously missing was any reference to supporting a war in Europe. They had left the door open for a decision to move in either direction on that matter.[17]

If push came to shove, in light of the group's past record, it would almost certainly have been against intervention. Although it had always been opposed to a war in the Pacific, that concern had always been secondary on its agenda.[18] On August 11, 1941, its executive committee had passed a resolution opposing war with both Germany and Japan, and insisting that if attacked by either it was essential, militarily, for the U.S. to avoid a two-front war: "Involvement in war on the Atlantic would make more difficult adequate defense on the Pacific. Involvement in war on the Pacific would make more difficult adequate defense on the Atlantic."[19]

Roosevelt and his advisers were well aware of how tenuous previous victories had been—sometimes they had been by a modest margin and other times by a paper-thin one. And these were for steps short of war.[20] Congressional leaders advised the president that there was major opposition to entering voluntarily a war with Germany when we already had one on our hands with Japan.[21] Contemporary press reporters also believed that the request for such an action would prove controversial and the result far from assured.[22]

The past political history of the bitter and divisive intervention debates makes T. R. Fehrenbach's judgment quite sound: "There would have been lengthy debate, most probably a filibuster in the Senate by Wheeler and his cohorts, and the resulting controversy and bitterness would have kept the nation divided even in the event of an enemy attack."[23]

4. Germany and Italy Join the War

Thus a military tragedy (Pearl Harbor) could have been easily transformed into a political one as well, with the nation's politicians and people at each other's throats when unity was imperative. Furthermore, there seemed no need for such a risky step as seeking a two-front war resolution. There was the widespread assumption that the Tripartite Pact among the Axis powers required German intervention.[24] Whether it actually did or not, many were convinced that Hitler's pride and arrogance would drive him to such a step.

At the night meeting of the cabinet on December 7th Secretary of War Henry L. Stimson urged Roosevelt that he ride the tide of war emotion and request congressional action against Germany: "I pointed out that we knew ... that Germany had pushed Japan into this and that we should ask for a declaration of war against Germany also."[25] No one else in the cabinet supported the proposal.[26] Cordell Hull noted in his diary that there was a consensus that there would be war on that front without the U.S. taking the initiative:

> There was some discussion of whether we should declare war on the other members of the Axis. We assumed, however, that it was inevitable that Germany would declare war on us. The intercepted Japanese messages passing back and forth between Berlin and Tokyo had given us the understanding that there was a definite undertaking on this point between the two Governments. We therefore decided to wait and let Hitler and Mussolini issue their declarations first. Meanwhile we would take no chances and would act, for example in the Atlantic, on the assumption that we were at war with the European section of the Axis as well.[27]

The president himself was among those who wanted to wait.[28] Roosevelt told the meeting that he was going to delay two days before tackling the matter,[29] probably implying that he thought the Germans would solve the problem for him by then. At the very least, the delay would imply that it would give time to assure that the wisest decision would be made.

At the following meeting of key political leaders that evening (for which the cabinet remained), the president speculated that a German declaration might occur even before he delivered his message to Congress concerning Japan initiating war.[30] Some of those attending speculated to the press that a declaration against Germany might be sought because everyone was convinced that Japan was acting as the agent of Germany in the assault.[31] If so, Germany's prompt intervention would be quite natural. The next day, as he proceeded through the day's business and prepared for his fireside chat with the nation that evening, the president still believed that a German announcement could come at any hour—as did other members of his staff.[32]

Even if it did not occur, the recurring military tensions in the Atlantic created the high probability of an open breach on that front. The only question in that approach was when it would happen.

State and Federal Officials Join In to Feed the Fire of Indignation at Germany

The afternoon of the attack, boisterous Mayor Fiorello H. LaGuardia went on WNYC radio to charge that the attack had been "master-minded by the thugs and gangsters who control the Nazi Government."[33] That evening Donald M. Nelson, who was the director of the Supply, Priorities and Allocations Board, spoke on an already-scheduled MBS (Mutual Broadcast System) war preparation program. He promptly added to his planned remarks the accusation that the Far Eastern attack had been "directed primarily from Berlin.... All important elements of the Axis are now in action—direct military action—against the United States."[34]

Not only did individual officials and spokesmen come out in damning Germany as (in some critical fashion) the cause of the Japanese attack, the government itself was not above a little official verbal eye-poking to convey its hostility to the German regime. The day after the attack, the 8th, the president released a statement stressing that the Germans had encouraged the conflict as a means of diverting attention from the European War:

> the German intention was to divert American resources into the Pacific War and thereby bringing to an end the lend-lease program that was doing so much to enable the British to continue their fight. The Germans were so certain that this would be the result that they repeatedly asserted it in both radio and printed propaganda. The fact that the aid was continuing exposed the propaganda as false and based on a misleading premise as to what would occur as the result of American involvement in the Pacific.[35]

An official German spokesman, speaking on what a later generation would call a not-for-attribution basis, dismissed these American accusations: "Nothing can change the fact that there is only one aggressor in the world—namely, Franklin D. Roosevelt."[36]

Others in the administration more openly stoked the verbal coals of war. Breckinridge Long, who served as assistant secretary of state, spoke before the American Farm Bureau Federation in Chicago on the 9th. He urged his audience not to become so preoccupied with the Pacific that it as diverted from the danger in Europe. "For Germany, in the very heart of Europe, is under the absolute rule of ruthless and ambitious men who live for war, have prepared for war, and finally forced war upon that continent."[37]

But how was that the affair of the U.S.? Because the Nazi regime was determined to cripple American aid to Britain and to intervene in the Western Hemisphere as well. "Hitler intends to prevent supplies from reaching the British Isles and thus make easier an invasion of England. He intends to intimidate us into a retreat from the high seas and ... blast a way for himself toward the conquest of the Western Hemisphere."[38]

Roosevelt Rhetorically Roasts Germany at Press Conferences and in a Major Radio Address

At a press conference in the Oval Office on the 9th, Roosevelt renewed the verbal censure. After stressing that bad news continued to come in, that the casualty lists were going to be large for the first days of the war, and that the war would be a long one, he turned his attention to the European situation. He noted that both Germany and Italy "consider themselves at war with the United States at this moment just as much as they consider themselves at war with Britain or Russia"[39]— a misrepresentation of those governments' official positions but a very realistic one as to their actual hostile sentiments. Germany had been promising, Roosevelt insisted, that if Japan came into the war it would gain "complete and perpetual control of the whole Pacific area."[40]

The Far Eastern and European wars were thus irretrievably linked. Whatever worked to the advantage of Japan inevitably assisted the German war effort and vice versa,

> That is their simple and obvious grand strategy. And that is why the American people must realize that it can be matched only with similar grand strategy. We must realize for example that Japanese successes against the United States in the Pacific are helpful to German operations in Libya; that any German success against the Caucasus is inevitably an assistance to Japan in her operations against the Dutch East Indies; that a German attack against Algiers or Morocco opens the way to a Japanese attack against South America, and the [Panama] Canal....[41]

Implicit is the theme that though no one had declared open war between the U.S. and the German-Italian alliance, such war—to all practical purposes—already existed. If such remarks encouraged making it official, that took the pressure off Roosevelt; if it didn't, it conceptually helped shape American opinion if he eventually had to risk taking the initiative.

The latter was one of the key objectives of the speech he gave later that evening of the 9th, one that went through five drafts in order to polish its thrust and argument.[42] (Domestically, the audience was estimated in the range of 80 million.[43] The speech was translated and broadcast by shortwave in a dozen languages.[44]) In it Roosevelt added further pressure on American (and potentially German) political opinion by linking Germany, Italy, and Japan into an alignment that was clearly manifesting certain attitudes and actions: "The course that Japan has followed for the past ten years in Asia has paralleled the course of Hitler and Mussolini in Europe and in Africa. Today, it has become far more than a parallel. It is collaboration, actual collaboration, so well calculated that all the continents of the world, and all the oceans, are now considered by the Axis strategists as one gigantic battlefield."[45]

The evidence for this accusation? At length Roosevelt pointed out the many cases when the two European powers had started a war "without warning. And now Japan has attacked Malaya and Thailand—and the United States—without warning."[46]

Much later in his speech he returned to this theme that the three Axis powers were acting in concert and that Germany was playing the dominant role:

> Your government knows that for weeks Germany has been telling Japan that if Japan did not attack the United States, Japan would not share in dividing the spoils with Germany when peace came. She was promised by Germany that if she came in she would receive the complete and perpetual control of the whole of the Pacific area—and that means not only the Far East, but also all of the islands in the Pacific, and also a stranglehold on the west coast of North and Central and South America.
>
> We know also that Germany and Japan are conducting their military and naval operations in accordance with a joint plan. That plan considers all peoples and nations which are not helping the Axis powers as common enemies of each and every one of the Axis powers.
>
> That is their simple and obvious grand strategy. That is why the American people must realize that it can be matched only with similar grand strategy....
>
> Remember always that Germany and Italy, regardless of any formal declaration of war, consider themselves at war with the United States at this moment just as much as they consider themselves at war with Britain or Russia. And Germany puts all the other Republics of the Americas into the same category of enemies....
>
> We expect to eliminate the danger from Japan, but it would serve us ill if we accomplished that and found the rest of the world was dominated by Hitler and Mussolini.[47]

When telegrams and letters began to arrive the next day, along with commentaries carried on the radio networks and editorials that appeared in the newspapers, it seemed clear to Roosevelt that a vast number of

Americans shared his conceptual linking of the Japanese with the Germans as all part of a joint world war.[48]

On the congressional level, some thought that the president was only stating the obvious. As Speaker of the House Sam Rayburn worded it, "Of course we all think that Germany and Italy are going to follow the Japanese as brothers in this Axis agreement."[49] Only a few openly stressed that American action hadn't improved the situation. Veteran critic Congressman Hamilton Fish reminded those who would listen, "Naturally, they've considered us their enemy ever since we passed the lend-lease bill and supplied arms to Britain and Russia. What I am interested in is whether we're going to have a war resolution against them."[50] That overt a step the president still carefully avoided.

On the other hand, the president was willing to keep the rhetorical fires burning and take limited actions to back them up. In a proclamation signed on the 8th but not released to the public until the following day, he authorized severe actions to be taken to limit the normal civil rights of German, Italian, and Japanese foreign nationals residing in the United States. Japanese restrictions were justified on the grounds that aggression had occurred.

Of Germany and Italy the document bluntly asserted, "An invasion or predatory incursion is threatened upon the territory of the United States."[51] Individuals owing loyalty to those nations would be more tightly restricted than native-born Americans.[52] This was also a way of signaling to Germany and Italy what the U.S. thought was going on. The cynic might even say it was an open invitation to declare war, though in the context of the time it was also certainly a reasonable evaluation of the probability of conflict as well.

Furthering the mind frame of the inevitability of war was Secretary Cordell Hull in his press conference of Tuesday the 9th. He spoke vaguely of how the U.S. was receiving unofficial reports of likely German intervention in the conflict. He urged Americans to be aware of that strong possibility so that it would not take anyone unprepared.[53]

The Japanese, of course, were also doing their part in encouraging German intervention as well. Tokyo spokesmen were heard by foreign radio monitors to say, "We have asked Germany to declare war on America."[54] Another reported to his countrymen, "We naturally expected Germany to declare war upon the United States."[55]

The Quick Shift in American Opinion

While all this was going on, American opinion was quietly fermenting, and those who had once vehemently opposed a European war were coming to realize that events had created a dynamic of their own and that it seemingly led—inevitably—toward intervention. After the declarations of war were adopted against Germany and Italy, the anti-war *Chicago Tribune* editorially referred to the shift in attitude that both it and others had observed in the preceding several days:

> Germany and Italy apparently found that their last reason for maintaining the pretext of non-belligerent relations with the United States disappeared with the attack upon Hawaii. America, then, could be given a war on two fronts. Our European enemies accepted the fact and declared the reality. They may have only anticipated action in Congress, where there was a growing sentiment for dismissing the fiction that we were not at war and by appropriate action conceding that we were.[56]

Only a few days had passed, but they were precious days necessary to permit, psychologically, those who once were vehement opponents of European war to become reconciled with the inevitable. Thanks to the delay, American unity could be preserved even when faced with the vast difficulty and complications of a two-front war.

The Tripartite Pact Background

Although the speculation was widespread that Germany lay behind the Japanese attack and would automatically feel obligated to come to the assistance of her ally, both the Tripartite Pact, which established the Rome-Berlin-Tokyo axis, and recent history made it more ambiguous.

The pact itself clearly mentioned only those situations when a member of the pact had been attacked by an outsider rather than the current situation in which a member had initiated the war. Furthermore, the events of recent history also justified a refusal to enter the fray. When Germany had launched her assault on the Soviet Union (an analogous situation in which an Axis partner had taken the initiative), Japan had declined to consider the pact as requiring her intervention.[57] In refusing to become immediately involved in a war with the U.S., Germany would be taking the same position.

On the other hand, German Foreign Minister von Ribbentrop readily conceded after the war that he had repeatedly tried to drag Japan into the war after Britain refused to concede defeat in the West:

> At the time I tried to induce Japan to attack Singapore, because it was impossible to make peace with England and I did not know what military measures we could take to achieve this end. In any case, the Fuhrer directed me to do everything I could in the diplomatic field to weaken England's position and thus achieve peace. We believed that this could

4. Germany and Italy Join the War

best be done through an attack by Japan on England's strong position in East Asia. For that reason I tried to induce Japan, at that time, to attack Singapore.[58]

Yet even here war with Britain was the issue, not war with the United States.

Herr von Erdmannsdorff served as special intermediary for the government at the Japanese Embassy in Berlin. There he constantly suggested various options and advantages for Japan in beginning a war against British possessions in the Far East.[59] One possibility that had been discussed by the Japanese, he informed his superiors, was that if such a war occurred that it would involve a pledge not to invade the Philippines—an obvious effort to minimize the danger of U.S. intervention.[60]

Due to the failure of such earlier efforts to expand the war, it is not surprising that von Ribbentrop was taken aback when Japan, unexpectedly and without notice to Germany, chose not simply to launch a war, but to do so not against the British (which the Germans desired) but against the Americans, whom Germany preferred to keep on the sidelines.[61]

Yet Germany had received hints that something serious might be brewing. Von Ribbentrop was requested by Japan on November 18 to agree to a treaty stating that neither nation would sign a peace treaty with any mutual enemy unless both agreed to it. Who the enemy was had been left ambiguous.[62] With the Germans' interest centering on Great Britain, that surely seemed to them the most natural (or, at least, self-serving) interpretation.

On November 20th, Japanese General Okamoto discussed with the German ambassador to Tokyo whether Germany would provide support in a war that Japan initiated. The ambassador cited Ribbentrop's commitment of two days earlier ruling out peace except by mutual agreement.[63]

The ambassador did his best to discourage any temptation to include the United States in any such commitment. He noted "that in view of American weakness, a hesitant attitude would be initially possible and suitable, in order to drive the U.S. to a decision, difficult from the domestic political standpoint, on entry into the war."[64] In other words it might be best to delay German entry in order to escalate America's internal political divisions.

A few days later, on the 25th, the 1936 Anti-Comintern Pact was formally renewed in Berlin with attendant publicity and mutual congratulations. Eight new countries were added to the alliance.[65] The official theme was that the renewal and expansion of membership proved the evolution of a new Europe in which national self-interests and regional mutual interests would both receive their just due. The underlying subtheme of meetings and rhetoric, however, was clearly that Europe now had a new master—Germany. As Italian Foreign Minister Galeazzo Ciano wrote at the time, "The Germans were masters of the house and they made us all feel it, even if they were especially polite to us [Italians]...."[66]

In the celebratory mood of the moment, von Ribbentrop made a commitment to Japanese Ambassador Oshima Hiroshi that seemed to undermine the German policy of avoiding a war with America—an alteration that had been neither discussed internally within his foreign office nor presented as the result of an ordered policy change coming from Hitler himself.[67] The Japanese relayed the statement to Tokyo,

> We have received advice to the effect that there is practically no hope of the Japanese-U.S. negotiations being concluded successfully, because of the fact that the United States is putting up a stiff front. If this is indeed the fact of the case, and if Japan reaches a decision to fight Britain *and the United States*, I am confident that that will not only be to the interest of *Germany and Japan jointly*, but would bring about favorable results for Japan herself [emphasis added].[68]

To make sure he had not misunderstood, Ambassador Oshima inquired whether this meant that Germany would actively enter such a war. This time von Ribbentrop became more evasive: "Roosevelt is a fanatic, so it is impossible to tell what he would do" if the Japanese launched such an attack.[69] After the war, von Ribbentrop found it impossible to believe that he had said the things he did even when presented with a transcript. In one sense this may have been self-serving.[70] On the other hand, as H. L. Trefousse suggests, the full significance of what he had said may simply not sunk have in at the time.[71] It would certainly not be the first nor the last time in diplomatic history that such imperfect perception has occurred.

To make certain that the Germans realized how dangerous things actually were, on the 30th Oshima was instructed to stress the extreme tenuousness and uncertainty of peace continuing.[72] Meanwhile, in Tokyo the German ambassador was being warned of much the same thing. The biggest stumbling block in the Japanese-American talks, the Japanese foreign minister insisted, was his nation's refusal to repudiate the Tripartite Pact. If war now erupted would Germany honor that pact and provide the needed assistance? The German ambassador promised his nation would.[73]

On December 1st, Oshima was instructed to begin negotiations with the Germans both in regard to the original promise not to agree to separate peace treaties and to guarantee full German involvement if war occurred. Receiving evasive answers as to how great was the near-term risk of war, von Ribbentrop replied equally evasively as to what written commitments his government would undertake. Besides, Hitler was not in Berlin and nothing definitive could be agreed to until his return.[74]

Von Ribbentrop did not wish Tokyo to be informed of his inability to negotiate the matter at the moment and requested, "please do not wire this to Japan."[75] This request was ignored and the American Magic decrypters read it on the 10th of the month.[76] In a separate message evaluating the reliability of the foreign minister's pro-war assurances, Oshima informed his superiors that "from my past experiences with Ribbentrop I feel fairly confident when I say that you will not be mistaken if you assume that there will be no objections" to any war plans against the United States.[77] This decrypt was in the hands of the State Department on December 6th, and may have contributed to Roosevelt's confidence as to the inevitability of Germany coming into the conflict once the United States was involved.[78]

On December 3rd, Oshima again pushed for an agreement. Again von Ribbentrop stonewalled, citing Hitler's absence until the following week.[79] By the 5th, however, things had changed and the Fuhrer had granted permission to negotiate the treaty. Provided with a draft, the Japanese were now confident that when war erupted the German response would be guaranteed—even though the final text had not been agreed to nor the signatures attached.[80]

Preliminary German agreement to such a step probably grew out of a desire to eliminate any remaining chance of a Japanese-American reconciliation.[81] Japan was being of at least limited value to Germany even while standing apart from the European War. Her uncertain ambitions had introduced the element of military uncertainty into the picture for the Americans and had caused a massive assignment of the limited U.S. naval resources into the Pacific. A reconciliation with the West would free most of these assets for possible use against the Germans.

Initial German Ambivalence to Japan's Action

In spite of the commitment to tighten their treaty bonds with Japan, Pearl Harbor still caught the power brokers in Germany by surprise. Foreign Minister von Ribbentrop immediately dismissed it as "a propaganda trick of the opposing side which has fooled my press department."[82] What would Germany do as this immediate reaction because untenable?

The immediate German government response in Berlin avoided committing the country to any specific policy—it "is not acting in haste," insisted one spokesman,[83] adding, "Suffice it to say that Japan and we are allies,"[84] an answer that could mean war but could equally well mean little more than continued support for Germany's Far Eastern compatriot.

Regardless of what was finally decided, it was a safe course for the German media to promptly side with their ally while blasting the Americans so long as they did not indicate that their nation was immediately entering the war. It was not surprising that German radio stations were quickly filled with praise for Japan's action and with criticisms of the United States.[85] Germany and the U.S. had been locked in a near-war situation in the Atlantic as the U.S. attempted to provide protection for ships carrying British war supplies, so the news of Japan's astounding success could only be viewed as highly justified comeuppance for the Americans.

The first German newspaper editions to be published after the attack were initially far more cautious than the radio: They avoided mention of the attack entirely.[86] This reticence quickly vanished as later editions provided all the details they could. Even the news of the vitally important Russian front was given less coverage than the information coming in from the Far East.[87] One Nazi publication excitedly described the success of the attack and asked its readers, "How's that for a starter?"[88]

The German people reacted with uncertainty and wonderment. It was not so much that they supported or opposed what had happened—it simply came so unexpectedly that they weren't sure how to react. To use the words of one American correspondent observing their responses, "Usually indifferent to what is printed in the newspapers, Berliners gathered to read the latest news and discuss it. It is not enough to say that the attack on Hawaii excited the people. It stupefied them.... I got the impression that they are completely bewildered. The war in Russia has been staggering enough to the prosaic imagination of the average German."[89] Now there was an even vaster war half the world away.

A single policeman continued to be sufficient to guard the main entrance to the American Embassy since no demonstrators of any type appeared.[90] A normally reliable Swedish informant resident in Berlin estimated that pro-intervention sentiment seemed to be running about 60 percent in favor and 40 percent against.[91] German public opinion did not matter greatly in a rigidly hierarchical power structure such as Germany's. On the other hand, if these numbers were approximately accurate, they are reflective of the fact that Hitler would have no major problems with even private public opinion regardless of the direction he chose to proceed.

German officials willing to discuss the matter off-the-record with foreign correspondents were divided as to which course to follow. Those favoring a delay argued that since the German military was already deeply involved in the Russian conflict that it was better to finish that piece of their foreign agenda before adding anything to it.[92] Those inclined toward immediate action argued that the United States was now so deeply involved in an Oriental quagmire that it could not divert any forces to shift the balance of power in the European conflict.[93]

One ominous straw in the wind came when German Foreign Office personnel began to disappear from their off-hours restaurants and bars.[94] A major decision of some kind was clearly in the works, and reporters for American news services spoke of the "ominous silence" that had descended in regard to their usual sources.[95]

Hitler Chooses Intervention

On December 6th, the Russians launched an unexpected massive offensive with no less than a hundred divisions, and quickly began to force the Germans back from the doors of Moscow.[96] Hitler was plotting strategy to deal with this deteriorating situation on the Russian front when his press officer, Otto Dietrich, rushed in with important news. Hitler immediately thought this would be word of yet another crisis on the Russian front. Discovering that it was a report of the Japanese entering the war, Hitler's spirits visibly lifted and he responded, "Is this report correct?" Dietrich assured him that he had already confirmed it by telephone with Berlin.[97]

Hitler's vision of Britain's future role openly collided with his instinct to take advantage of the situation. Reverting to his sentimental attachment to preserving the British Empire, he is said to have told Heinz Lorenz, "Now the British will lose Singapore. That was never my intention. We are fighting the wrong people. We ought to have the Anglo–American powers for our allies,"[98] not the emphatically non–Nordic and racially suspect Japanese.[99] But that view of Britain represented a world that could not be, and which Hitler would probably have detested if it had occurred. In the here and now he had a war to fight and this utilitarian need promptly caused him to think of how the Japanese action might be turned to the long range German advantage.

Hitler rushed to the bunker where Generals Keitel and Jodl were plotting strategy to cope with the Russian advances. Entering without even a coat on, Hitler appeared to them both startled and relieved as he shared the telegram.[100] Immediate joy had to soon yield to military necessity, and Hitler began to draft a directive ordering the German army to go on the defensive for the remainder of the winter. The severity of the supply situation had fatally compromised the capacity for further offensive action. This instruction was issued on Dec 8th, and the necessary implementing orders were left for Hitler's subordinates to issue after he returned to Berlin on that day.[101]

Late on the night of the Pearl Harbor attack, Ambassador Oshima received the surprising news of the attack on the Americans. Around 11:00 P.M. (Berlin time), he met with von Ribbentrop about the matter.[102] Von Ribbentrop promised him that "Germany and Italy's immediate participation can be assumed to be a matter of course."[103] To reinforce this point, Oshima said that "while I was in the room von Ribbentrop immediately passed on the gist of our conversation by telephone to Ciano," the Italian Foreign Minister.[104]

Ciano refers to this call in his diary: "A night call from Ribbentrop; he is joyful over the Japanese attack on the United States. He is so happy, in fact, that I can't but congratulate him, even though I am not so sure about the advantage."[105]

From von Ribbentrop's standpoint, at the minimum the new front would diminish military and economic supplies being poured into Britain and, at the maximum, it might even bring Japan into the anti–Russia war. Either would benefit the prospects of the Third Reich.

When Hitler reached Berlin on the 9th, one of his first visitors was von Ribbentrop, who carried with him the Japanese request for a prompt war declaration. Whatever enthusiasm he had manifested to the ambassador, von Ribbentrop now exercised the traditional diplomat's right to speak considerably differently to his own superior: He chose to stress that, legally, there was no obligation to intervene, since Japan had initiated the attack rather than been its victim. Furthermore, "although we welcomed a new ally against England, it meant we had a new opponent to deal with as well, or would have one to deal with if we declared war on the United States."[106]

Hitler rejected such caution on both political grounds as well as expedience: "If we don't stand on the side of Japan, the pact is politically dead. But that is not the main reason. The chief reason is that the United States already is shooting at our ships. They have been a forceful actor in this war and through their actions have already created a situation of war."[107]

As von Ribbentrop remembered the meeting on a different occasion, Hitler stressed that "the United States had already fired upon our ships and thereby had practically created a state of war; that it was therefore only a question of form, or, at least, that this official state of war might supervene at any moment, as a result of an incident; and that in the long run it was impossible that this state of affairs in the Atlantic continue without a German-American war."[108]

There was even something in the manner of the attack that struck an emotional chord in Hitler's heart. American newspapers castigated the unannounced beginning of the war as duplicating Hitler's own approach. To them it was censure; to Hitler it was praise. As he told the Japanese ambassador a few days later, "You gave the right declaration of war. This method is the only proper one ... one should strike—as hard as possible—and not waste time declaring war."[109]

When Oshima and von Ribbentrop met again, the foreign minister was the bearer of good news. This time von Ribbentrop could definitively tell the ambassador that Hitler had returned and was deciding the most useful manner to announce the war decision to the world.[110] He assured Oshima that the first vital steps had already been taken: Hitler had "issued orders to the entire German navy to attack American ships whenever and wherever they meet them."[111] Although such a policy—when carried out—would inevitably create a war, a formal declaration had not yet been prepared for publication.[112]

Although the decision had been made, Hitler wanted to assure that it was presented in a manner that most effectively dramatized the decision. This was the apparent reason that he delayed from the 9th to the 11th—it provided him time to work on the presentation and to arrange for the receptive audience of the Reichstag to hear his address.[113]

Hitler's decision was a carefully guarded one until he announced it to the Reichstag. A few signals had, however, been sent. The announcement that the Kroll Opera House was canceling its next performances so the Reichstag could use its facilities was one of those indications that a major policy decision of some kind was about to be announced.[114] The German Foreign Office spokesman continued to dodge any concrete answer: "The situation has not changed," he insisted.[115]

If one were to judge by the intensity of the rhetoric, however, the signs were also not good. United Press reported that the government-controlled German press "continued its campaign of attacks on President Roosevelt with almost unparalleled violence."[116]

Hitler's Defense of Intervention before the Reichstag

By November 21st at the latest, Hitler was discussing the need for a major policy address as a means of summarizing the war's course and encouraging the nation's belief in ultimate victory in spite of the unexpected resiliency of the Russian forces.[117] The inability to deliver the anticipated quick knockout blow was both alarming and depressing and clearly had to be dealt with.[118] Worse yet, indications of inadequate German planning were beginning to emerge. Stories had already begun to circulate (by front line soldiers' letters, for example) of the ferocity of the resistance and the failure of the German army to provide the necessary clothing and supplies for winter fighting.[119] Morale had slumped and the Japanese action gave a tool whereby, at least rhetorically, to give it a needed boost.

Hitler addressed the Reichstag at 2 P.M. local time (8 A.M., Eastern Standard, in the United States). After an introduction by Reich Marshal Hermann Goering, Hitler spoke for 88 minutes.[120] After speaking for a while defending his own peaceful intentions and pointing to the vast number of Russian prisoners as evidence that the decision to invade the Soviet Union had been a wise one, he then turned to the United States.[121] As far back as the diplomacy preceding the outbreak of war the U.S. had encouraged Poland to resist the German demands, he insisted.

Although there would be inevitable difficulties posed by the varying forms of government in the U.S. and the Third Reich this was not the fundamental problem. At the root of the problem were the two American Presidents that had followed the most actively anti–German foreign policy, first Woodrow Wilson and now Franklin D. Roosevelt. Wilson had betrayed his promise of a just and equitable peace while Roosevelt had pursued a policy of confrontation with Germany both by opposing her foreign policy and supporting Britain in her resistance to German plans and actions.

Since the U.S. claimed to be a neutral power and not at war it was "particularly despicable" that two German POWs who had escaped to the United States from Canada "were handcuffed and handed back to Canadian authorities contrary to all international agreement and custom."

But actions far more directly confrontational had been adopted as well. War equipment was provided Britain. German submarines were attacked at sea. American forces seized Iceland in a step to neutralize the effectiveness of German submarine operations. In July, the American Secretary of the Navy had instructed his forces to attack German vessels in the Atlantic.

The American policy toward Japan was similarly hypocritical and confrontational. How then should one explain Roosevelt's actions toward both Germany and Japan? He suggested that Roosevelt was nothing short of "insane." Furthermore, "We know, of course, that the eternal Jew is behind all this. Roosevelt himself may not realize it, but then that only shows his own limitations."

In light of what had happened, diplomatic relations were now being broken. Such was inevitable: Roosevelt had planned a war against Germany to begin no later than 1943 regardless of what Germany did. To enhance the cooperation among the Axis powers it was necessary to enter a new agreement with Italy and Japan; Hitler read its text to those present.

As Hitler characterized events, nothing was happening but the inevitable. A number of factors created this reality. There was the Jewish element involved in all this, of course. There nearly always was when

4. Germany and Italy Join the War

Hitler interpreted events. But there were other forces at work as well that could hardly be underestimated in creating the German-American tension.

One lay in the politics of envy or distraction. Germany had worked its way out of the Depression, Hitler stressed. Since the New Deal had failed to solve America's domestic economic disaster, Roosevelt had to seek out foreign controversies to distract attention from his policy failures.

Then there was something far more personal, the class element that created an unbridgeable socioeconomic gap between men like Roosevelt and men like Hitler and the worldview they adopted as the result. Although Hitler's movement was called "National Socialism" (though he was always willing to downplay the latter element to maximize his support from business), his conception of himself and of his American foe represented the kind of economically determined analysis one would expect from a socialist:

> I understand only too well that a world-wide distance separates Roosevelt's ideas and mine. Roosevelt comes from a rich family and belongs to the class whose path is smoothed in the democracies. I was only the child of a small, poor family and had to fight my way by work and industry.
>
> When the Great War came, Roosevelt occupied a position where he got to know only its pleasant consequences, enjoyed by those who do business while others bleed. I was only one of those who carried out orders as an ordinary soldier and actually returned from the war just as poor as I was in the autumn of 1914. I shared the fate of millions, and Franklin Roosevelt only the fate of the so-called upper ten thousand. [122]

Could it be any surprise that Roosevelt could neither understand, accept, nor tolerate the aspiring national ambitions of Germanic people such as Hitler? And because of that unbridgeable gap, and the other reasons already mentioned, war now doomed the two peoples into a blood battle to the death. Such was Hitler's interpretation of why Germany was entering the war against the U.S.

In a postscript to Hitler's lengthy address, Hermann Goering spoke briefly concerning how there now was "in the truest sense of the word—a world war between the powers of construction and the powers of decay."[123]

In private the mentality of this address was going to have repercussions far beyond the mere entry into a new war. Hitler's heaping of responsibility of the war upon the Jews in his Reichstag speech was but the tip of the iceberg: The expansion of the conflict into, literally, a world-war "because of" them provided the crucial moral justification for their extermination. Even he was not foolhardy enough to put that on the public record, however. In private and with the right listeners it was a different matter. Before a private meeting with some 50 Reichsleiter and Gauleiter held on Dec. 12th, he all but directly ordered the destruction of the ethnic foe that bedeviled his ideology and imagination. As Goebbels summed up that address,

> With regard to the Jewish Question, the Fuhrer is determined to make a clear sweep of it. He prophesied that, if they brought about another world war, they would experience their annihilation. That was no empty talk. The world war is there. The annihilation of Jewry must be the necessary consequence. This question is to be viewed without any sentimentality. We're not there to have sympathy with the Jews, but only sympathy with our German people. If the German people has again now sacrificed around 160,000 dead in the eastern campaign, the originators of this bloody conflict will have to pay for it with their own lives.[124]

Why Did Hitler Make His Decision?

Although in retrospect Hitler's choosing war with the U.S. seems incredibly misguided, at the time the question was less clear-cut. It was an inescapable fact that the United States was fully determined to keep Britain in the war and prevent a German military victory even if she herself could not, for domestic political reasons, enter the fray. The United States was far from neutral, and by such actions as attempting to provide a protected zone for British shipping around North America and by aggressively seeking out German submarines was a belligerent in everything but name. Sooner or later the Americans were going to enter the war directly. True, diplomatically and militarily Hitler had, uncharacteristically, attempted to avoid a final break. But for how much longer was that policy advantageous? Was not now as rational a time as any to openly take up the challenge?

Furthermore, massive damage clearly had been inflicted by the Japanese.[125] Even the Americans were admitting it in their radio broadcasts. True, the Americans were attempting to build up their military. Yet they were nowhere near ready for a major conflict[126]—certainly far less so than they were likely to be even a few years in the future.

In addition, even a pessimistic scenario meant that American resources would have to be divided between two far-flung regions, which could only work to Germany's advantage.[127] True, the U.S. insisted such would not occur but how could one regard these claims as credible? Japan's powerful advances simply could not be ignored and would have to be dealt with even at the cost of not sending the resources to Europe that the Americans wished to provide.

Propaganda Minister Joseph Goebbels echoed that sentiment when

4. Germany and Italy Join the War

he said, "Through the outbreak of war between Japan and the USA, a complete shift in the general world picture has taken place. The United States will scarcely now be in a position to transport worthwhile material to England let alone the Soviet Union."[128]

Although these arguments seemed realistic at the time, the decision was not just an intellectual one for Hitler. It was a gut reaction and, in this case, Hitler's instincts would steer him wrong.

The long-harbored anger over American support of Britain and its barely concealed war against the German navy contributed heavily to the psychological equation. Now Hitler could openly retaliate and demonstrate what he really thought of such actions, especially since Hitler took great pleasure at his American foe being so obviously blooded on a major scale. To strike at such a moment cost him nothing in new obligations in the short term, allowed him to portray himself as defender of the Axis alliance, and permitted him to vent long pent-up spleen at the Americans.[129]

Even more importantly, it fit in so well with his blame-everything-on-the-Jews mentality, which he manifested clearly in his Reichstag speech. He regarded both the Soviet Union and the United States as dominated and controlled in all pivotal matters by a cabal of Jews: the infernal, eternal, hated Jew. It was his divine destiny to rescue the world from that menace, and since "the Jew" had now successfully managed to bring the Americans into war with Japan, it was part of his holy duty and obligation to take up the challenge. That this analysis was fatally flawed by the fact that it was his ally Japan rather than the supposedly Jew-controlled Americans who had started the war was irrelevant on the psychological level. That the Jews were openly *in* it was sufficient to justify his conclusion. Ultimately, somehow, the Jew had to be responsible. Racial theory demanded it.[130]

Certainly their anti–Semitic premises dangerously encouraged Hitler and others to underestimate the U.S. potential. Von Ribbentrop encouraged an Italian delegation that visited in Berlin the following year with exactly this type of reasoning: "I know them—I know their country. A country devoid of culture, devoid of music—above all, a country without soldiers, a people which will never be able to decide the war from the air. When has a Jewified nation like that ever become a race of fighters and flying aces?"[131]

By a year after entry into the war, the evidence was clear that Hitler had opened a Pandora's box that would cause him far more harm than good: By then American forces were proceeding to dent and defeat the Axis Forces in North Africa. Less than three years later, they were in continental Europe in the hundreds of thousands. Just as the German leadership in 1917 had disastrously underestimated the American capacity for successful intervention, so did Hitler a quarter century later.[132]

Hitler had boasted the day he received word of the Pearl Harbor attack, "We can't lose the war at all. We now have an ally which has never been conquered in 3,000 years."[133] He was about to learn that though history does repeat itself, changing personalities, economies, and national structures can still produce different endings than had occurred in the past. History provides illustrations and probabilities, not iron-clad guarantees.

Italy Avoids a War Commitment

Italian radio avoided any mention of Pearl Harbor for 12 hours after the attack. German radio broke the store at 9 A.M. local time. Italian radio avoided the matter until after the story broke about noon in the afternoon edition of the newspapers.[134] In light of this silence, morning papers in Italy would likely have been prohibited from discussing it also. Since it was not the Italian custom to publish Monday morning editions, a formal decision had not been required.[135]

When Italian radio finally began to provide commentary, as it described the situation, America had reaped what it had sown: it had sown interventionism in the European war through the Lend-Lease Act and it had reaped Japanese intervention in areas the U.S. considered important. One broadcast argued that, "Thanks to the Japanese, the Americans, enemies of progressive humanity, must pay with their blood for the crimes of the Anglo-Saxon peoples."[136]

At least one broadcast monitored by CBS in New York implied that all three Axis powers were now in the war. That broadcast argued that "the declaration of war was made some time before actual operations had taken place, and it involves, in accordance with the three-power pact the existence of a state of war between the two Axis powers and the United States."[137]

Possibly there had been an overzealous misstatement on the Italian end or something was lost or misunderstood in translation. Nevertheless, as soon as Roman radio began receiving reports that it had referred to such an intervention, it broadcast a denial that such a decision had been reached.[138] It stressed that the treaty commitments covered a different situation from that which had occurred: "Although Japan was bound by the three-power pact to make war should the United States wage war against Germany and Italy she did not wait for this."[139]

The newspaper *Piccolo* carried the commentary of its New York correspondent Francesco Romano:

4. Germany and Italy Join the War 121

As he saw it, President Roosevelt had pulled a very unwilling America into the conflict through a foreign policy that embarrassed Japan endlessly in one matter after another; this ultimately put her in a position of surrendering to the extreme demands of the United States or having to fight. Evidence of the on-going determination of the Americans to act contemptuously of even the dignity of the Japanese could be seen in Secretary of State Hull's blatant assertion that the final Japanese diplomatic note was not merely wrong on a single point but was completely erroneous and misleading. All this amounted to what Romano called a "refined hypocrisy" that masked FDR's aggressive purposes.[140]

As both newspaper and radio sources began to pour out voluminous verbiage about the peace-seeking intentions of the Japanese and Italy's historically friendly ties with that country, what all carefully avoided was any prediction as to whether the European axis members would enter the war on Japan's behalf.[141] Some edged up to the brink without going over it. *Corriere Della Sera* proclaimed that, "Japan is at our side. We are beside it, with all our soul, all our forces."[142] Did this statement refer to moral support, or battlefield assistance?

War was a political decision that had to be made at the highest levels and, though it would be embraced when given, an insufficient time had passed for the government to come to a conclusion as to the future. The situation was further complicated because, Italian pride notwithstanding, Italy was the junior member of the European fascist coalition and would need to interact and respond to the German decision rather than initiate an independent policy of her own.

The government, however, could praise Japan and heap blame on the United States as a safe interim approach—keeping options open for whatever it ultimately decided. At noon Rome time a press briefing was provided for the foreign correspondents. By a careful editing and omission of the time of the Japanese attack, the implicit critique was that the Japanese had been directly responding to the Anglo-American war-making movements of the previous day. After all, at 8:15 (Rome time) a mobilization was ordered in Hong Kong. Then at midnight, President Roosevelt issued the order for the American Navy to carry out its orders. Then at 2:10 A.M. came word that Roosevelt would ask for a declaration of war, followed minutes later by a statement that war now existed.[143]

When word began to appear in the press of the actual chronology of the events, Italy dealt with the fact that Japan had committed the first act of war by shifting the underlying responsibility onto the United States for allegedly provoking the assault. *Virginio Gayda* stressed the argument that, "When a criminal with manifest homicidal tendencies raises his arm to strike the designated victim, one cannot say he is the innocent party if at the last instant the chosen victim reacts and shoots him to death."[144]

In a similar vein the paper *Resto del Carlino* conceded that, "The American newspapers clamor about surprise and unexpected attacks. The fact is that Japan, which had been patient in the face of provocations up to the limit possible, acted with promptness, rapidity and timeliness when the decision came and reversed the positions. It was not the provoked and besieged party that sustained the first shock, but the provoker."[145]

Mussolini Follows Hitler's Lead

Benito Mussolini was as receptive to a war with America as was Hitler. On December 3, the Japanese ambassador met with Mussolini and noted that the negotiations between Japan and the Americans were in tenuous shape. He anticipated a total rupture at any time, and his nation wished to invoke the Tripartite Pact's pledge of mutual assistance when that happened. Although that obligation was limited to situations where participants were the victims of an attack, it took Mussolini only a little thought before he responded that Italy would promptly enter the war if conflict erupted with the Americans, regardless of who initiated the war.[146] The only wiggle room he left for himself was that the Germans would have to concur in the same policy.[147]

After the ambassador left, he shared his enthusiasm with Count Galeazzo Ciano, not only his relative but also the Italian foreign minister: "Thus we arrive at war between continents, which I have foreseen since September, 1939."[148]

Ciano was not so optimistic. He noted in his diary that the interpreter was literally trembling when translating Japan's request for a declaration of war.[149] Ciano's contacts in Berlin indicated that the Germans were far from enthused about the supposed opportunity given them. "Perhaps they will accept because they cannot get out of it, but the idea of provoking America's intervention pleases the Germans less and less."[150] When on the 5th the Germans submitted a proposed text for the agreement, Ciano was amazed at the abrupt about-face: "After delaying two days, now [von Ribbentrop] cannot wait a minute to answer the Japanese...."[151]

Such reservations, of course, were unknown to Mussolini. When war actually erupted, he had no difficulty in arriving at his own decision, nor did he attempt to find a way verbally to worm his way around Hitler's preference in the matter. "Mussolini was happy. For a long time now he has been in favor of clarifying the position between America and the Axis," explained an unenthusiastic Ciano in his diary.[152]

4. Germany and Italy Join the War

Yet what made Missolini commit such a blunder? The Americans had clearly been doing their best to inflict damage on the German submarine force and, through assistance to Britain, help Britain survive and damage the Reich. The Italians did not have a major submarine force at risk in the Atlantic, and whatever indirect hindrance the Americans may have been it was not of such a visible nature as what the Germans faced.

"It is difficult to account for the lightheartedness with which he viewed this dangerous extension of the conflict," remarks Ivone Kirkpatrick. "But things were going so badly in Russia and Libya that he may have been ready to clutch at any straw."[153]

Dennis M. Smith finds the explanation in two factors. The first was prejudice: Mussolini viewed the U.S. as "a country of Negroes and Jews."[154] He considered it vastly amusing that such a supposedly great country would be ruled by a man with paralyzed legs.[155] It became both the content of vulgar jokes[156] and symbolic of America's fundamental weakness. The latter idea was especially dangerous, for it caused Missolini to underestimate fatally the potential American danger.[157]

In the short term the pro-war decision created a propaganda problem for the Italian government. The Latin American nations generally responded to the war by sympathy with the United States and by more overt means such as by freezing Japanese commercial accounts, by declarations of war, by seizing Axis commercial vessels, and by opening ports to U.S. war ships.

Routinely the Italian government and its controlled media had depicted those nations as highly mistreated by the U.S.; the positive response simply did not reflect the image that had been carefully cultivated over the years.[158] The very large Italian immigrant community in Brazil made that country's response especially embarrassing.[159] After initially avoiding any mention of hostile Latin American actions, the press then turned to a two-edged explanation. First of all, the decisions were the result of American economic pressure.[160] Secondly, the Latin American pro–U.S. stance was militarily meaningless.[161]

By the end of the following year, Mussolini was aware that he had made a very unwise decision. As he himself admitted, "In Italy the moral repercussions of the American landing in Algiers were immediate and profound.... The country began to feel the strain. As long as only the English were in the Mediterranean, Italy, with Germany's help, could hold firm and resist, though at the cost of ever greater sacrifices; but the appearance of America disturbed the weaker spirits and increased by many millions the already numerous band of listeners to enemy radio."[162]

But first came the moment of glory and optimism—the official announcement of the war.

Mussolini Announces His Decision

The American chargé d'affaires, George Wadsworth, received word of Italy's course on the 11th in a 2:30 P.M. meeting with Ciano at his foreign ministry office. Ciano considered Wadsworth "a good but rather timid man with whom I have had little to do. He thinks that I have called him to discuss the arrest of certain journalists, but I disabuse him immediately. He listens to the declaration of war, and turns pale. He says, 'It is very tragic.'"[163]

Wadsworth recounted it a bit differently when describing the meeting to reporters. First of all, he had been perfectly aware what was going to be the subject.[164] Furthermore,

> When I walked into his office he halted me half-way to his desk by rising, making it quite clear that I was not to sit down. With a scowl on his face he recited his piece as though he had learned it by heart, saying in one sentence that he must inform me that Italy considered herself at war with the United States. I bowed my head and said, "I'm very sorry to hear it." "May I give you a message before I take leave of you?" Ciano replied coldly, "I don't think there is anything more to be said."[165]

Informed that it was a message from former American Ambassador Phillips, Ciano yielded. It turned out to be a message of appreciation for the courtesy shown to him by the Foreign Office while he had served in Italy. "Count Ciano then relaxed somewhat in his manner and said with the suspicion of a friendly smile, 'Thank you.'"[166]

Although no official word had been issued of what was going to be said, rumor spread quickly on the 11th that Mussolini would be giving a major policy speech of some type. With that in mind, word was sent to Fascist party members to gather together and march to the Piazza Venezia. Over several hours various groups including school children were also brought to the site to assure an abundant audience for the address.[167]

Speaking to a crowd of a 150,000 people, the Premier emphatically declared to both the crowd and his radio audience that it was a somber day that would ultimately alter the history of entire continents: the Trioartite Pact, previously only an abstract treaty between nations, now became an active military alliance in which no less than 250,000,000 people were united to defeat their joint foes.[168]

Mussolini carefully put the entire blame on FDR for what had happened, "Neither the Axis nor Japan wanted an extension of the conflict. One man, one man only, a real tyrannical democrat, through a series of infinite provocations, betraying with a supreme fraud the population of his country, wanted the war and had prepared for it day by day with diabolical obstinacy."[169]

Perhaps to reassure any skeptics who viewed Italy as being forced into yet another war to satisfy Hitler, Mussolini pointed to the power of the Japanese: "The formidable blows that on the immense Pacific expanse have been already inflicted on American forces show how prepared are the soldiers of the Empire of the Rising Sun. I say to you, and you will understand, that it is a privilege to fight with them."[170]

Ciano was impressed by the speech and by the crowd but felt that the timing—to beat Hitler to the punch in publicly announcing the war first—undercut some of the enthusiasm that otherwise would have been present.

> Mussolini made a speech from the balcony—a brief and cutting speech, which fell on a great crowd. A very pro–Japanese setting. News of the naval victories has excited the Italian imagination. The demonstration, however, was not very enthusiastic. We must not forget that it was three o'clock in the afternoon, the people were hungry, and the day was quite cold. These are all elements which do not make for enthusiasm.[171]

In an historical irony (since Germany was the dominant party in the alliance), Mussolini's short four or five minute speech was begun shortly before Hitler began his own war declaration speech.[172] Courtesy of the Führer's wordiness, Mussolini's brevity and head start, the Italian premier could claim to have announced war to the world before Hitler did.

After Mussolini's speech a large and enthusiastic crowd made its way to the Japanese Embassy to demonstrate its support for the decision. The ambassador appeared to thank them on behalf of his government.[173]

The Second Tripartite Pact

About noon of the day of the public announcements, the representatives of Germany, Italy, and Japan signed a new pact bringing them into a formal wartime alliance. The introduction put the responsibility for the conflict solely on Roosevelt's shoulders. It stressed that the warmongering approach of the U.S. was the same as that of the British, and praised each other's "patient and conciliatory attitude" in response to the alleged ongoing provocations.[174]

Then followed the new agreement itself, divided into four sections. Article 1 stated that the Axis powers would engage in the conflict wholeheartedly and with all their resources; Article 2, that none would make a peace treaty or armistice with the West except by agreement with the other parties; Article 3 promised that after the successful conclusion of the war, the Axis would continue its course of collaboration "in order to realize and establish an equitable new order in the world." Finally, Article 4 made the agreement effective immediately.¹⁷⁵

The Japanese were ecstatic. Shigenori Tori, foreign minister, spoke of how the new agreement "together with the marvelous achievements of the Imperial [Japanese] armed forces unfold a bright future for the Japanese Empire, which is proceeding resolutely with the construction of a New World Order."¹⁷⁶

5

The Senate: Declaring War on Germany and Italy

The Formalities Observed: Germany and Italy Inform the State Department

The American chargés d'affaires based in Rome and Berlin received the declarations of war on behalf of their government[1] before either Hitler[2] or Mussolini[3] made the war announcement to their own publics. In addition, the German declaration was delivered in Washington to the State Department at 8:15 A.M. on December 11th.[4]

When a German diplomatic team consisting of the chargé d'affaires Hans Thomsen and the First Secretary of the Embassy Heribert von Strempel arrived at the State Department, they were startled to find three newspaper photographers pushing their way into the elevator to accompany them. Thomsen complained to his associate, "This is not very dignified."[5]

The State Department was not prepared to give anything but the barest token of courtesy either. Not invited to utilize the formal diplomatic reception room, the Germans were kept waiting in the outer office of the American secretary of state. When Hull arrived an hour later he ignored them, entered his office, and kept them waiting for an hour. Then he sent out word that he was "otherwise engaged" and they were sent to the chief of the European Division to deliver the formal notification of hostilities.[6]

The text of the note delivered was identical to that delivered to the chargé d'affaires in Berlin and began with the assertion,

> The government of the United States, having violated in the most flagrant manner and in ever-increasing measure all rules of neutrality in

favor of the adversaries of Germany and having continually been guilty of the most severe provocations toward Germany ever since the outbreak of the European war, provoked by the British declaration of war against Germany on September 3, 1939, has finally resorted to open military acts of aggression.[7]

With this opening one would anticipate the specification of something dramatic having occurred in the last few days and as having irrevocably widened the diplomatic breach. Instead the note then surveys anti–German military orders issued the American military in September and October,[8]

First there was the announcement on September 11 that the President had ordered the American military to attack any German naval craft they encountered. If this were not sufficient to make his policy crystal clear, in a speech in late October he emphasized that the policy remained in effect. Furthermore the American military took full advantage of this opportunity. The American warships *Greer*, *Kearny*, and *Reuban James* had all attacked warships of the Germany navy—submarines in particular. Secretary of the Navy Knox informed the press that such attacks had occurred so it was not merely a matter of trusting the German version of events.

The U.S. had gone so far as to openly seize vessels of the German merchant marine which in no way had acted against it. By such repeated behavior the American Government had produced a situation that differed virtually nothing from open warfare.[9]

Hence the German government felt it necessary to cease diplomatic relations and resort to an open state of war.

Nothing distinctly new is noted in the declaration, nor is there even an explanation or rationale for why Germany had waited so long to take a step that had been available from the day the Americans had first acted against their interests. This itself is an oddity since the gap between initial American provocation and ultimate German reaction could easily have been cited as evidence of German forbearance, peaceful intentions, and determination against broadening the war—all the types of self-justifying diplomatic rhetoric that is typical of such international correspondence and which can actually be anything from the completely truthful to the thoroughly disingenuous.

Interestingly, not one reference appears in the entire document as to the Pacific War. The Japanese are not mentioned. The Tripartite Pact is not mentioned. As far as this document is concerned, the attack on Pearl Harbor might not have occurred. The war declaration is presented strictly in terms of German national self-interest and as a justified response to American military and other action at a time it claimed to be neutral in the war.

At the European Division office, Ray Atherton accepted the message as merely making official what had been a long-time reality: It "was merely formalizing the realization that the Government and people of this country had faced since the outbreak of war in 1939 of the threat and purposes of the German Government and the Nazi regime toward this hemisphere and our free American civilization."[10]

Leaving the diplomatic meeting that day, Thomsen recognized both the seriousness of the occasion and the personal difficulties that were sure to follow in light of the diplomatic breach. Turning to the reporters outside the State Department, he playfully enquired, "Anybody want to buy a nice car?"[11] That trip was the last time he drove it. Before being moved along with other German diplomats to the Greenbrier Hotel in White Sulphur Springs, West Virginia, he was able to sell it to the owner of a nightclub near the embassy.[12]

In the kind of nonchalance toward the seriousness of war that sometimes drove the Germans to distraction, the Italian government did not bother to order steps to inform directly the U.S. government in Washington. After radio broadcasts began to come in from Italy announcing the Duce's decision, reporters rang the bell at the embassy in an attempt to gain some type of comment from Ambassador Ascanio dei principi Colonna. His male servant who answered the door responded that no one could be of any assistance yet; "The boss is still in bed."[13]

When the ambassador arrived later in the day at the State Department, he was also diverted to someone besides the secretary of state. In this case it was James C. Dunn who served as political adviser on European affairs.

The Italian ambassador had taken the initiative on his own to visit the State Department. He arrived without a diplomatic notification of war to deliver and had not yet, he indicated, received any formal word on the subject from Rome. Without any documentation to present, he came, he said, to asked about the status of those attached to the embassy in light of the apparent rupture between the two countries.[14]

After being told that the declaration of hostilities had been delivered in Rome, he inquired as to the arrangements that would be made for his personnel to leave the country. The response was that they would be exchanged when practical for their American counterparts in Italy. Similar assurances had been given the Germans as well.[15] In light of the subservient political relationship between Italy and Germany, Dunn could not resist the temptation to suggest that "we fully anticipated that Italy would obediently follow along" by also declaring war.[16]

At the White House, Roosevelt took no time out of his schedule to listen to the war addresses of either Hitler or Mussolini.[17] He took it so in stride that one national newsmagazine referred to how "thereafter, he penned Congress an almost perfunctory note requesting it to recognize the existence of war between the United States and the Axis Powers."[18]

As the document was being prepared to inform Congress of the actions by the European Axis powers, Stephen Early, the spokesman for the president, confirmed that these decisions were "as expected." Germany had acted and "Italy had goose-stepped along, apparently following orders."[19]

Press Reaction

Except for the most optimistic, there had been a growing sense of inevitability since Pearl Harbor had been struck. The *Boston Herald* described it "as an anticlimax after Sunday's thunderous events."[20] Others implicitly wondered how war had been delayed as long as it had been: The *Atlanta Constitution,* for example, spoke of how "we have long realized" that such a collision was inescapable.[21]

Editorialists typically considered it a time for grim determination. The *New York Post* summed it up in two sentences: "It looks to us like a long war and a tough one, but with an Allied victory waiting at the end of the rocky road. We think it is going to get worse before it gets better, and that all of us would be wise to steel our minds to that probability."[22] The *Philadelphia Inquirer* called it "the hour of crisis, the hour of high resolve."[23]

The *San Francisco Chronicle* asked, "Doubtless by this time we realize that it is serious, but do we appreciate how serious?"[24] Unlike World War I, when American optimism viewed the outcome as unquestionable, this time there was the recognition that the task, though doable, would be difficult. The *St. Louis Globe Democrat,* though confident in American strength, felt compelled to add, "may God grant us the strength to carry through."[25]

As the *New York Sun* stressed, there seemed no precedent for a fascist state to start war this way. Their normal mode was to follow the example of Japan and drop the bombs first and then, only afterwards, to inform the victims that war had been begun.[26] In similar manner, the *Los Angeles Times* spoke of how no other fascist power had ever bothered to declare war before beginning it.[27]

Although Germany's proven military strength required that a type of respect be accorded that powerful (albeit vicious and dangerous) foe, the unimpressive and bungling record of Italy on the battlefield made it the ready object of ridicule. Perhaps an editorial cartoon in a major Southern newspaper summed up the contempt best: It pictured Mussolini with a black eye, a wounded and wrapped foot, a broken arm and on crutches. Raised defiantly in his right hand is a wooden sword with the proclamation of war on it. In the lower left corner is a startled crow muttering, "et tu Benito!"[28]

War Declared Against Germany

At approximately 12:30 P.M. on December 11, the vice president (the presiding officer of the Senate) laid before its members a message the president had sent to Congress earlier that day:

> On the morning of December 11 the Government of Germany, pursuing its course of world conquest, declared war against the United States.
> The long known and the long expected had thus taken place. The forces endeavoring to enslave the entire world now are moving toward this hemisphere.
> Never before has there been a greater challenge to life, liberty, and civilization.
> Delay invites greater danger. Rapid and united effort by all the peoples of the world who are determined to remain free will insure a world victory of the forces of justice and of righteousness over the forces of savagery and of barbarism.
> Italy also has declared war against the United States.
> I therefore request the Congress to recognize a state of war between the United States and Germany and between the United States and Italy.[29]

The treatment of the two foes provides a revealing commentary on what the president and most Americans thought of them. Germany was a danger. Italy is mentioned almost as an afterthought. All the rhetoric is targeted at Germany; none at Italy. Germany was the force to be reckoned with; by its bare mention almost mute testimony was given to the common view of Italy as more of a farce than a true military power.

Furthermore, there were other profound differences between what was now happening and what had occurred concerning Japan. A *Richmond (Virginia) News Leader* editorial observed,

> The text of a declaration of war on Germany and a similar one against Italy was drafted and, even before the President's message reached Congress, was approved unanimously by the Senate Foreign Relations Committee. Mr. Roosevelt himself did not honor the new belligerents with so much as the personal appearance he had made to urge the declaration against Japan. He simply forwarded a brief message which was read separately in the two chambers and was then, under suspension of rules, adopted unanimously.[30]

The vice president referred the letter to the Committee on Foreign Relations. Senator Tom Connally of that committee promptly stood up with the text of the proposed declaration of war against Germany:

> Whereas the Government of Germany has formally declared war against the Government and the people of the United States of America: Therefore be it
> *Resolved, etc.,* That the state of war between the United States and the Government of Germany, which has thus been thrust upon the United States, is hereby formally declared; and the President is hereby authorized and directed to employ the entire naval and military forces of the United States and the resources of the Government to carry on war against the Government of Germany; and, to bring the conflict to a successful termination, all of the resources of the country are hereby pledged by the Congress of the United States.[31]

Having had the text read, Connally explained how it was possible for the committee already to have considered the matter and agreed to a common stance as to policy and wording:

> I shall presently ask unanimous consent for the immediate consideration of the joint resolution just read to the Senate. Before the request is submitted, however, I desire to say that, being advised of the declaration of war upon the United States by the Governments of Germany and Italy, and anticipating a message by the President of the United States in relation thereto, and after a conference with the Secretary of State, as chairman of the Committee on Foreign Relations, I called a meeting of the committee this morning and submitted to the committee the course I expected to pursue as chairman and the request which I expected to make.
> I am authorized by the Committee on Foreign Relations to say to the Senate that after consideration of the text of the joint resolution which I have reported and after mature consideration of all aspects of this matter, the membership of the Committee on Foreign Relations unanimously approve and agree to the course suggested. One member of the committee was absent, but I have authority to express his views.[32]

Since the request for unanimous consent to consider immediately the joint resolution brought no protest, the resolution was read for the required three times. Connally requested the yeas and nays. No one had spoken for or against the recommendation nor concerning the merits of the text itself. As the roll call proceeded different individuals took opportunity to explain why specific fellow members were not present (see below), but otherwise the vote proceeded in a normal, straightforward manner.

The result was 88 for, 0 against, and seven not present. The seven not in the chamber passed word to colleagues and reporters that if they had been present they would have voted in the affirmative as well.[33]

The isolationists now had the war they so bitterly opposed. That fact did not convince them that they had been in the wrong, only that the worst had occurred in spite of their good-faith efforts to avoid it. Senator Vandenberg is representative in the entry of his diary for December 11th:

> We "asked for it" and "we got it." The interventionist says today—as the President virtually did in his address to the nation—"See! This proves we were right and that this way was *sure* to involve us." The non-interventionist says (and I say)—"See! We have insisted from the beginning that this course would lead to war and it has done exactly that." ... Perhaps, in a sense, we are *both* right.... I say that when, at long last, Germany turned upon us and declared war against her most aggressive enemy on earth, it is no contribution to "historical accuracy" (to put it mildly) for us to pretend to say that this war has been "thrust upon us." ... But if this war is worth fighting it is worth accepting for what it is—namely, a belligerent cause which we openly embraced long ago and in which we long since nominated ourselves as active participants. The "thrusting" started two years ago when we repealed the Arms Embargo.[34]

More important, of course, were the immediate difficulties that lay ahead. Charles A. Lindberg, though an isolationist, shared feelings of national unpreparedness with his private journal on December 11th, feelings that a majority of those pushing for an earlier war would have shared:

> Now, all that I feared would happen has happened. We are at war all over the world, and we are unprepared for it from either a spiritual or a material standpoint. Fortunately, in spite of all that has been said, the oceans are still difficult to cross; and we have the time to adjust and prepare, which France lacked and which England has had only in part since aviation has spanned the barrier of her Channel.[35]

War Declared Against Italy

With the German war resolution officially adopted, the House next turned to Italy. The chairman of the Committee on Foreign Relations, Senator Connolly, introduced the text of the resolution it was recommending:

> Whereas the Government of Italy has formally declared war against the Government and the people of the United States of America: Therefore be it
> *Resolved, etc.,* That the state of war between the United States and the Government of Italy which has thus been thrust upon the United States is hereby formally declared; and the President is hereby authorized and directed to employ the entire naval and military forces of the United States and the resources of the Government to carry on war against the Government of Italy; and, to bring the conflict to a successful termination, all of the resources of the country are hereby pledged by the Congress of the United States.[36]

After alluding to how his committee had decided upon this wording earlier in the day, the text was formally read three times per accepted procedure. At that point the yeas and nays were called for by the same senator and the roll called of all present. Nothing had been said in behalf of or against the resolution. During the vote itself (see below) only explanations for various members' absences and the announcement of the way they would have voted slowed the procedure.

When all was over the vote was 90 in favor of war, 0 against, and five not present. Two of the senators who had not made it in time for the anti–German vote had arrived in time to cast their endorsement of the new war.[37]

As in the case with the vote concerning Germany, the senators did not even take time for speech making. They heard the proposals and they voted. For pro-intervention forces it had always seemed inevitable; for those opposed war was now unavoidable. Recriminations in either direction were withheld for the future.

The Missing Members

Although seven senators had missed the anti–German vote, only five were absent for the proposal against Italy. Senator Charles O. Andrews (Democrat, Florida) arrived in time to cast a vote for war with Mussolini's regime. Afterwards he explained that "on the vote of the joint resolution declaring the existence of a state of war with Germany, I was unavoidably detained as chairman of a committee conducing hearings involving national defense. I ask unanimous consent that I be recorded as voting 'yea.' "[38]

The fabled "senatorial courtesy" will permit members to bend considerably the rules and normal customs in order to maintain harmony among the relatively small number of individuals making up the body. On this point, however, Robert M. La Follette of Wisconsin (Progressive) felt compelled to object: "I understand the desire of the Senator from Florida to be recorded, but I believe that to grant his request would be contrary to the rules and practices of the Senate and would establish a very bad precedent." Because of his "personal affection for the Senator from Florida" he hesitated to object, but saw no choice but to "make the point of order that what he asks to have done is contrary to the rules and practices of the Senate."[39]

This placed the vice president in the unenviable position of having to make a ruling on a matter involving the personal pride of the members. In effect he tried to throw the matter back to the Senate itself. "There is no question about the rules of the Senate in this matter. The only question is whether, on an occasion of absolute unanimity, the rule might be abrogated by unanimous consent."[40]

La Follette responded that much as he hated to pursue the matter that he feared "establish[ing] a precedent for suspending the rules by unanimous consent in cases of unanimity. Such a precedent might be used as an argument in favor of suspending the rules when there is a majority of two-thirds, and perhaps even when there is only a bare majority."[41]

Upon this insistence the vice president sustained the point of order and Andrews continued to be carried on the record simply as not voting in regard to the matter of war with Germany.

Senator William H. Smathers (Democrat, New Jersey) had shown up in time to vote for the Italian war. (On the earlier vote he had been described as "unavoidably detained.")[42] Either out of the feeling that there was no need to modify the *Record* to add his vote in the affirmative column or out of a recognition that the rejection of Andrews's request had already made the effort futile, he did not make a similar effort to alter the vote count.

This left a core group of five individuals who were not present for either tally: Senators Bone, Lee, Tydings, Wagner, and Wheeler. Senator Robert F. Wagner of New York (Democrat) is simply described as "unavoidably absent today."[43]

Senator Josh Lee of Oklahoma (Democrat) and Senator Tydings of Maryland (also a Democrat) were both reported as "unavoidably detained" at the time of the German vote.[44] When Tydings arrived, he noted in the *Record* that "I was detained by a late train and regret that I was not in the Chamber when the recent votes were taken. Had I been present, I should have voted 'yea' on all three joint resolutions passed by the Senate in answer to the challenge of the countries which have made war upon us."[45]

Homer T. Bone (Democrat) was reported as ill, Burton K. Wheeler (Democrat) was "absent because of the serious illness of his brother."[46] The illness of Wheeler's kin was, in fact, life-threatening: Wheeler's brother was "in a hospital in Brookline, Massachusetts, so desperately ill that the Senator from Montana had to leave Washington yesterday for Massachusetts."[47]

6

The House of Representatives Responds to War with Germany and Italy

War Against Germany

At shortly after 12:30 on the afternoon of Thursday the 11th, the president's formal message informing Congress that Germany and Italy had declared war was read to the House. Congressman John D. McCormack moved that "the message of the President be referred to the Committee on Foreign Affairs, and ordered printed."[1] Having done so, he requested that the rules be suspended and that immediate action be taken upon a joint resolution authorizing war.

Without comments either for or against and with no remarks as to why various individuals were absent, the roll call tallied 393 endorsing war, 36 not present, and 1 simply answering "present" (Rankin of Montana).

A little later, after disposing of a few other matters of business, word was received that the Senate had passed its own war authorization. Congressman McCormack then arose and asked for unanimous consent for the House to adopt that measure as its own. Since there was no objection, the measure was read the required three times. In light of the silence of objections, it was deemed as accepted unanimously, the Speaker announced. Having once again secured technical unanimity for war by the means of substituting the Senate's measure for its own, McCormack then asked that the House's own resolution "be vacated and that the resolution be laid on the table" and removed from discussion, which was immediately done.[2]

War Against Italy

Immediately Congressman McCormack brought forth the House war resolution targeting Italy, with a text identical to that of the Senate. The Speaker asked whether the "House suspend the rules and pass the resolution," and McCormack promptly requested a vote.

Some members who had been absent for the earlier count had now drifted in, increasing the pro-war vote accordingly. The final tally was 399 in favor, 30 still absent, and one (Rankin) voting as merely "present."

Again, there had been no discussion of the merits or possible demerits of the measure—and at this stage of the degeneration of the situation into full world war, the most that would likely have been imaginable would have been taking issue with some technical fault in the wording. Again, there was no explanation of why members were absent nor comments as to how they would have voted if present. At this stage everyone certainly knew it would have been in the affirmative.

The Audience

The galleries in both the Senate and House had been crowded for the vote concerning Germany. Public attention had been centered there for years. Since Italy was viewed as but a footnote to the other action, the crowds began to loudly discuss the matter and then leave after the German vote was completed in the Senate.[3] The interested and respectful silence that had been present disappeared.[4]

In the House gallery, the noise was so pervasive that the Speaker temporarily stopped the Italian vote in order to re-establish a reasonable degree of quiet for the proceedings.[5] Some thought those in the galleries had misinterpreted the demand for silence as an order to clear the galleries, since about two-thirds of the audience left.[6] More likely they recognized that the most important and pivotal action of the day was completed.

Lord Halifax, the British ambassador, was again present. After the voting in the Senate was completed, he made his way over to the house galleries and observed the House's endorsement of the anti–German war as well.[7]

Post-Vote Denunciations

It was only after both war resolutions were accepted that the congressmen took time to put their feelings on the record. Members were granted, by unanimous consent, permission to expand their remarks for publication in either the next day's Record or in the appendix that would ultimately be published with supplemental materials.[8]

Congressman Warren G. Magnuson (Democrat, Washington) began the succession of speakers but was content to simply remark that, "I favor the resolution and declaration against Germany."[9] However enjoyable the political rhetoric was and no matter how deeply felt, Magnuson clearly felt that this was one occasion upon which it was not needed.

The incredible bridging of previously existing divisions was illustrated by a cartoon in the *Chicago Sun*, which Laurence F. Arnold of Illinois (a Democrat) cited to his listeners: "It depicts the strong hand of isolationism clasped in the strong hand of interventionism, with the ugly and treacherous face of Nippon in the background." This unity of purpose was especially essential since Germany and Italy had openly "today declared it is their intention to destroy us." The result of this hostile alliance was "the greatest danger that ever confronted this Nation."[10]

Owen Harris (Democrat) of Arkansas thought it highly appropriate that the European fascists were now openly in the war. After all, they had also utilized "detestable and infamous acts." In fact he saw behind the action of Japan the manipulation of the German leader: "It is evident that the conquest and aggression by Germany, Italy, and Japan is directed and moved by the forces in Berlin, under the control and dictatorship of Hitler."[11]

The United States had been guilty of excessive forbearance toward the European dictators in the past. "The President and the people of America have been patient, even though for the past two years war appeared inevitable." It had even been patient after war broke out when severer action would have been far more appropriate: "In our declaration of war against Japan last Monday many of us felt then, as we do now, that Germany and Italy should have been included, because the attack of the Japanese was in actuality an attack by all of the Axis Powers."[12]

As far as Congressman Thomas D'Alesandro of Maryland was concerned, "we have been at war with Germany and Italy for some time.... President Roosevelt saw what was coming when other people did not. I am happy to say that upon every occasion since I have been in Congress, he had my full and complete support."[13]

D'Alesaudro made a drastic distinction between Mussolini and the people of his land though conspicuously not applying the same reasoning to Germany:

> It is a pity that two mad men, Hitler and Mussolini, could upset the whole world. They must be put down. If the Italian people could express

6. The House Responds to War with Germany and Italy

themselves they would say the same thing. I am convinced that if the ordinary citizen of Italy saw the chance, he would destroy Mussolini and Italy would soon become the ally of America in its war for freedom and democracy.[14]

The implied distinction between nation and leader, historically speaking, was clearly valid. Furthermore, the Italians were far less enthused about the prospect of war than the Germans and supported it with less enthusiasm. Even Mussolini himself was motivated far more by personal ego and the ties he had created years earlier with Hitler than by any genuine passion for general war in Europe or with the Americans. His own forces had been humiliated years earlier in Ethiopia and, however reluctant he was to ever to concede the matter openly, it was impossible for him to have totally blinded himself to the inadequacies in his own military forces and its leadership.

Louisiana's Vance Plauche (Democrat) began by speaking of Japan's "treacherous and dastardly act" of attacking "America while still pretending to seek understanding and to want peace." In light of what had happened, "now, as expected, its partners in infamy, Germany and Italy, have declared war on these United States." There was no choice but to "destroy those nations who have embarked upon a course of world dominion and who have been properly classified as 'international desperadoes and assassins.'"[15]

American Labor Congressman Vito Marcantonio of New York spoke of how "this is a war of defense, a just war, an anti–Fascist war, and a war of liberation."[16] Whatever ethnic and racial divisions existed, victory in this global conflagration was the goal shared by one and all: "I have the honor to represent the Twentieth Congressional District of New York. It is composed of Americans of all races, colors, and creeds: Americans of Italian extraction, Puerto Ricans, Negroes, and Jews. They have lived and worked for America. In keeping with the great tradition of Washington, Lincoln, Garibaldi, De Diego, and Frederick Douglass, they will fight and die for America."[17]

Joseph R. Bryson (South Carolina Democrat) cited his letter to the president on the day of the vote declaring hostilities with Japan as evidence that he had anticipated that Italy and Germany would openly enter the war as well. Although he does not come out and say it, he gives every indication of having in mind the contrast of the current conflict with more controversial ones of the past. In this case there was no question that, "History will record that this war was not of our making. We take up the challenge with clean hands."[18]

Nor does he explicitly mention how in some past conflicts (the American Civil War in particular) a disproportionate burden was placed on the poorer segments of society while the richer ones were able to escape the draft and combat entirely. Yet that thought seems likely to have been in his mind as he warns that such would not be the case in the current war: "Even the poorer ones of us enjoy blessings undreamed of by the peoples of any other country or clime. We are admonished [by the Bible], however, from those who receive much, much in like manner is expected."[19]

The non-voting delegate of Alaska, Anthony J. Dimond (Democrat), argued that since others had forced the issue by either direct attack or by declaring war that there was no alternative. "Under these circumstances, no loyal citizen can have the least doubt of the course of action to be taken."[20]

He laid down Alaska's commitment in rhetoric that could easily be used to demean anyone who did not agree with his own definition of the terms: "In Alaska we are, in my judgment, singularly blessed in the absence of 'fifth columnists,' saboteurs, and traitors, and for that we are profoundly thankful."[21]

He confessed that there was a considerable skittishness in his home territory: "the people of Alaska are apprehensive because they know that, if not on the firing line, they are only one step removed from it...."[22] His concern was better placed than he could have imagined. Soon Japanese forces would seize a few of the outer islands of the Aleutians and bring the war, effectively, to the doorstep of the North American continent.

The Ideological Element in the War

Although Democrat Eugene J. Keogh of New York was willing to cast the war in terms of national survival, he stressed that this was also an ideological conflict. It involved two very different attitudes toward the relationship of the state to its people, two world-views that vied for control of the world:

> There is now a direct and awful clash of conflicting philosophies of life and government. Those philosophies are, on the one hand, that of the totalitarian states in which as a principal component is the view that the individual is subservient to the state and, on the other hand, that of the free, democratic, representative governments, the cardinal keystone of which is that such governments are created by men; derive their just powers from the consent of the governed; and are charged with the responsibility of insuring to their citizens the freedom of speech, the freedom of religion, the freedom from want, and the freedom from fear.... Our way of life, our liberty, and our civilization have very definitely and insidiously been challenged.[23]

However true this was in the abstract, the victory would require laboring with the Soviet Union's form of totalitarianism. In that system these fundamental freedoms had been equally destroyed as in Nazism, and millions had perished on the most nebulous of charges. Keogh does not deal with the historical irony that the practicalities of both survival and victory required seeking allies where one could find them, even if they themselves were guilty of vast evils.

William T. Pheiffer of New York (Republican) echoed the common theme that the American Congress and government had labored to avoid hostilities and that the war had created a consensus "to win the war as quickly and decisively as possible." Desirable as such a victory was, he stressed that it had to be a clear-cut Western triumph rather than a negotiated peace: "This war must not, and shall not, end until we have ridded the world of the horrible scourge of Nazism and until we have made assurance doubly sure that the sun will be setting very early in the Land of the Rising Sun."[24]

When Congressman Hamilton Fish, Jr. (Republican, New York) next rose, he rejected such talk of a quick victory as exaggerated optimism. Instead the three-fold alliance against the United States "probably means a long, bloody, and costly war. We are now confronted with war on two oceans, and with the armed forces of Germany, Italy, Japan, and their allies and satellites."[25]

America had long been a hybrid country, with significant minorities from around the world. In this highly dangerous war there was no room for any of them to be sitting on the sidelines nonaligned. "I appeal to all American citizens of foreign origin to unite with one hundred percent loyalty in defense of the United States and our free institutions," said Fish.[26] Earlier in the day and off the floor of the House he had stressed that, "From now on politics is out and only unity of action to achieve victory is vital to America."[27]

Thomas F. Ford (a member of the all–Democratic Mississippi delegation) conceded that "for the moment" the other side was in the ascendancy. "The battle will be long. The cost in blood and treasure will be tremendous." Yet there was cause for optimism. "It is the final battle that wins a war. That victory will be ours."[28]

He also saw a profound ideological cast to the war:

> What are we fighting for? The answer is plain. We are fighting not for territorial gains, not for commercial supremacy, not for the right to hold subject peoples in thrall, but for the right of free people to remain free, for the right of freedom of expression; for the right of every man to worship his God as he sees fit; for the right to live in peace and security; and for the reestablishment of, and the practicing of, honor and faith and good intent among all peoples.[29]

The opposition to seeking "commercial supremacy" and, even more so, to colonialism ("territorial gains" and "hold[ing] subject peoples in thrall") were to create tensions with the British throughout the war. As time progressed, the Americans saw victory as the opportunity for a new beginning for colonial nations, while the British (and French) labored for a recreation of their pre-war and traditional spheres of influence and control. The Americans were visionary and idealistic and were disappointed at the determination of others to cling to imperialism over less-developed countries. The British, in turn, thought the Americans were totally unrealistic about what real-world conditions required, and considered restoring their prior rights and privileges as a natural outcome and reward for their role in producing the victory.

The Difficulties Faced by the U.S.

Democratic Congressman Robert L. F. Sikes of Florida began by stressing that the Japanese had attacked "viciously, without warning." He emphasized the prolonged effort of the United States to stay out of the war. "We leaned over backward in that effort. So diligently did our Government seek accord with Japan that its apparent appeasement of the Japs brought strong protests from patriotic citizens."[30]

At the moment the enemy was extremely strong and Americans must not delude themselves on this matter:

> Let no person mistake the magnitude of the task that lies ahead of us. This will not be an easily won war. Japan has a seasoned, well-trained war machine. It is a thoroughly ruthless machine. Back of it stand all the resources and the cunning and the might of her Axis partners, Germany and Italy. Their strength, too, is directed against us, and in every conceivable way they will wage war upon us.[31]

To win this kind of battle meant that there could be no passive individuals even on the home front. The danger was too great and the task too formidable to permit such. It would be a war involving both human brawn but also collective will power:

> Our people must work together and stand together. Every shoulder must be put to the wheel. There must be unity in every walk of life. Personal differences and politics must be forgotten.
> Every person can help in this struggle. Many will proudly wear our country's uniform. Those who cannot can still bear its colors. We can produce food, or we can produce fighting equipment. We can help to make every idle acre bring forth food. We can help to make every wheel and every lathe turn out materials for war. We can invest in defense bonds.
> And wherever we may be or whatever our task may be, we can talk for

6. The House Responds to War with Germany and Italy

our Nation. We can believe in the things our boys are fighting for. We can let our neighbors know that we, in the best way we can, are fighting for those things, too."[32]

Pete Jarman (part of the all–Democratic Alabama delegation) reminded his listeners that the people of the nation "are confronted with a situation which affords no choice except to indulge in a declaration of war...." Three declarations in just four days had turned into reality "the fears of so many of our people who have for several years feared the necessity of our fighting Germany and Italy."[33]

It was not going to be an easy war and the nature of its beginning was symbolic of the unexpected and painful turns that would lie in the future. "The very treachery of this attack in the midst of these negotiations in our Capital cause it to be quite natural for our armies to have lost the first battle and the first several skirmishes. America has lost battles before and will, doubtless, lose others before this unfortunate war, which has been thrust upon us, is concluded, but America never has lost and will not now lose the last battle."[34]

George M. Grant (Democrat, Alabama) stressed that "every man, woman, and child in America, whether it be on the home front, farm, in the mill, mines, or armed forces" could contribute something to the ultimate victory. "All that we hold dear is at stake."[35]

California Republican Congressman Thomas Rolph spoke of the American antipathy for war and how when "arrogant, self-seeking war lords" launch a war such as this there was no choice but to resist with "every ounce of strength at our command such unwarranted and wanton violations of all we hold dear."[36]

He saw in Hitler and Mussolini power gone to rot. He suggested that the words of the poet Shelley well described such men:

> Power like a desolating pestilence,
> Pollutes whatever it touches; and obedience,
> Bane of all genius, virtue, freedom, and truth,
> Makes slaves of men, and of the human frame
> A mechanized automaton.[37]

When Mrs. Frances P. Bolton (Republican, Ohio) spoke, she conceded that she had not always agreed with the policies of the Roosevelt administration. But that was past history. "We are at war and there is no place in our lives for anything that will not build our strength and power, and build it quickly."[38] It was a time for all to rise above their traditional prejudices and pettiness—even members of Congress. "Let us not permit ourselves any littleness, any selfishness, any intolerance. Rather let us assume a greatness beyond ourselves, reconsecrating ourselves daily to the ideal of brotherhood that is America...."[39]

She astutely recognized that if this war was going to be won, it would be as much due to American industry and innovation as to the soldier on the front line:

> Nothing could have been done that would have united this country more completely than Japan's mode of attack. But this initial spirit of unity will fail if there be less than united action too.
> This war is like no other war in history. Methods used in 1918 will not serve now—weapons must be adapted to the new war, and those weapons must be produced with a speed which looks impossible and which must be increased constantly with unfaltering strides. Victory will be won on the production line—uncountable numbers of lives will be lost if that line fails.[40]

Congressman Stephen M. Young (Democrat, Ohio) spoke of how victory would not be obtained by empty rhetoric ("by wearing V buttons nor by boasts of our might") but through national unity behind the president, "loyalty, work, consecration, and combined determination to win or die." He expressed support for Roosevelt in virtually religious terms: "I have confidence in our President and gladly yield deference and devotion to him and unselfish support of his leadership."[41]

He reminded his fellow members that "In recent months I have no numerous occasions said that only Congress may declare war and that only one man, Adolf Hitler, can put us into war against Germany." That he had now done. What America had been going through since Sunday was horrendous. "This is our Gethsemane."[42]

Americans much preferred peace, New York Democrat Donald L. O'Toole emphasized. "We Americans detest war, but down to the lowliest citizen we are grateful that our beloved Nation will not sell her soul for peace." He pictured the conflict as a clash of civilization itself with the forces of anarchy and destruction. "The jackals are now running in the pack with the Asiatic wolves, but we shall stand our ground and wipe out forever these menaces to morality, religion, respectability, and civilization."[43]

It was not a time for internal grudge holding: "We must be forgiving to those of our citizenry who, in the past, were taken in by the European propagandists and who, perhaps, contributed in some manner against the defense of our country. They, too, are fully cognizant of the danger that now confronts us and of the value of the American way of life."[44]

Martin J. Kennedy of New York City spoke broadly of the commitment of his metropolis's willingness "to act as the first line of defense along the east coast. In the present crisis, regardless of racial origin, religion, or politics, we stand united squarely behind our Commander in Chief, President Roosevelt."[45]

An Unrepentant Anti-Interventionist

The opposition in recent years to intervention abroad was regarded as wrong headed by a goodly number and some (as we have seen here and in previous chapters) took the opportunity to get in a few verbal censures at their opponents. Charles A. Wolverton (Republican, New Jersey) saw nothing to apologize for.

> I would have avoided it if it had been possible. Until we had war thrust upon us, first, by Japan, and now by Germany and Italy, I have voted upon every measure presented to this House during the war emergency period, upon the basis of whether the particular measure would tend to take us into war. If, in my opinion, it had such a tendency then I voted against it. And, with the same desire to protect our people from the ravages of war I have voted, without exception for every appropriation that would build up and make stronger our defense.[46]

Carefully re-emphasizing his opposition to war while protecting himself against any accusation that his actions had left the nation militarily weak—note the emphasis on having consistently voted for increased defense expenditures—he spoke in neither jubilation nor shame, only in sadness.

> It is needless to say that my regret is deep and sincere that the course we have followed, for the more than two years the war has raged, has not saved us from participation in the war. I am deeply disappointed. But with a realization that our national safety and security is threatened there is but one duty for all of us and that is to support to the fullest extent our Government, in the fulfillment of its duty to provide for the security and safety of our people.... In the fulfillment of this task may we have the help of the divine hand that has never failed us in the past as a source of strength.[47]

Congressional Democrat James F. O'Connor of Montana recalled the deliberations concerning declaring war on Japan: "Little was said. No arguments or speeches were necessary for the passage of this resolution. The atrocious acts of Japan, like a sudden calamitous stroke, united the American people as never before."[48]

Faced with a declaration of hostilities from both Germany and Italy, the choice was equally obligatory.

> I, for one, have fought every move that I thought would cause us to enter a war unnecessarily, but when nations assault us and declare war

against our people and our country there was and is but one answer.... Whatever arguments, contentions, and maybe mistakes that have taken place or occurred in the past are water under the bridge and we must stand together as one in this hour of America's greatest crisis.[49]

The repeated efforts of the United States to avoid a foreign conflict were heavily stressed by Ohio Republican George H. Bender:

> We have done everything humanly possible to insulate ourselves against the temptations and provocations which might lead to war. Our consciences are clear. We have gone further in the pursuit of peace than any other nation in history.
> We have tried to keep our ships at home.
> We have kept our citizens from war zones.
> We have restricted our commerce and closed our eyes to events.
> These pathways are henceforth closed to us. Germany and Italy have declared themselves at war with the United States.[50]

If the international situation was to be reversed, it was up to the United States to make the decisive difference. "The enslaved millions of Europe and Asia are looking to America, the last great hope on earth, for salvation.... We shall make war upon the land, upon the seas, and in the air with the bravery and courage of a free people to the end that mankind may realize in our lifetime the ideals of humanity for which all decent men must strive."[51]

Congressman Allen T. Treadway (Republican, Massachusetts) emphasized the quickness with which Congress had moved in response to the declarations of war. "Within an hour after being formally advised of it by the President, the Congress, without a dissenting vote, accepted the challenge thus laid down.... Hitler has contemptuously referred to democracies as being unable to function speedily and efficiently in a crisis. Today we have demonstrated that the greatest democracy on earth can act in a constitutional manner with the utmost dispatch...."[52]

He concurred in the judgment of other speakers that the task was not going to be easy. It would be foolish to forget that this was "a worldwide, all-out war"[53] that would inevitably bring its share of defeats before final victory.[54] The American people should not delude themselves. They were going to bear a tremendously heavy burden that would change their normal ways of living in the most drastic manner:

> Production must be doubled and redoubled. Home defenses must be organized. We must give up many of the material things of life to which we have become accustomed. There can be no more "business as usual." Heavier and heavier taxes must be borne. All our effort must be concentrated on the defense of our homeland and on the destruction of Hitlerism. Everything else must be subjugated to these purposes.[55]

6. The House Responds to War with Germany and Italy

The series of short speeches was brought to an end by the words of Democrat John A. Meyer of Maryland. Aggression had been launched by Japan. War had been declared by Germany and Italy. America was simply responding to what they had done.[56]

Perhaps it was more relevant than Meyer realized at the time that in his closing two paragraphs he appealed to the political and spiritual memory of the American people, citing famous words from both sources:

> North and south, east and west, Americans of every class, creed, and color are united as never before. We, their Representatives, stand here rallying around our dead and we are "highly resolved that these dead shall not have died in vain; that this Nation, under God, shall have a new birth of freedom; and that government of the people, by the people, and for the people shall not perish from this earth."
>
> I pray that Almighty God may bless our arms; I know that we shall achieve ultimate victory. Then once more "peace on earth, good will to men" will be the cherished possession of all.[57]

The Absentees

Six House members arrived between the two votes, enabling them to cast their decision for war with Italy though not with Germany: Allen, Flannery, Magnuson, Scanlon, Tinkham, and Weiss. Later in the day Tinkham and Allen both spoke of how they had been "unavoidably absent" during the first vote, though without spelling out why their absence had been unavoidable.[58]

That left 30 counted as not voting on either measure:

> Joe B. Bates (Kentucky, Democrat,)
> J. Jasper Bell (Missouri, Democrat,)
> Richard T. Buckler (Farm Labor, Minnesota)
> William T. Byrne (Democrat, New York)
> Arthur P. Cannon (Democrat, Florida)
> John W. Costello (Democrat, California)
> John J. Delaney (Democrat, New York)
> Charles L. Gerlach (Republican, Pennsylvania)
> Ward Johnson (Republican, California)
> Augustine B. Kelley (Democrat, Pennsylvania)
> John H. Kerr (Democrat, North Carolina)
> Michael J. Kirwan (Democrat, Ohio)
> William H. Larrabee (Democrat, Indiana)
> Joseph A. McArdle (Democrat, Pennsylvania)
> Donald H. McLean (Republican, New Jersey)
> Joseph J. Mansfield (Democrat, Texas)

Noah W. Mason (Republican, Illinois)
John R. Murdock (Democrat, Arizona)
Caroline O'Day (Democrat, New York)
James A. O'Leary (Democrat, New York)
Frank C. Osmers, Jr., (Republican, New Jersey)
Joseph L. Pfeifer (Democrat, New York)
J. W. Robinson (Democrat, Utah)
Edwin M. Schaefer (Democrat, Illinois)
Henry B. Sheridan (Democrat, Alabama)
Joe L. Smith (Democrat, West Virginia)
Henry B. Steagall (Democrat, Alabama)
Richard J. Welch (Republican, California)
Compton I. White (Democrat, Idaho)
James Wolfenden (Republican, Pennsylvania,)

Some of the reasons for the absences were recorded in the *Record* and are representative of the kinds of delays inherent in bringing together, quickly, any large group for prompt legislative action.

McArdle, for example, had left Washington because of illness after voting for the war resolution concerning Japan. "I returned to Pittsburgh to again seek the medical services of my physician, and advised my office to keep me informed of anything of importance which might come up in the House." When he received word of the likely war votes that Thursday, the early plane out of Pittsburgh had already left and the afternoon flight would get him there too late. Having missed the train connection as well he drove to the District, arriving over an hour too late for the votes.[59]

Others also found transportation difficulties impossible to overcome. Kelley, Scanlon, and Weiss had jointly chartered a plane back to Washington.[60] Oddly, though the latter two had been able to reach the House floor in time for the Italian vote, Kelley missed both.

Kelley's problem began when he did not receive the phone call announcing that day's vote. "I got the message indirectly from Congressmen Weiss and Scanlon and I attempted to engage a private plane from my home town, but due to the weather conditions, which were very bad west of the Allegheny Mountains, the pilot deemed it inadvisable so it was necessary for me to drive thirty miles to catch a plane at the Pittsburgh airport." He provided no explanation of how he still managed to miss both votes while the other two members had missed only one.[61]

Congressman Delaney had been on a military inspection tour:

> Mr. Speaker, today, when the vote was taken declaring a state of war to exist between Germany and Italy and the United States, I was on my way to the naval airport at Floyd Bennett Field, Brooklyn, N.Y., con-

cerning the preparations being made at that field for the protection of the New York Harbor. When I was informed of the action of Germany and Italy declaring war on the United States I immediately left for Washington, arriving a few minutes late.[62]

In the greater scheme of things such absences did not matter, since none of them was intending to vote against the war resolutions. Yet, given the opportunity, they preferred to put on the public record the reasons for their absences and thereby avoid potential misunderstandings.

Miss Rankin Dissents Again—More Discretely

Congresswoman Jeannette Rankin had voted against the war with Japan. In this case she merely had herself recorded as "present." In many ways this is odd: Neither the Germans nor the Italians—for all their bellicose animosity toward the United States and naked aggression in Europe and Africa—had directly assaulted the American military forces. (At least not under circumstances where critics were certain that the United States did not have at least partial responsibility for the hostile encounters.) In contrast, the Japanese forces had directly assaulted major American military installations without even breaking diplomatic relations.

Being able to vote against war when faced with such direct aggression would, seemingly, force the consistent individual to vote against it where nothing direct had yet occurred. Perhaps the political pressure had become too great on her, or she had begun to have second thoughts about her own wisdom earlier in the week.

Before the presidential message was received, Rankin had spent some time in the gallery of the House observing both the onlookers and the members already on the House floor. As the time came for the vote she descended to the legislative floor itself. Several of those present spoke with her briefly to urge her not to vote against the measure.[63] Congressman Everett Dirksen (Republican, Illinois) sat to her left and was among this number,[64] and pleaded with her at length.[65] When the time came for the German vote, her voice was so soft that the Speaker asked her to repeat her response. Again it was a mere, "Present."[66]

The reaction to Rankin's vote was considerably different this time and the shift from "no" to effective abstention—by having herself recorded just as "present"—likely made the difference. Not to mention that, unlike Pearl Harbor, the European war was not ignited by an inflammatory direct assault on American territory. As a *New York Herald Tribune* correspondent reported, the "present" vote "was interpreted as a sign that she had yielded somewhat in her convictions as to the necessity of war, and eight or ten persons applauded her. Several Representatives stopped to pat her on the shoulder or shake her hand."⁶⁷ This time the boos and wrath were missing.

After casting a second "present" on the Italian declaration, Rankin retired to a nearby a cloakroom. She drank some milk and consumed an apple while remaining off floor for the vote legalizing the sending of American forces abroad to implement the war declarations.⁶⁸

British Relief and Japanese Caution

From the standpoint of anti-interventionists, the British had plotted zealously and unscrupulously to draw the United States into the European War. From the standpoint of those favoring intervention, Britain had only done the right thing, yet the general British reaction to the declaration was far more restrained than it had been at the time of the First World War. Upon that occasion, the mood of celebration had become so rowdy that American Ambassador John G. Winant had to curb the enthusiasm of his guests with a pointed rebuke: "Gentlemen, we are in danger of making fools of ourselves."⁶⁹

This time the emotions were subdued. As one correspondent reported, everyone was happy—more than that, they felt a heavy burden had been removed from their backs. Yet once the week's events had begun they all felt that the result was inevitable, just like in the kind of ancient tragedy the Greeks were famous for. So he concluded, they accepted it on those terms rather than with an outburst of enthusiasm."⁷⁰

Meanwhile, a world away, the Japanese were pleased with Germany's entrance into the war but its leaders also urged caution and calm. Premier-General Hideki Tojo urged a large public rally not to fall into a state of "intoxication by initial victories."⁷¹ The future held a lengthy and vigorous struggle between East and West.⁷²

The moral case for the war was also emphasized. Tojo argued that "I am convinced that right is on our side, and that in the end right will win."⁷³ In addressing a luncheon in honor of the revised Tripartite Pact, Foreign Minister Shigenori Togo reminded his audience that "Justice alone promises victory."⁷⁴

The President Signs the Declaration

The president's actions had been far different than in regard to Japan. Then Roosevelt had traveled to Capitol Hill to rally Congress. This time the German and Italian action seemed so natural and expected, that the official notification to Congress was simply typed and read to the legislative body. Less than three hours later the necessary paperwork was

6. The House Responds to War with Germany and Italy   151

presented by a congressional delegation to the president. At 3:05 P.M. the war declaration concerning Germany was signed, and a minute later so was that targeting Italy.[75] Roosevelt remarked, "I've always heard things came in threes. Here they are."[76]

Senator Carter Glass (Democrat, Virginia) vigorously responded with a reference to how certain members had wanted to make the resolution more restrained. He spoke of how "some men in the Senate Foreign Relations Committee wanted to soften the resolutions so as not to hurt the feelings of civilians in the Axis countries. I said, 'Hell, we not only want to hurt their feelings but we want to kill them.'"[77]

Notes

Preface

1. Chesly Manly, "Congress Votes War on Japan in Speedy Session," *Chicago Tribune*, December 9, 1941, 7.

Chapter 1

1. George Gallup, "Majority in Poll Expected War," *Richmond (Virginia) Times Dispatch*, December 10, 1941, 2.
2. Harrison E. Salisbury, *A Journey for Our Times: A Memoir* (New York: Harper & Row, 1983), 61.
3. Including the military. Future Secretary of State Dean Rusk was on duty that morning and his superiors in G-2 shared with him an intelligence document that they intended to promptly destroy but which they thought he should see first, "a memorandum prepared five days earlier by the Japanese section of G-2 listing targets in the Pacific which the Japanese might attack. Pearl Harbor was not on the list" (Dean Rusk, *As I Saw It* [New York: W.W. Norton 1990], 102). The chief of naval operations sent out a warning to naval commands on November 25, 1941, "Preparations are becoming apparent in China, Formosa, and Indo China for an early aggressive movement of some character although as yet there are no clear indications as to its strength or whether it will be directed against the Burma Road, Thailand, Malay Peninsula, Netherlands East Indies or the Philippines" (Richard Connaughton, *MacArthur and Defeat in the Philippines* [Woodstock, NY: Overlook Press, 2001], 150). Again, the absence of Pearl Harbor is notable. The most serious contingency ever contemplated even in war gaming was a small or major air raid at some point during the war—not half the Japanese carrier fleet available attacking at once.
4. Cordell Hull noted in his diary that after the surprise began to wear off, the next reaction was how absurdly "unwise" the attack had been from the long-range Japanese standpoint. "However, as reports came in of the tremendous damage suffered at Hawaii, this feeling became somewhat diluted" (Cordell Hull, *The Memoirs of Cordell Hull*, vol. 2, [New York: Macmillan, 1948], 1099).
5. Dorothy Thompson, "On the Record," *Richmond (Virginia) Times Dispatch*, December 11, 1941, 15.
6. "Radio Flashes News of Attack during Quiet Sunday Afternoon," *New York Herald Tribune*, December 8, 1941, 4.
7. Ibid.
8. "It Is a Real War," *Baltimore Sun*, December 7, 1941 (special edition), 1. See the same source for additional observations made sporadically by the same observer.

9. For a survey of the timing of a number of the new reports that were issued in Washington that day, see James M. Minifie, "Roosevelt Calls Congress Chiefs to War Parley," *New York Herald Tribune*, December 8, 1941, 6.
10. Gerald Griffin, "Tempo of War Apparent at White House," *Baltimore Sun*, December 8, 1941, 3.
11. *Ibid.*
12. Frances Perkins, *The Roosevelt I Knew* (New York: Viking Press, 1946), 379.
13. *Ibid.*
14. Elliott Roosevelt, *As He Saw It* (New York: Duell, Sloan and Pearce, 1946), 50–51.
15. C. P. Trussell, "Congress Decided," *New York Times*, December 8, 1941, 1.
16. Samuel I. Rosenman, *Working with Roosevelt* (New York: Harper & Brothers, 1952), 305–306.
17. For her personal account, see Grace Tully, *F.D.R. My Boss* (New York: Charles Scribner's Sons, 1949), 256.
18. Robert E. Sherwood, *Roosevelt and Hopkins: An Intimate History* (New York: Harper & Brothers, 1948), 433.
19. Trussell, "Congress Decided," 6.
20. William D. Leahy, *I Was There: The Personal Story of the Chief of Staff to Presidents Roosevelt and Truman Based on His Notes and Diaries Made at the Time* (New York: Whittlesey House, 1950), 64.
21. *Ibid.*
22. "Archbishop Curley and the War," *Baltimore Sun*, December 8, 1941, 28.
23. Trussell, "Congress Decided," 1.
24. *Ibid.*
25. *Ibid.*
26. Frank L. Kluckhorn, "President Fears 'Very Heavy Losses' on Oahu—Churchill Notifies Japan that a State of War Exists," *New York Times*, December 8, 1941, 4.
27. "'No Choice' Says Landon," *New York Times*, 6.
28. "Wilkie Calls for Unity," *New York Times*, December 8, 1941, 6.
29. "Hoover Calls to Arms," *New York Times*, December 8, 1941, 6.
30. "Hoover Sees War 'Forced Upon Us,'" *Richmond [Virginia] Times Dispatch*, December 9, 1941, 5.
31. "Isolation Groups Back Roosevelt," *New York Times*, December 9, 1941, 44.
32. Justus D. Doenecke, *The Battle against Intervention, 1939–1941* (Malabar, FL: Krieger Publishing Co., 1997), 95.
33. Wayne S. Cole, *Roosevelt & the Isolationists, 1932–45* (Lincoln, Nebraska: University of NE Press, 1983), 503.
34. Trussell, "Congress Decided," 6.
35. "Action Against Japs Demanded by U.S. Leaders," *Chicago Tribune*, December 8, 1941, 14.
36. Trussell, "Congress Decided," 6.
37. *Ibid.*
38. *Ibid.*
39. For one of the larger collections of immediate reactions carried by the press of the day, see "Action Against Japs Demanded," 14.
40. All quotes in this paragraph from, "Wheeler Backs a War on Japan," *New York Times*, December 8, 1941, 6.
41. "Declaration of War Urged by Wheeler," *Baltimore Sun*, December 8, 1941, 2.
42. "Japs Didn't Ask U.S. to 'Pink Tea,' Wheeler Warns," *Chicago Tribune*, December 10, 1941, 10.
43. "Clark of Missouri Asks Unity," *New York Times*, December 8, 1941, 6.
44. "'No Choice,' Says Walsh," *New York Times*, December 8, 1941, 2.
45. Jack Beall, "Congress United in Call for War, Vote Due Today," *New York Herald Tribune*, December 8, 1941, 8.
46. "Attack Arouses Indignation in Congress," *Richmond (Virginia) Times Dispatch*, December 8, 1941, 5.
47. *Ibid.*
48. Beall, 8.
49. "Most Congressmen Seem to Favor a Declaration," *Baltimore Sun*, December 8, 1941, 2.
50. "Attack Arouses Indignation," 5.
51. Rorin Morse Platt, *Virginia in Foreign Affairs, 1933–1941* (Lanham, MD: University Press of America, 1991), 221. For a survey of contemporary Southern opinion as to why the region was more

Notes—Chapter 1

militant in foreign affairs than others, see "Fighting South Tells Why It Is More Bellicose," *New York Times,* December 14, 1941, 28.

52. "Most Congressmen," 2.

53. "Gen Wood Gives Support," *New York Times,* December 8, 1941, 6.

54. "America First to Back War if Congress Does," *New York Herald Tribune,* December 8, 1941, 14.

55. Chalmers M. Roberts, "A Day That Will Live...." *Washington Post,* December 7, 2001, A41.

56. Cole, *Roosevelt and the Isolationists,* 502.

57. James J. Martin, *American Liberalism and World Politics, 1931–1941: Liberalism's Press and Spokesmen on the Road Back to War between Mukden and Pearl Harbor,* vol. 2 (New York: Davin-Adair, 1964), 1268.

58. "United Support of War Is Asked by Lindbergh," *New York Herald Tribune,* December 9, 1941, 18.

59. Wayne S. Cole, *Charles A. Lindbergh and the Battle against American Intervention in World War II* (New York: Harcourt Brace Jovanovich, 1974), 207.

60. "Lindbergh Keeps Silence," *Richmond Times Dispatch,* December 8, 1941, 2.

61. "Lindbergh Remains in Seclusion; Gives No Views on Japan," *Richmond [Virginia] News Leader,* December 9, 1941, 1.

62. "Isolation Groups Back Roosevelt," 44.

63. "'We Will Support It,' Says America Firster," *Richmond (Virginia) Times Dispatch,* December 9, 1941, 5.

64. Wayne S. Cole, *America First: The Battle against Intervention, 1940–1941* (Madison: University of Wisconsin Press, 1953; reprint, New York: Octagon Books, 1971), 196.

65. "Isolation Groups, Back Roosevelt," 44.

66. Doenecke, *Battle,* 95. On his prewar, publicly announced conviction that if we thought that a war was inevitable in the Far East that we needed to massively enhance the military facilities in the Philippines, see Cole, *Lindbergh,* 208–209.

67. Cole, Charles A. Lindbergh, 210.

68. Cole, *America First,* 196.

69. "America First Acts to End Organization," *New York Times,* December 12, 1941, 22.

70. Jack Steele, "America First Votes to Quit and Back War," *New York Times,* December 12, 1941.

71. Cole, *Roosevelt & the Isolationists,* 504–505.

72. For example, the Maryland chapter suspended operations in anticipation of closing down. See "State America First Group to Suspend Action, Gwyer Says," *Baltimore Sun,* December 8, 1941, 8. The Pittsburgh chapter went even further and announced its dissolution in a meeting that required "less than fifteen minutes." See "America First Group in Pittsburgh Dissolves," *Baltimore Sun,* December 9, 1941, 3.

73. Cole, *America First,* 197.

74. *Ibid.,* 198–199.

75. For a perceptive analysis of how the movement should not be interpreted in the naïve and one-dimensional manner it often is, see Martin, 1270.

76. Arthur Krock, "Unity Clicks into Place," *New York Times,* December 8, 1941, 6.

77. *Congressional Record: Proceedings and Debates of the 77th Congress, First Session,* vol. 87, Part 9: November 26, 1941 to January 2, 1942 (Washington, D.C.: United States Government Printing Office, 1941), 9511.

78. "Japanese Note Full of Infamous Falsehoods, Secretary Hull Declares," *Baltimore Sun,* December 7, 1941 (special edition), 2.

79. Kluckhorn, "President Fears," 4.

80. "Mr. Hull's Statement," *New York Times,* December 8, 1941, 10.

81. Irwin F. Gellman, *Secret Affairs: Franklin Roosevelt, Cordell Hull, and Sumner Welles* (Baltimore, MD: Johns Hopkins University Press, 1995), 269.

82. Joseph C. Grew, *Turbulent Era: A Diplomatic Record of Forty Years, 1904–1945,* edited by Walter Johnson, vol. 2 (Boston: Houghton Mifflin, 1952), 1253.

83. *Ibid.*

84. Charles E. Bohlen, *Witness to His-*

Notes—Chapter 1

tory: 1929–1969 (New York: W. W. Norton 1973), 112.

85. CR 9509.
86. CR 9510. For the full text, see the editorial, "We Shall Win," *Baltimore Sun,* December 8, 1941, 16.
87. "Newspapers Call for Meeting Foe," *New York Times,* December 8, 1941, 5.
88. *Ibid.*
89. "Nation's Press Assaults Japan's Attack on U.S.," *New York Herald Tribune,* December 8, 1941, 14.
90. Beall, 8.
91. CR 9511.
92. CR 9513.
93. "Japan Strikes and America Answers," Editorial, *Richmond (Virginia) Times Dispatch,* December 8, 1941, 10.
94. "Clean Hands; United Hearts," Editorial, *Richmond (Virginia) News Leader,* December 8, 1941, 12.
95. "America First Now!," *New York Times,* December 8, 1941, 19.
96. Mark L. Chadwin, *The Hawks of World War II* (Chapel Hill, NC: University of North Carolina Press, 1968), 264–265.
97. "United Support," 18.
98. "Nazi-Japanese Influence," *Newsweek,* December 15, 1941, 11.
99. "Nation's Press," 14.
100. "Editorial Comment on Japanese Attack," *Baltimore Sun,* December 8, 1941, 6.
101. "War with Japan," Editorial, *New York Times,* December 8, 1941, 22.
102. "Nation's Press," 14.
103. Thomas J. Hamilton, "Japanese Seizure Ordered by Biddle," *New York Times,* December 8, 1941, 6.
104. "President Authorizes Arrest of Nipponese," *Richmond (Virginia) Times Dispatch,* December 8, 1941, 4.
105. Hamilton, 6.
106. *Ibid.*
107. *Ibid.*
108. "Number Put at Less than 1,000," *New York Times,* December 8, 1941, 6.
109. "Tokyo Businesses in U.S. Are Seized," *Baltimore Sun,* December 9, 1941, 10.
110. *Ibid.*

111. "Japanese Taken to Ellis Island in F.B.I. Raids," *New York Herald Tribune,* December 8, 1941, 11.
112. *Ibid.*
113. *Ibid.*
114. "Morgenthau Bans Dealings with Japanese," *Baltimore Sun,* December 8, 1941, 3.
115. "Aliens in America," *Chicago Tribune,* December 9, 1941, 10. For comparison, 416,892 Mexicans, 442,551 Poles, 291,451 British, and 158,202 Swedish nationals lived in the U.S. though retaining their original foreign citizenship.
116. Tokyo "Businesses," 10.
117. "F.B.I. Arrests 900 Japanese in U.S. and Hawaii," *New York Herald Tribune,* December 9, 1941, 11.
118. "108 Germans, 54 Italians Held in City Roundup," *New York Herald Tribune,* December 10, 1941, 14.
119. *Ibid.*
120. For a detailed listing of the restrictions on these groups, see "Axis Nationals All Classed as Enemy Aliens," *New York Herald Tribune,* December 10, 1941, 15.
121. *Ibid.*
122. "Monday to Be Observed as Bill of Rights Day," *New York Herald Tribune,* December 10, 1941, 15.
123. "Round-Up on West Coast," *New York Times,* December 9, 1941, 40.
124. "F.B.I. Active in Connecticut," *New York Times,* December 9, 1941, 40.
125. *Ibid.*
126. 108 Germans, 14.
127. *Ibid.*
128. "2,303 Are Held in Roundup of Axis Nationals," *New York Herald Tribune,* December 10, 1941, 10.
129. "2,541 Axis Aliens Now in Custody," *New York Times,* December 13, 1941, 8.
130. *Ibid.*
131. *Ibid.*
132. "Japanese Taken to Ellis Island," 11.
133. Cf. *Ibid.*
134. "2,541," Axis Aliens, 8.
135. Cabell Phillips, *The 1940s: Decade of Triumph and Trouble* (New York: New York Times, 1975), 63.

Notes—Chapter 1

136. "Tokio Embassy 'Passes Hat' to Pay Food Bill," *New York Herald Tribune*, December 9, 1941, 28.
137. David Brinkley, *Washington Goes to War: The Extraordinary Story of the Transformation of a City and a Nation* (New York: Alfred A. Knopf, 1988), 93.
138. "U.S. Releasing Funds for Japanese Envoys," *Baltimore Sun*, December 11, 1941, 2.
139. Paul W. Ward, "Japanese Embassy Guarded by Washington Police Squad," *Baltimore Sun*, December 8, 1941, 3.
140. *Ibid.*
141. *Ibid.*
142. *Ibid.*
143. For New Orleans, see the description in "Japanese Consulate Staffs Burn Papers," *Baltimore Sun*, December 8, 1941, 17.
144. "Papers Set Wall Afire," *Baltimore Sun*, December 8, 1941, 17.
145. "War Surprises Jap Consulate; Destroy Papers," *Chicago Tribune*, December 8, 1941, 4.
146. "Japanese News Offices in New York Shut Down," *Baltimore Sun*, December 8, 1941, 3.
147. "Sell, D.N.B. Reporter, Loses Capital Privileges," *New York Herald Tribune*, December 9, 1941, 13.
148. "German Reporters Held for Inquiry," *Richmond (Virginia) Times Dispatch*, December 11, 1941, 7.
149. "Sell, D.N.B. Reporter," 13.
150. *Ibid.*
151. "Navy Shuts Off News to Japan, Germany, Italy," *New York Herald Tribune*, December 9, 1941, 17.
152. "Nazi Pilots in Jap Blitz?," *Baltimore Sun*. December 9, 1941, 16.
153. "Navy Shuts Off News," 17.
154. "Navy Halts News Stories to Four Axis Countries," *Baltimore Sun*, December 9, 1941, 10.
155. *Ibid.*
156. "U.S. Is 'Investigating.'" *New York Times*, December 11, 1941, 6.
157. "U.S. Seizes Five Nazi Reporters, Cuts News Line," *New York Herald Tribune*, December 10, 1941, 16. Also see this article for biographical information on certain of the individuals.
158. For the case of one in particular, see, "Italian Reporter in Custody," *New York Herald Tribune*, December 10, 1941, 16.
159. "Berlin and Rome Curb U.S. Writers," *New York Times*, December 11, 1941, 6.
160. "State Department Explains," *Chicago Tribune*, December 11, 1941, 11.
161. "Berlin and Rome Curb U.S.," 6.
162. *Ibid.*
163. "Exchange to Be Arranged," *New York Herald Tribune*, December 12, 1941, 9.
164. "Berlin and Rome Curb U.S.," 6.
165. *Ibid.*
166. For example, "Exchange," and "U.S. May Free Writers If Axis Does Likewise," *New York Herald Tribune*, December 12, 1941, 12.
167. "Japanese on Coast Call War 'Hara-Kiri,'" *Richmond (Virginia) Times Dispatch*, December 9, 1941, 28.
168. "Jap American League Affirms Loyalty to U.S.," *Chicago Tribune*, December 8, 1941, 5.
169. "Japanese on Coast," 28.
170. *Ibid.*
171. "Wisconsin Germans Back U.S.," *New York Herald Tribune*, December 12, 1941, 6.
172. "Steuben Society Pledges Loyalty in War on Nazis," *New York Herald Tribune*, December 12, 1941, 10.
173. For examples, see "Italo-American Bloc Here Calls for Axis Defeat," *New York Herald Tribune*, December 12, 1941, 12.
174. "Poletti Cites Loyalty of Italian-Americans," *New York Herald Tribune*, December 12, 1941, 15.
175. "Steuben Society," 10.
176. "Americans in Japan," *New York Times*, December 9, 1941, 15.
177. *Ibid.*
178. "Americans, Britons Rounded Up," *New York Times*, December 9, 1941, 15.
179. "Japanese Announce Pact," *New York Times*, December 12, 1941, 4.
180. *Ibid.*
181. "Japanese Holding 1,270 in Cus-

tody." *Richmond (Virginia) Times Dispatch,* December 11, 1941, page 7.
182. "Japan to Protect Enemy Nationals," *New York Times,* December 9, 1941, 15.
183. *Ibid.*
184. Bohlen, 112–113.
185. Richard M. Ketchum, *The Borrowed Years, 1938–1941: America on the Way to War* (New York: Random House, 1989), 790.
186. *Ibid.*
187. "Nazis Retaliate for Arrests of Germans in U.S," *New York Herald Tribune,* December 12, 1941, 9.

Chapter 2

1. F. R. Kent, Jr., "Two War Declarations: A Marked Difference," *Baltimore Sun,* December 9, 1941, 2.
2. *Ibid.*
3. CR 9504.
4. James B. Reston, "Capital Swings into War Stride; Throngs Cheer for the President," *New York Times,* December 9, 1941, 5.
5. *Ibid.*
6. *Ibid.*
7. *Ibid.*
8. *Ibid.*
9. F. R. Kent, Jr., "Notables Pack Capitol for War Declaration," *Baltimore Sun,* December 9, 1941, 2.
10. "Tokio Embassy 'Passes Hat,' to Pay Food Bill," *New York Herald Tribune,* December 9, 1941, 28.
11. "War Declared on Japan," *Richmond (Virginia) News Leader,* December 8, 1941, 2.
12. "Tokio Embassy 'Passes Hat,'" 28.
13. Reston, 5.
14. *Ibid.*
15. James M. Minifie, "Roosevelt Seen by 2,000, Heard by 80,000,000," *New York Herald Tribune,* December 9, 1941, 8.
16. Frank L. Kluckhorn, "Unity in Congress," *New York Times,* December 9, 1941, 5.
17. *Ibid.*
18. Reston, 5.
19. *Ibid.*
20. Kent, "Notables," 2.
21. *Ibid.*
22. Reston, 5.
23. Kent, "Notables," 2.
24. Minifie, "Roosevelt," 8.
25. *Ibid.*
26. *Ibid.*
27. Margaret Truman, *Harry S. Truman* (New York: William Morrow, 1973), 145.
28. Kluckhorn, "Unity," 5.
29. Kent, "Notables," 2.
30. Minifie, "Roosevelt," 8.
31. Kent, "Notables."
32. Bert Andrews, "President Fears U.S. Losses at Hawaii Base Are Heavy," *New York Herald Tribune,* December 8, 1941, 1.
33. Minifie, "Roosevelt."
34. "Millions in City Halt Tasks to Hear President," *New York Herald Tribune,* December 8, 1941, 8.
35. "Tokio Embassy 'Passes Hat,'" 28.
36. The full text of Roosevelt's speech can be found in many sources. In the current case, it is taken from CR 9504–9505.
37. Samuel I. Rosenman, *Working with Roosevelt* (New York: Harper and Brothers, 1952) 307.
38. Joseph P. Lash, *Roosevelt and Churchill, 1939–1941: The Partnership that Saved the West* (New York: W. W. Norton, 1976), 491.
39. Wayne S. Cole, *Roosevelt & the Isolationists, 1932–45* (Lincoln, NE: University of Nebraska Press, 1983), 505.
40. Harold L. Ickes, *The Secret Diary of Harold L. Ickes;* Vol. 3: *The Lowering Clouds, 1939–1941* (New York: Simon and Schuster, 1954), 664.
41. Grace Tully, *F.D.R. My Boss* (New York: Charles Scribner's Sons, 1949), 256.
42. Cole, *Roosevelt & the Isolationists,* 505–506.
43. Tully, 256.
44. Reston, 5.
45. Mark L. Chadwin, *The Hawks of World War II* (Chapel Hill, NC: University of North Carolina Press, 1968), 264.
46. *Ibid.*
47. William D. Leahy *I Was There: The*

Personal Story of the Chief of Staff to Presidents Roosevelt and Truman Based on His Notes and Diavies Made at the Time (New York: Whittlesey House, 1950), 44.

48. Tully, 255.

49. Lee Kennett, *For the Duration: The United States Goes to War—Pearl Harbor-1942* (New York: Charles Scribner's Sons, 1985), 17.

50. Breckinridge Long, *The War Diary of Breckinridge Long: Selections from the Years 1939-1944* (Lincoln, NE: University of Nebraska Press, 1966), 227–228.

51. Ickes, 661.

52. Ibid., 663.

53. Justus D. Doenecke, *In Danger Undaunted: The Anti-Interventionist Movement of 1940-1941 as Revealed in the Papers of the America First Committee* (Stanford, CA: Hoover Institution Press, 1990), 454–455.

54. CR 9505.

55. Dewey L. Fleming, "Nation Moves Swiftly to Avenge War Losses, Meet Japanese Attack," *Baltimore Sun*, December 9, 1941, 3.

56. CR 9505.

57. Burton W. Folsom, "Senator Arthur Vandenberg: A Profile in Courage," *Mackinac Center for Public Policy Research*, available: http://www.mackinac.org/article.asp?ID=349 [May 2003].

58. Ibid.

59. "Arthur Vandenberg," *Hoover & Truman: A Presidential Friendship*, a site sponsored by the Hoover Presidential Library & Museum and the Truman Presidential Library and Museum. Available: http://www.trumanlibrary.org/hoover/vandenbio.htm [May 2003].

60. CR 9505.

61. Ibid.

62. Cole, *Roosevelt & the Isolationists*, 504.

63. Ibid.

64. Richard E. Darilek, *A Loyal Opposition in Time of War: The Republican Party and the Politics of Foreign Policy from Pearl Harbor to Yalta* (Westport, CT: Greenwood Press, 1976), 27.

65. C. David Tompkins, *Senator Arthur H. Vandenberg: The Evolution of a Modern Republican, 1884-1945* ([East Lansing, MI]: Michigan State University Press, 1970), 189.

66. Ibid.

67. Ibid., 190.

68. Ibid.

69. "Arthur Vandenberg."

70. CR 9505–9506.

71. CR 9505.

72. Unless otherwise noted, the biographical information on the various senators and representatives is taken from the internet edition of the *Biographical Directory of the United States Congress, 1774–Present*, (http://bioguide.congress.gov/biosearch/biosearch.asp.) Information on any individual may be obtained by entering the individual's name, branch of Congress served in, and state represented. Party affiliations come from Linda S. Hubbard, ed., *Notable Americans: What They Did, from 1620 to the Present*. 4th ed. (Detroit: Gale Research, 1988), 206–209, who provides a convenient compendium of this information on all members from the first Congress onward.

73. George N. Green, "Thomas Terry Connally (1877–1963)," at *The Handbook of Texas Online*. (http://www.tsha.utexas.edu/handbook/online/articles/view/CC/fco36.html). [May 2003].

74. Ibid.

75. "Most Congressmen Seem to Favor a Declaration," *Baltimore Sun*, December 8, 1941, 2.

76. Ibid.

77. Ibid.

78. "All-Out War Sure Now, Says Tydings," *Baltimore Sun*, December 8, 1941, 28.

79. "Congress Leaders Take Part in Cabinet Session to Discuss U.S. Act," *Baltimore Sun*, December 8, 1941, 2.

80. Ibid.

81. "Miss Rankin's Lone 'No' Vote Booed in House," *New York Herald Tribune*, December 9, 1941, 7.

82. C. P. Trussell, "Unanimous Senate Acts in 15 Minutes," *New York Times*, December 9, 1941, 6.

83. Richard Lowitt, *George W. Norris: The Triumph of a Progressive, 1933–1944* (Urbana, IL: University of Illinois Press, 1978), 364.

84. *Ibid.*, 365.
85. George W. Norris, *Fighting Liberal: The Autobiography of George W. Norris* (New York: Macmillan, 1945), 190.
86. Norman L. Zucker, *George W. Norris: Gentle Knight of American Democracy* (Urbana, IL: University of Illinois Press, 1966), 135.
87. On the apparently insurmountable economic costs of trying to wage an anti–Nazi war without Britain to assist, see Zucker, 134.
88. *Ibid.*, 134–135.
89. Miss Rankin's Lone 'No' Vote, 7.
90. Patrick J. Maney, *"Young Bob" La Follette: A Biography of Robert M. La Follette, Jr., 1895-1953* (Columbia, MO: University of Missouri Press, 1978), 248.
91. *Ibid.*, 249.
92. *Ibid.*
93. *Ibid.*
94. *Ibid.*, 249–250.
95. *Ibid.*, 249.
96. *Ibid.*, 250.
97. *Ibid.*
98. "Urges Change of Vote," *New York Herald Tribune*, December 9, 1941, 7.
99. For a detailed discussion of the meeting, see Cole, *Roosevelt & the Isolationists*, 501–502, and Ketchum, 782–783.
100. Wayne S. Cole, *Senator Gerald P. Nye and American Foreign Relations* (Minneapolis, MN: University of Minnesota Press, 1962), 198.
101. *Ibid.*, 198–199.
102. "Opinions of Senator Nye," *New York Times*, December 8, 1941, 6.
103. Richard M. Ketchum, *The Borrowed Years, 1938-1941: America on the Way to War* (New York: Random House, 1989), 783.
104. Cole, *Senator Gerald P. Nye*, 199.
105. "Opinions," 6.
106. Cole, *Roosevelt & the Isolationists*, 502.
107. Cole, *Senator Gerald P. Nye*, 199.
108. *Ibid.*, 200.
109. CR 9504.
110. CR 9505.
111. CR 9506.
112. CR 9504.
112. CR 9539.
113. CR 9504.
114. CR 9505.
115. CR 9504.
116. CR 9506.
117. *Ibid.*
118. *Ibid.*
119. *Ibid.*
120. CR 9504, 9506.
121. CR 9506.
122. CR 9504.
123. CR 9506.
124. *Ibid.*
125. *Ibid.*
126. CR 9505–9506.
127. Trussell, "Unanimous Senate Acts," 6.

Chapter 3

1. CR 9519.
2. CR 9520.
3. *Ibid.*
4. Hannah Josephson, *Jeanette Rankin: First Lady in Congress—A Biography* (Indianapolis, IN: Bobbs-Merrill, 1974), 161.
5. Dewey L. Fleming, "Nation Moves Swiftly to Avenge War Losses, Meet Japanese Attack," *Baltimore Sun*, December 9, 1941, 3.
6. For a concise description of the very different atmosphere before the preceding war declaration see, "Unity on War Contrasts with Confusion '17," *New York Herald Tribune*, December 9, 1941, 13.
7. Josephson, 161.
8. "Miss Rankins Lone 'No' Vote Booed in the House," *New York Herald Tribune*, December 9, 1941, 7.
9. Josephson, 161. Stanley Weintraub, *Journey into War: December 7, 1941* (New York: Dutton, 1991), 634, attributes the remark to Congressman John M. Dingell.
10. CR 9520.
11. *Ibid.*
12. *Ibid.*
13. *Ibid.*
14. *Ibid.*
15. Richard E. Darilek, *A Loyal Op-*

position in Time of War: The Republican Party and the Politics of Foreign Policy from Pearl Harbor to Yalta (Westport, CT: Greenwood Press, 1976,) 20.

16. Jack Beall "Congress United in Call for War, Vote Due Today," *New York Herald Tribune*, December 8, 1941, 8.

17. Kenneth S. Davis, *FDR: The War President, 1940–1943* (New York: Random House, 2000), 349.

18. CR 9520.
19. *Ibid.*
20. CR 9521.
21. *Ibid.*
22. *Ibid.*

23. Hamilton Fish, *FDR: The Other Side of the Coin—How We Were Tricked into World War II* (New York: Vantage Press, 1976), 157.

24. *Ibid.*, 158–159.
25. *Ibid.*, 159.
26. *Ibid.*
27. CR 9521.
28. *Ibid.*
29. *Ibid.*
30. *Ibid.*

31. "Edith Nourse Rogers," available: http://clerkweb.house.gov/105/womenbio/ ExtendedBio/Rogersexb.htm [May 2003].

32. *Ibid.*

33. Dorothy M. Brown, "Edith Nourse Rogers," *American National Biography*, edited by John A. Garraty and Mark C. Carnes (New York: Oxford University Press, 1999). As available: http://www.rice.edu/fondren/woodson/exhibits/wac/rogers.html+Edith%2BRogers&hl=en&ie=UTF-8 [May 2003].

34. CR 9521.
35. *Ibid.*
36. *Ibid.*
37. *Ibid.*
38. *Ibid..*
39. *Ibid.*
40. *Ibid.*
41. CR 9522.
42. *Ibid.*
43. *Ibid.*
44. *Ibid.*
45. *Ibid.*
46. *Ibid.*
47. *Ibid.*

48. Wally Edge, "New Jersey's Greatest Generation," *PoliticsNJ.com—New Jersey's Online Political Network* available: http://www.politicsnj.com/September20_2001.htm [May 2003].

49. Robert A. Caro, *The Years of Lyndon Johnson*, vol. 1: *The Path to Power* (New York: Alfred A. Knopf, 1982), 757.

50. *Ibid.*

51. The right to expand remarks was granted to all those present and permission also given for those not present to insert their views on the resolution in the *Record* (see CR 9537). Since even the expanded version had to be submitted promptly so that day's *Record* could be available the next day, even this form reflects immediate sentiments of the various speakers. Hence we gain a wider survey of congressional opinion by quoting the official version of the proceedings, though it also permits some individuals to participate in the debate who actually did not do so at the time or who did so in greater brevity. In this trade-off of breadth of opinion versus strict historical accuracy as to amount of participation, the former seems more important to future students of the subject in determining the attitudes and opinions of the time.

52. CR 9522.
53. *Ibid.*
54. CR 9523.
55. *Ibid.*
56. *Ibid.*
57. *Ibid.*
58. *Ibid.*
59. *Ibid.*
60. *Ibid.*
61. *Ibid.*
62. CR 9523–9524.
63. CR 9524.
64. *Ibid.*
65. *Ibid.*
66. *Ibid.*
67. *Ibid.*
68. *Ibid.*
69. CR 9524–9525.
70. CR 9525.
71. *Ibid.*
72. *Ibid.*
73. *Ibid.*
74. *Ibid.*

75. *Ibid.*
76. *Ibid.*
77. *Ibid.*
78. CR 9525–9526.
79. Dennis S. Nordin, *The New Deal's Black Congressman: A Life of Arthur Wergs Mitchell* (Columbia, MO: University of Missouri Press, 1997), 240–244.
80. CR 9526.
81. *Ibid.*
82. *Ibid.*
83. *Ibid.*
84. *Ibid.*
85. *Ibid.*
86. *Ibid.*
87. *Ibid.*
88. CR 9527.
89. *Ibid.*
90. *Ibid.*
91. *Ibid.*
92. *Ibid.*
93. *Ibid.*
94. *Ibid.*
95. CR 9528.
96. CR 9527–9528.
97. *Ibid.*
98. *Ibid.*
99. *Ibid.*
100. *Ibid.*
101. *Ibid.*
102. *Ibid.*
103. CR 9528–9529.
104. CR 9529.
105. *Ibid.*
106. *Ibid.*
107. *Ibid.*
108. *Ibid.*
109. *Ibid.*
110. CR 9530.
111. CR 9529.
112. CR 9530.
113. *Ibid.*
114. *Ibid.*
115. *Ibid.*
116. CR 9530–9531.
117. CR 9531.
118. *Ibid.*
119. *Ibid.*
120. *Ibid.*
121. *Ibid.*
122. CR 9532.
123. *Ibid.*
124. *Ibid.*
125. *Ibid.*
126. *Ibid.*
127. "Rep. Van Zandt Returns Japanese Decoration," *Baltimore Sun*, December 13, 1941, 3.
128. *Ibid.*
129. CR Appendix, A5504.
130. CR 9532.
131. *Ibid.*
132. CR 9532–9533.
133. CR 9533.
134. *Ibid.*
135. *Ibid.*
136. *Ibid.*
137. *Ibid.*
138. *Ibid.*
139. *Ibid.*
140. *Ibid.*
141. *Ibid.*
142. *Ibid.*
143. For the impact of the embargo, see this writer's, *No Choice but War: The United States Embargo against Japan and the Eruption of War in the Pacific* (Jefferson, NC: McFarland & Company, 1995). In July and August of 1941 the fear of war erupting as a result of the embargo was widely acknowledged. By December the embargo's potential importance as a war-initiating motive had vanished from the American press and public consciousness. If war had broken out in early August there would have been intense questioning of the degree of American culpability.
144. CR 9534.
145. *Ibid.*
146. *Ibid.*
147. *Ibid.*
148. CR 9535.
149. *Ibid.*
150. *Ibid.*
151. *Ibid.*
152. CR 9536.
153. CR 9535.
154. *Ibid.*
155. CR 9536.
156. *Ibid.*
157. *Ibid.*
158. *Ibid.*
159. *Ibid.*
160. Sam Rayburn, "*Speak, Mister Speaker*," edited by H. G. Dulaney and Edward H. Phillips (Bonham, TX: Sam Rayburn Foundation, 1978), 86.

Notes—Chapter 3

161. "Miss Rankin Voted 'Present' in Weak Voice; Clerk Had to Call Her Name a Second Time," *New York Times*, December 12, 1941, 6.
162. F.R. Kent, Jr., "Notables Pack Capitol for War Declaration," *Baltimore Sun*, December 9, 1941, 2.
163. CR 9537.
164. "For War: 470–1," *Newsweek*, December 15, 1941, 24.
165. CR 9537.
166. *Ibid.*
167. Frank L. Kluckhorn, "Unity in Congress," *New York Times*, December 9, 1941, 5.
168. "Four-Hour Chronology of Declaration of War," *New York Times*, December 9, 1941, 3.
169. Kluckhorn, "Unity," 1.
170. Samuel W. Bell, "War Declaration Swiftly Voted, Congress Took 4 Days in 1917," *New York Herald Tribune*, December 9, 1941, 7.
171. "Aids Twice in War Steps," *New York Times*, December 9, 1941, 5.
172. Kluckhorn, "Unity," 5.
173. *Ibid.*
174. CR 9531.
175. CR 9538.
176. *Ibid.*
177. *Ibid.*
178. *Ibid.*
179. CR 9537.
180. MargaretTruman, *Harry S Truman* (New York: William Morrow & Co., 1973), 145.
181. CR 9537.
182. Stanley Weintraub, *Journey into War: December 7, 1941* (New York: Dutton, 1991), 634.
183. "8 Middle West Congressmen Miss War Vote," *Chicago Tribune*, December 9, 1941, 4.
184. Kent, "Notables."
185. For an analysis of her life-time work, see Josephson *Jeannette Rankin's*.
186. *September 11, 2001: Two Who Voted against War, 60 Years Apart*, available: http://www.loper.org/~george/trends/2001/Oct/67.html [December 2001].
187. Kent, "Notables."
188. Huntington Library, *Important People: Jeannette Rankin (1880–1973)*, available: http://www.huntington.org/vfw/imp/rankin.html [December 2001].
189. Megan McNamer, *Votes: Not Violets—The Legacy of Jeannette Rankin*, http://www.umt.edu/comm/s99/votes.html [December 2001].
190. Jeannette Rankin Foundation, *The Story of Jeannette Pickering Ranking, 1880-1973*, available: http://www.rankin-foundation.org/story.htm [December 2001].
191. Josephson, 153.
192. *September 11, 2001*.
193. Josephson, 154–155.
194. For details, see *Ibid.*, 158–159.
195. *Jeannette Rankin (1917–1919 & 1941–1943)*, available: http://www.senate.gov/member/mt/baucus/general/bios/JeannetteRankin.htm [December 2001].
196. "Miss Rankin's Lone 'No' Vote Booed."
197. Josephson, 160.
198. *Ibid.*
199. D. B. Hardeman and Donald C. Bacon, *Rayburn: A Biography* (Austin, TX: TexasMonthly Press, 1987), 276.
200. McNamer, *Votes*.
201. William "Fishbait" Miller, *Fishbait: The Memoirs of the Congressional Doorkeeper* (Englewood Cliffs, NJ: Prentice-Hall, 1977), 61.
202. Josephson, 162.
203. Kent, "Notables."
204. *Ibid.*
205. Chesly Manly, "Congress Votes War on Japan in Speedy Session, *Chicago Tribune*, December 9, 1941, 7.
206. Josephson, 162.
207. Everett M. Dirksen, *The Education of a Senator* (Urbana, IL: University of Illinois Press, 1998), 249.
208. McNamer, *Votes*.
209. Miller, 61.
210. "For War: 470–1," 24.
211. "Miss Rankin Urged to 'Redeem Honor' of Native State," *Richmond (Virginia) Times Dispatch*, December 9, 1941, 5.
212. "America Will See It Through," Editorial, *Richmond (Virginia) Times Dispatch*, December 9, 1941, 12.
213. *September 11, 2001*.
214. Miller, 61.

215. See the summary of her remarks in Josephson, 165–167. The quotation comes from 167. In my own perusal of the *Congressional Record* I could not find this speech either on that date or even several days afterwards, although there was a reference to her wishing to "expand" her remarks on one occasion—though neither the original nor expanded form of her remarks seemed to be included.

216. Josephson, 167.

217. *Ibid.*, 168.

Chapter 4

1. David Lawrence, "Hitler's Japanese War," *Richmond (Virginia) News Leader,* December 8, 1941, 7.

2. Westbrook Pegler, "Fair Enough," *Richmond (Virginia) Times Dispatch,* December 9, 1941, 13.

3. Walter Lippmann, "Wake Up, America," *Richmond (Virginia) News Leader,* December 9, 1941, 6.

4. Wayne S. Cole, *Roosevelt & the Isolationists, 1932–45* (Lincoln, NE: University of Nebraska Press, 1983), 503.

5. *Ibid.*

6. Jack Beall "Congress United in Call for War, Vote Due Today," *New York Herald Tribune,* December 8, 1941, 8.

7. *Ibid.*

8. *Ibid.*

9. "Norman Thomas Urges War Be Localized in Far East," *Baltimore Sun,* December 10, 1941, 6.

10. *Ibid.*

11. *Ibid.*

12. *Ibid.*

13. Keith Sainsbury, *Churchill and Roosevelt at War: The War They Fought and the Peace They Hoped to Make* (NY: New York University Press, 1994), 18.

14. *Ibid.*, 19.

15. Cf. the remarks on Robert A. Taft's position in William S. White, *The Taft Story* (New York: Harper & Brothers, 1954), 156–157.

16. William R. Hearst, "Hearst Asserts U.S. Will Knock Marauders Out," *New York Herald Tribune,* December 9, 1941, 13. The *Tribune* reprinted the text of the entire editorial.

17. Wayne S. Cole, *America First: The Battle Against Intervention, 1940–1941* (New York: Octagon Books, 1953), 193–194, and Cole, *Roosevelt & the Isolationists,* 504.

18. Cole, *America First* 193. For quotations on its anti–Far East war statements, see 190–192, and Wayne S. Cole, *Charles A. Lindbergh, and the Battle against American Intervention in World War II* (New York: Harcourt Brace Jovanovich), 208.

19. Cole, *America First,* 192.

20. T. R. Fehrenbach, *F.D.R.'s Undeclared War, 1939 to 1941* (New York: David McKay, 1967), 318.

21. *Ibid.*

22. For example, William L. Shirer, *The Rise and Fall of the Third Reich: A History of Nazi Germany* (New York: Simon and Schuster, 1960), 894.

23. Fehrenbach, 318.

24. For example, Frank L. Kluckhorn, "Unity in Congress," *New York Times,* December 9, 1941, 5, and "U.S. to Continue Aid to Britain," *New York Times,* December 9, 1941, 1.

25. Robert A. Divine, *The Reluctant Belligerent: American Entry into World War II* (New York: John Wiley & Sons, 1965), 157.

26. *Ibid.*

27. Cordell Hull, *Memoirs of Cordell Hull,* vol. 2 (New York: Macmillian, 1948), 1099–1100.

28. David Reynolds, *The Creation of the Anglo-American Alliance, 1937–41: A Study in Competitive Co-operation* (Chapel Hill, NC: University of North Carolina Press, 1982), 220.

29. Patrick J. Hearden, *Roosevelt Confronts Hitler: America's Entry into World War II* (Dekalb, IL: Northern Illinois University Press, 1987), 221.

30. Harold L. Ickes *The Secret Diary of Harold L. Ickes,* vol. 3, *The Lowering Clouds, 1939–1941* (New York : Simm & Schuster, 1954), 664.

31. Bert Andrews, "President Fears U.S. Losses at Hawaii Base Are Heavy," *New York Herald Tribune,* December 8, 1941, 1.

Notes—Chapter 4

32. Samuel I. Rosenman, *Working with Roosevelt* (New York: Harper & Brothers, 1952), 308.
33. "New Yorkers Are Warned by Mayor LaGuardia," *Baltimore Sun*, December 8, 1941, 2.
34. "'Directed from Berlin,' Donald Nelson Charges," *Baltimore Sun*, December 8, 1941, 11.
35. "U.S. to Continue Aid to Britain," *New York Times*, December 9, 1941, 17.
36. "Berlin Calls Roosevelt World's Only Aggressor," *Richmond (Virginia) Times Dispatch*, December 10, 1941, 2.
37. "We Must Not Forget Hitler during Pacific War, Says Long," *Richmond (Virginia) Times Dispatch*, December 10, 1941, 6.
38. *Ibid.*
39. James M. Burns, *Roosevelt: The Soldier of Freedom* (New York: Harcourt Brace Jovanovich, 1970), 173.
40. *Ibid.*
41. *Ibid.*
42. Kenneth S. Davis, *FDR: The War President, 1940–1943* (New York: Random House, 2000), 349.
43. "No Lights Show at White House during Address," *New York Herald Tribune*, December 10, 1941, 2.
44. *Ibid.*
45. "The President's [Radio] Address: December 9, 1941," as *The New York Times*, December 10, 1941, 4.
46. *Ibid.*
47. *Ibid.*
48. Davis, 350.
49. "Rayburn Calls Roosevelt Talk 'Frank, Lucid,'" *New York Herald Tribune*, December 10, 1941, 3.
50. *Ibid.*
51. "German-Italian Invasion Perils U.S., Says F.D.R.," *Chicago Tribune*, December 10, 1941, 20.
52. *Ibid.*
53. Wilfrid Fleisher, "Reports to Hull Indicate Nazis May War on U.S.," *New York Herald Tribune*, December 10, 1941, 9.
54. "Reich Urged to Declare War on U.S.," *Richmond (Virginia) Times Dispatch*, December 10, 1941, 1.
55. "Nazi Declaration Imminent," *Richmond (Virginia) Times Dispatch*, December 10, 1941, 6.
56. "At War with Germany, Italy, and Japan," Editorial, *Chicago Tribune*, December 12, 1941, 18.
57. "Allies of Tokyo Evade War Issue," *New York Times*, December 9, 1941, 16.
58. International Military Tribunal, *Trial of the Major War Criminals before the International Military Tribunal, Nuremberg, 14 November 1945–1 October 1945*, vol. 10 (Germany: International Military Tribunal, 1947), 296–297.
59. H. L. Trefousse, *Germany and American Neutrality, 1939–1941* (New York: Octagon Books, 1969), 139–140.
60. *Ibid.*
61. International Military Tribunal, 297. For an argument that Ribbentrop's effort to bring Japan into the war with Russia was an approach Hitler only tolerated rather than embraced, see Michael Bloch, *Ribbentropp* (New York: Crown Publishers, 1992), 343–344.
62. Trefousse, 140.
63. *Ibid.*, 140–141.
64. *Ibid.*, 140.
65. For an interesting description of the internal tensions in this odd grouping of nations and the public relations problems the event caused for the Nazi regime, see Joseph P. Lash, *Roosevelt and Churchill, 1939–1941: The Partnership that Saved the West* (New York: W.W. Norton, 1976), 342–343.
66. Bloch, 343.
67. Trefousse, 142–143.
68. *Ibid.*, 142.
69. *Ibid.*
70. *Ibid.*, 144.
71. *Ibid.*, 144–145.
72. *Ibid.*, 143.
73. *Ibid.*, 144.
74. *Ibid.*, 145.
75. Carl Boyd, *Hitler's Japanese Confidant: General Oshima Hiroshi and Magic Intelligence, 1941–1945* (Lawrence, KS: University of Kansas Press, 1993), 36.
76. *Ibid.*
77. *Ibid.*
78. *Ibid.*
79. Trefousse, 145.
80. *Ibid.*, 147.
81. David Reynolds, *The Creation of the Anglo-American Alliance, 1937–41: A Study in Competitive Cooperation* (Chapel

Hill, NC: University of North Carolina Press, 1982), 220.
82. Trefousse, 148.
83. George Axelsson, "Nazi Course Not Revealed," *New York Times,* December 9, 1941, 17.
84. "Nazis Declare 'World Curse' on Roosevelt," *New York Herald Tribune,* December 8, 1941, 14.
85. Frank L. Kluckhorn, "President Fears 'Very Heavy Losses' on Oahu—Churchill Notifies Japan that a State of War Exists," *New York Times,* December 8, 1941, 1.
86. "Reich Awaiting Word from Japan," *New York Times,* December 8, 1941, 4.
87. George Axelsson, "Pledge by Hitler to Ally Awaited," *New York Times,* December 10, 1941, 9.
88. "Roosevelt Vilified by Nazis; Decision of War on U.S. Waits in Both Berlin and Rome," *Richmond (Virginia) Times Dispatch,* December 9, 1941, 3.
89. Alex Small, "U.S.–Japan War Stuns Berlin's Man in Street," *Chicago Tribune,* December 9, 1941, 17.
90. Axelsson, "Pledge," 9.
91. "Hitler to Address Reichstag Today," *New York Times,* December 11, 1941, 14.
92. *Ibid.*
93. *Ibid.*
94. "Declaration of War Urged by Wheeler," *Baltimore Sun,* December 8, 1941, 1.
95. *Ibid.*
96. Alan Bullock, *Hitler: A Study in Tyranny,* Revised Edition (New York: Harper & Row, 1962), 661.
97. John Toland, *Adolf Hitler* (Garden City, New York: Doubleday & Co. 1976), 694.
98. Werner Maser, *Hitler,* translated from the German by Peter and Betty Ross (London: Allen Lane, 1973), 299.
99. On Hitler's private conversations after the Tripartite Pact in which he expressed regret about being in an alliance with an Oriental people, see Albert Speer, *Inside the Third Reich,* translated from the German by Richard and Clara Winston (Toronto, Canada: Macmillan, 1970), 121.

100. Toland, 694.
101. *Ibid.,* 695.
102. Boyd, 36.
103. *Ibid.*
104. *Ibid.*
105. Donald F. Drummond, *The Passing of American Neutrality, 1937–1941* (New York: Greenwood Press, 1968), 369.
106. International Military Tribunal, 297.
107. Toland, 695.
108. International Military Tribunal, 298.
109. Bullock, 662. For additional praise by Hitler for waging war before declaring it, see Shirer, 896.
110. Boyd, 36.
111. *Ibid.,* 37.
112. Shirer, 893.
113. *Ibid.,* 897.
114. "Nazis Prepare Statement on U.S. Relations," *New York Herald Tribune,* December 10, 9.
115. *Ibid.*
116. "War Declaration Doubted," *New York Herald Tribune,* December 10, 1941, 9.
117. Ian Kershaw, *Hitler—1936–1945: Nemesis* (New York: W.W. Norton, 2000), 444.
118. *Ibid.,* 445.
119. *Ibid.,* 447.
120. Daniel T. Brigham, "Germany and Italy Declare War on U.S.," *New York Times,* December 12, 1941, 4.
121. For lengthy extracts of the speech, see, "Textual Excerpts from the War Speech of Reichsfuehrer in the Reichstag," *New York Times,* December 12, 1941, 4. All quotations come from this source unless otherwise indicated.
122. Bullock, 663.
123. "Hitler Blames Roosevelt as He Declares War," *New York Herald Tribune,* December 12, 1941, 7.
124. Kershaw, 490. On how his listeners interpreted the address as encouraging or demanding a campaign of annihilation, see pages 491–492.
125. Stanley Weintraub, *Journey into War: December 7, 1941* (New York: Dutton, 1991), 648. 648.
126. *Ibid.*
127. Waldo Heinrichs, *Threshold of*

War: Franklin D. Roosevelt and American Entry into World War II (New York: Oxford University Press, 1988), 220.

128. Kershaw, 442.
129. Klaus P. Fischer, *Nazi Germany: A New History* (New York: Continuum, 1995), 475.
130. *Ibid.*
131. Bloch, 345.
132. Bullock, 662.
133. Kershaw, 442. Cf. Toland, 694.
134. Herbert L. Matthews, "Rome Backs Japan, Dodges War Issue," *New York Times*, December 9, 1941, 10.
135. "'Sympathy with Japan' Italian Attitude," *Richmond (Virginia) News Leader*, December 8, 1941, 6.
136. "Italy Predicts a Delay," *New York Times*, December 8, 1941, 4.
137. "Rome Radio Denies Alleged Broadcast," *Baltimore Sun*, December 9, 1941, 11.
138. *Ibid.*
139. *Ibid.*
140. Matthews, "Rome Backs Japan," 10.
141. *Ibid.*
142. "Japan's War Is Ours, Italian Press Brags," *Richmond (Virginia) Times Dispatch*, December 10, 1941, 1.
143. Matthews, "Rome Backs Japan," 10.
144. Hebert L. Matthews, "Rome Is Secretive on Pending Policy," *New York Times*, December 10, 1941, 10.
145. *Ibid.*
146. Ivone Kirkpatrick, *Mussolini: A Study in Power* (New York: Hawthorn Books, 1964), 503.
147. Ray Moseley, *Mussolini's Shadow: The Double Life of Count Galeazzo Ciano* (New Haven: Yale University Press, 1999), 138.
148. Kirkpatrick, 503.
149. Trefousse, 146.
150. *Ibid.*
151. *Ibid.*, 147.
152. Galeazzo Ciano, *The Ciano Diaries: 1939–1943*, edited by Hugh Gibson (Garden City, New York: Doubleday & Co., 1946), 416.
153. Kirkpatrick, 503.
154. *Ibid.*, 273.
155. *Ibid.*, 127.

156. *Ibid.*
157. Denis M. Smith, *Mussolini* (New York: Alfred A. Knopf, 1982), 273, 274. The last sentence of this paragraph refers to sentiments he voiced shortly after war began with the United States.
158. Matthews, "Rome Is Secretive," 10.
159. *Ibid.*
160. "See Vichy Aiding Axis," *New York Times*, December 11, 1941, 14.
161. *Ibid.*
162. Kirkpatrick, 127.
163. Moseley, 138.
164. *Ibid.*
165. *Ibid.*
166. *Ibid.*, 138–139.
167. "Italians Massed to Hear of War," *New York Times*, December 9, 1941, 4.
168. Brigham, 4.
169. "Duce Declares War on U.S. in 5-Minute Talk," *New York Herald Tribune*, December 12, 1941, 7.
170. For full text of the brief speech, see Benito Mussolini, "Mussolini War Speech," *New York Times*, December 12, 1941, 4.
171. Ciano, 417.
172. Brigham, 4. Brigham speaks of the speech being four minutes long. Official Italian Radio Broadcast Received by Associated Press, "Duce Declares War on U.S." makes it only slightly longer.
173. "War Declared by Mussolini on the U.S," *Richmond (Virginia) Times Dispatch*, December 12, 1941, 10.
174. Brigham, 4.
175. For the full text of the four sections, see *Ibid.*
176. "Japanese Announce Pact," *New York Times*, December 12, 1941, 4.

Chapter 5

1. Frank L. Kluckhorn, "War Opened on U.S.," *New York Times*, December 12, 1941, 1.
2. "Hitler Blames Roosevelt as He Declares War," *New York Herald Tribune*, December 12, 1941, 7.

3. "Duce Declares War on U.S. in 5-Minute Talk," *New York Herald Tribune*, December 12, 1941, 7.
4. Kluckhorn, "War Opened," 5.
5. Bertram D. Hulen, "Hull Very Frigid to Visiting Envoys," *New York Times*, December 12, 1941, 3.
6. *Ibid.*
7. "German Notification to U.S," *New York Herald Tribune*, December 12, 1941, 6.
8. "Charges in German Note," *New York Times*, December 12, 1941, 5.
9. *Ibid.*
10. William L. Langer and S. Everett Gleason, *The Undeclared War, 1940–1941* (New York: Harper & Brothers, 1953), 940.
11. David Brinkley, *Washington Goes to War: The Extraordinary Story of the Transformation of a City and a Nation* (New York: Alfred A. Knopf, 1988), 93.
12. *Ibid.*
13. James M. Minifie, "Hull Is Not In as Nazis Call to Tell Him of War," *New York Herald Tribune*, December 12, 1941, 8.
14. Hulen, 3.
15. *Ibid.*
16. James M. Minifie, "Hull Is Not In as Nazis Call to Tell Him of War," *New York Herald Tribune*, December 12, 1941, 8.
17. "The White House," *Newsweek*, December 22, 1941, 21.
18. *Ibid.*
19. Kluckhorn "War Opened," 1.
20. "Press as a Unit Backs War on Axis," *New York Times*, December 12, 1941, 5.
21. *Ibid.*
22. *Ibid.*
23. *Ibid.*
24. *Ibid.*
25. *Ibid.*
26. *Ibid.*
27. *Ibid.*
28. Fred O. Seibel, "The Most Unkindest Cut of All," *Richmond (Virginia) Times Dispatch*, December 12, 1941, 22.
29. CR 9652 and Franklin D. Roosevelt, *Development of United States Foreign Policy: Addresses and Messages of Franklin D. Roosevelt* (Washington, D.C.: United States Government Printing Office, 1942), 133, available: http://www.ibiblio.org/pha/7-2-188/188-title.html [May 2003].
30. "The Week," Editorial *Richmond (Virginia) News Leader*, December 13, 1941, 8.
31. CR 9652.
32. *Ibid.*
33. Bert Andrews, "Congress War Vote Is Given in 75 Minutes," *New York Herald Tribune*, December 12, 1941, 1.
34. Wayne S. Cole, *Roosevelt & the Isolationists, 1932–45* (Lincoln, NE: University of Nebraska Press, 1983), 507.
35. Wayne S. Cole, *Charles A. Lindbergh, and the Battle Against American Intervention in World War II* (New York: Harcourt, Brace, Jovanovich, 1974), 210.
36. CR 9553.
37. Andrews, "War Vote," 1.
38. CR 9652.
39. CR 9653.
40. *Ibid.*
41. *Ibid.*
42. *Ibid.*
43. *Ibid.*
44. *Ibid.*
45. CR 9654.
46. CR 9653.
47. CR 9652.

Chapter 6

1. CR 9665.
2. CR 9666.
3. "Silent Galleries Watch War Vote," *New York Times*, December 12, 1941, 5.
4. *Ibid.*
5. *Ibid.*
6. Bert Andrews, "Congress War Vote Is Given in 75 Minutes," *New York Herald Tribune*, December 12, 1941, 5.
7. *Ibid.*
8. CR 9672.
9. CR 9667.
10. *Ibid.*
11. *Ibid.*
12. *Ibid.*
13. *Ibid.*
14. *Ibid.*

15. *Ibid..*
16. CR 9668.
17. *Ibid.*
18. *Ibid.*
19. *Ibid.*
20. *Ibid.*
21. *Ibid.*
22. *Ibid.*
23. *Ibid.*
24. *Ibid.*
25. *Ibid.*
26. *Ibid.*
27. "Silent Galleries," 5.
28. CR 9668.
29. *Ibid.*
30. CR 9669.
31. *Ibid.*
32. *Ibid.*
33. *Ibid.*
34. *Ibid.*
35. *Ibid.*
36. CR 9670.
37. *Ibid.*
38. *Ibid.*
39. *Ibid.*
40. *Ibid.*
41. *Ibid.*
42. *Ibid.*
43. *Ibid.*
44. *Ibid.*
45. *Ibid.*
46. CR 9671.
47. *Ibid.*
48. *Ibid.*
49. *Ibid.*
50. *Ibid.*
51. *Ibid.*
52. *Ibid.*
53. *Ibid.*
54. CR 9672.
55. CR 9671.
56. CR 9672.
57. *Ibid.*
58. *Ibid.*
59. CR 9669.
60. CR 9672.
61. CR 9669.
62. CR 9668.
63. "Miss Rankin Voted 'Present' in Weak Voice; Clerk Had to Call Her Name a Second Time," *New York Times*, December 12, 1941, 6.
64. *Ibid.*
65. "Congress Vows Fight to Finish Against Axis," *Chicago Tribune*, December 12, 1941, 5.
66. Miss Rankin Voted 'Present' in "Weak Voice," 6.
67. Andrews, "Congress War Vote," 5.
68. Miss Rankin Voted 'Present' in "Weak Voice," 6.
69. Robert P. Post, "British Relieved by Declarations," *New York Times*, December 12, 1941, 13.
70. *Ibid.*
71. "Tojo Warns Japan of Long, Hard War," *New York Times*, December 14, 1941, 6.
72. *Ibid.*
73. *Ibid.*
74. *Ibid.*
75. Frank L. Kluckhorn, "War Opened on U.S." *New York Times*, December 12, 1941, 5. For a detailed chronology of the day's events, see "Congress Timetable on War Declaration," *New York Herald Tribune*, December 12, 1941, 6.
76. Kluckhorn, "War Opened," 5.
77. *Ibid.*

Bibliography

Primary Sources

Bohlen, Charles E. *Witness to History: 1929–1969.* New York: W. W. Norton, 1973.
Ciano, Galeazzo. *The Ciano Diaries: 1939–1943.* Edited by Hugh Gibson. Garden City, New York: Doubleday & Co. 1946.
Congressional Record: Proceedings and Debates of the 77th Congress, First Session. Vol. 87, Part 9: November 26, 1941 to January 2, 1942 (pages 9143–10152). Washington, D.C.: United States Government Printing Office, 1941.
Dirksen, Everett M. *The Education of a Senator.* Urbana, IL: University of Illinois Press, 1998.
Doenecke, Justus D. *In Danger Undaunted: The Anti-Interventionist Movement of 1940–1941 as Revealed in the Papers of the America First Committee.* Stanford, CA: Hoover Institution Press, 1990.
Farley, James A. *Jim Farley's Story: The Roosevelt Years.* New York: McGraw-Hill, 1948.
Fish, Hamilton. *FDR: The Other Side of the Coin—How We Were Tricked into World War II.* New York: Vantage Press, 1976.
Grew, Joseph C. *Turbulent Era: A Diplomatic Record of Forty Years, 1904–1945.* Edited by Walter Johnson. Vol. 2. Boston: Houghton Mifflin 1952.
Hull, Cordell. *The Memoirs of Cordell Hull.* Vol. 2. New York: Macmillan, 1948.
Ickes, Harold L. *The Secret Diary of Harold L. Ickes.* Vol. 3; *The Lowering Clouds, 1939–1941.* New York: Simon and Schuster, 1954.
International Military Tribunal. *Trial of the Major War Criminals before the International Military Tribunal, Nuremberg, 14 November 1945–1 October 1945.* Vol. 10. Germany: International Military Tribunal, 1947.
Keitel, Wilhelm. *The Memoirs of Field-Marshal Keitel.* Translated from the German by David Irving. New York: Stein and Day, 1966.
Leahy, William D. *I Was There: The Personal Story of the Chief of Staff to Presidents Roosevelt and Truman Based on His Notes and Diaries Made at the Time.* New York: Whittlesey House, 1950.

Long, Breckinridge. *The War Diary of Breckinridge Long: Selections from the Years 1939–1944.* Lincoln, NE: University of Nebraska Press, 1966.
Miller, William "Fishbait." *Fishbait: The Memoirs of the Congressional Doorkeeper.* Englewood Cliffs, NJ: Prentice-Hall, 1977.
Mussolini, Benito. "Mussolini War Speech." *New York Times,* December 12, 1941, 4.
Norris, George W. *Fighting Liberal: The Autobiography of George W. Norris.* New York: Macmillan, 1945.
Perkins, Frances, *The Roosevelt I Knew.* New York: Viking Press, 1946.
Rayburn, Sam. *"Speak, Mister Speaker."* Edited by H. G. Dulaney and Edward H. Phillips. Bonham, TX: Sam Rayburn Foundation, 1978.
Roosevelt, Elliott. *As He Saw It.* New York: Duell, Sloan and Pearce, 1946.
Roosevelt, Franklin D. *Development of United States Foreign Policy: Addresses and Messages of Franklin D. Roosevelt.* Washington, D.C.: United States Government Printing Office, 1942. Available: http://www.ibiblio.org/pha/7-2-188/188-title.html [May 2003].
Rosenman, Samuel I. *Working with Roosevelt.* New York: Harper & Brothers.
Rusk, Dean. *As I Saw It.* As told to Richard Rusk. Edited by Daniel S. Papp. New York: W.W. Norton, 1990.
Salisbury, Harrison E. *A Journey for Our Times: A Memoir.* New York: Harper & Row, 1983.
The Secret Conferences of Dr. Goebbels: The Nazi Propaganda War, 1939–1943. Selected and edited by Willi A. Boelcke. Translated from the German by Ewald Osers. New York: E. P. Dutton & Company, 1970.
Speer, Albert. *Inside the Third Reich.* Translated from the German by Richard and Clara Winston. Toronto, Canada: Macmillan, 1970.
Truman, Margaret. *Harry S Truman.* New York: William Morrow, 1973.
Tully, Grace. *F.D.R. My Boss.* New York: Charles Scribner's Sons, 1949.

Newspapers

Baltimore Sun. December 7–13, 1941.
Chicago Tribune. December 7–12, 1941.
New York Herald Tribune. December 8–14, 1941.
New York Times. December 8–14, 1941.
Richmond (Virginia) News Leader. December 8–13, 1941.
Richmond (Virginia) Times Dispatch. December 8–13, 1941.
Washington Post. December 7–13, 1941, and December 7, 2001.

Secondary Sources

"Arthur Vandenberg." *Hoover & Truman: A Presidential Friendship,* Site sponsored by the Hoover Presidential Library & Museum and the Truman Presidential Library and Museum. Available: http://www.trumanlibrary.org/hoover/vandenbio.htm [May 2003].

Biographical Directory of the United States Congress, 1774–Present. Available: http://bioguide.congress.gov/biosearch/biosearch.asp [December 2001].

Bloch, Michael. *Ribbentropp.* New York: Crown Publishers, 1992.

Boyd, Carl. *Hitler's Japanese Confidant: General Oshima Hiroshi and Magic Intelligence, 1941–1945.* Lawrence, KS: University of Kansas Press, 1993.

Brinkley, David. *Washington Goes to War: The Extraordinary Story of the Transformation of a City and a Nation.* New York: Alfred A. Knopf, 1988.

Brown, Dorothy M. "Edith Nourse Rogers." *American National Biography.* Edited by John A. Garraty and Mark C. Carnes. New York: Oxford University Press, 1999. Available: http://www.rice.edu/fondren/woodson/exhibits/wac/rogers.html+Edith%2BRogers&hl=en&ie=UTF-8 [May 2003].

Bullock, Alan. *Hitler: A Study in Tyranny.* Revised Edition. New York: Harper & Row, 1962.

Burns, James M. *Roosevelt: The Soldier of Freedom.* New York: Harcourt Brace Jovanovich, 1970.

Caro, Robert A. *The Years of Lyndon Johnson.* Vol. 1, *The Path to Power.* New York: Alfred A. Knopf, 1982.

Chadwin, Mark L. *The Hawks of World War II.* Chapel Hill, NC: University of North Carolina Press, 1968.

Cole, Wayne S. *America First: The Battle against Intervention, 1940–1941.* Madison: University of Wisconsin Press, 1953; reprint New York: Octagon Books, 1971.

_____. *Charles A. Lindbergh and the Battle against American Intervention in World War II.* New York: Harcourt Brace Jovanovich, 1974.

_____. *Roosevelt & the Isolationists, 1932–45.* Lincoln, NE: University of Nebraska Press, 1983.

_____. *Senator Gerald P. Nye and American Foreign Relations.* Minneapolis, MN: University of Minnesota Press, 1962.

Connaughton, Richard. *MacArthur and Defeat in the Philippines.* Woodstock, NY: Overlook Press, 2001.

Darilek, Richard E. *A Loyal Opposition in Time of War: The Republican Party and the Politics of Foreign Policy from Pearl Harbor to Yalta.* Westport, CT: Greenwood Press, 1976.

Davis, Kenneth S. *FDR: The War President, 1940–1943.* New York: Random House, 2000.

Divine, Robert A. *The Reluctant Belligerent: American Entry into World War II.* New York: John Wiley & Sons, 1965.

Doenecke, Justus D. *The Battle against Intervention, 1939–1941.* Malabar, FL: Krieger Publishing Co., 1997.

Drummond, Donald F. *The Passing of American Neutrality, 1937–1941.* New York: Greenwood Press, 1968.

Edge, Wally. "New Jersey's Greatest Generation." *PoliticsNJ.com—New Jersey's Online* Political Network. Available: http://www.politicsnj.com/september 20_2001.htm [May 2003].

"Edith Nourse Rogers." Available: http://clerkweb.house.gov/105/womenbio/ExtendedBio/Rogersexb.htm [May 2003].

Fehrenbach, T. R. *F.D.R.'s Undeclared War, 1939 to 1941.* New York: David McKay, 1967.

Fischer, Klaus P. *Nazi Germany: A New History.* New York: Continuum, 1995.

Folsom, Burton W. "Senator Arthur Vandenberg: A Profile in Courage." *Mack-*

inac Center for Public Policy Research. Available: http://www.mackinac.org/article.asp?ID=349 [May 2003].

Gellman, Irwin F. *Secret Affairs: Franklin Roosevelt, Cordell Hull, and Sumner Welles.* Baltimore, MD: Johns Hopkins University Press, 1995.

Green, George N. "Thomas Terry Connally (1877–1963)." *The Handbook of Texas Online.* Available: http://www.tsha.utexas.edu/handbook/online/articles/view/CC/fco36.html. [May 2003].

Hardeman, D.B., and Donald C. Bacon. *Rayburn: A Biography.* Austin, TX: TexasMonthly Press, 1987.

Hearden, Patrick J. *Roosevelt Confronts Hitler: America's Entry into World War II.* Dekalb, IL: Northern Illinois University Press, 1987.

Heinrichs, Waldo. *Threshold of War: Franklin D. Roosevelt and American Entry into World War II.* New York: Oxford University Press, 1988.

Hubbard, Linda S., ed. *Notable Americans: What They Did, from 1620 to the Present.* 4th Edition. Detroit, Michigan: Gale Research, 1988.

Huntington Library. *Important People: Jeannette Rankin (1880–1973).* Available: http://www.huntington.org/vfw/imp/rankin.html [December 2001].

Irving, David. *Goring: A Biography.* New York: William Morrow and Co., 1989.

Jeannette Rankin Foundation. *The Story of Jeannette Pickering Ranking, 1880–1973.* Available: http://www.rankinfoundation.org/story.htm [December 2001].

Jeannette Rankin (1917–1919 & 1941–1943). http://www.senate.gov/ member/mt/baucus/general/bios/JeannetteRankin.htm [December 2001].

Josephson, Hannah. *Jeanette Rankin: First Lady in Congress—A Biography.* Indianapolis, IN: Bobbs-Merrill, 1974.

Kendrick, Alexander. *Prime Time: The Life of Edward R. Murrow.* Boston: Little, Brown, 1969.

Kennett, Lee. *For the Duration: The United States Goes to War—Pearl Harbor-1942.* New York: Charles Scribner's Sons, 1985.

Kershaw, Ian. *Hitler—1936–1945: Nemesis.* New York: W.W. Norton, 2000.

Ketchum, Richard M. *The Borrowed Years, 1938–1941: America on the Way to War.* New York: Random House, 1989.

Kirkpatrick, Ivone. *Mussolini: A Study in Power.* New York: Hawthorn Books, 1964.

Langer, William L., and S. Everett Gleason. *The Undeclared War, 1940–1941.* New York: Harper & Brothers, 1953.

Lash, Joseph P. *Roosevelt and Churchill, 1939–1941: The Partnership that Saved the West.* New York: W. W. Norton 1976.

Lingeman, Richard R. *Don't You Know There's a War On? The American Home Front, 1941–1945.* New York: G. P. Putnam's Sons, 1970.

Lowitt, Richard. *George W. Norris: The Triumph of a Progressive, 1933–1944.* Urbana, IL: University of Illinois Press, 1978.

Maney, Patrick J. *"Young Bob" La Follette: A Biography of Robert M. La Follette, Jr., 1895–1953.* Columbia, Missouri: University of Missouri Press, 1978.

Martin, James J. *American Liberalism and World Politics, 1931–1941: Liberalism's Press and Spokesmen on the Road Back to War between Mukden and Pearl Harbor.* Vol. 2. New York: Davin-Adair, 1964.

Maser, Werner. *Hitler.* Translated from the German by Peter and Betty Ross. London: Allen Lane, 1973.

McNamer, Megan. *Votes: Not Violets—The Legacy of Jeannette Rankin.* Available: http://www.umt.edu/comm/s99/votes.html [December 2001]

Melosi, Martin V. *The Shadow of Pearl Harbor: Political Controversy over the Surprise Attack, 1941–1946.* College Station, TX: Texas A&M University Press, 1977.

Moseley, Ray. *Mussolini's Shadow: The Double Life of Count Galeazzo Ciano.* New Haven: Yale University Press, 1999.

Nordin, Dennis S. *The New Deal's Black Congressman: A Life of Arthur Wergs Mitchell.* Columbia, MO: University of Missouri Press, 1997.

Phillips, Cabell. *The 1940s: Decade of Triumph and Trouble.* New York: New York Times, 1975.

Platt, Rorin Morse. *Virginia in Foreign Affairs, 1933–1941.* Lanham, MD: University Press of America, 1991.

Reynolds, David. *The Creation of the Anglo-American Alliance, 1937–41: A Study in Competitive Co-operation.* Chapel Hill, NC: University of North Carolina Press, 1982.

Sainsbury, Keith. *Churchill and Roosevelt at War: The War They Fought and the Peace They Hoped to Make.* New York: New York University Press, 1994.

September 11, 2001: Two Who Voted against War, 60 Years Apart. Available: http://www.loper.org/~george/trends/2001/Oct/67.html [December 2001].

Sherwood, Robert E. *Roosevelt and Hopkins: An Intimate History.* New York: Harper & Brothers, 1948.

Shirer, William L. *The Rise and Fall of the Third Reich: A History of Nazi Germany.* New York: Simon and Schuster, 1960.

Smith, Denis M. *Mussolini.* New York: Alfred A. Knopf, 1982.

Toland, John. *Adolf Hitler.* Garden City, New York: Doubleday & Co., 1976.

Tompkins, C. David. *Senator Arthur H. Vandenberg: The Evolution of a Modern Republican, 1884–1945.* [East Lansing, MI]: Michigan State University Press, 1970.

Trefousse, H. L. *Germany and American Neutrality, 1939–1941.* New York: Octagon Books, 1969.

Weintraub, Stanley. *Journey into War: December 7, 1941.* New York: Dutton, 1991.

White, William S. *The Taft Story.* New York: Harper & Brothers, 1954.

Worth, Roland, Jr. *No Choice but War: The United States Embargo against Japan and the Eruption of War in the Pacific.* Jefferson, NC: McFarland & Company, 1995.

Zucker, Norman L. *George W. Norris: Gentle Knight of American Democracy.* Urbana, IL: University of Illinois Press, 1966.

Index

Abbreviations as follows: D = Democrat; R = Republican;
I = Independent; P = Progressive; A-L = American Labor;
H = House of Representatives; S = Senate

Alaska 140
Aleutians 140
America First: accepts need for war in the Pacific 17–20; Congressman Hamilton Fish and 56; initial silence regarding war with Germany 102; local chapters suspend operations; opposes two front war 102; Senator Robert M. La Follette, Jr., and 50; Senator Gerald P. Nye and 51
American Farm Bureau Federation 104
Andrews, Charles O. (S/D) 134
Anti-Comintern Pact (1936): expansion of membership 109–110
anti-interventionists: attitude toward a Pacific war 9; a by-product of World War One 19; effective death of movement after attack 19; interpretation of fundamental foreign policy errors of the FDR administration 73–74; interpretations of the Pearl Harbor attack 13–16; post-war bridging of gap with interventionists in foreign policy assumptions 47; pre-war opposition to arming Japan 83; problems a Pacific war posed for 6; resolving how to support war in Pacific while opposing one in the Atlantic 6; Senator Arthur H. Vandenberg defending their approach 45–46; support of increased pre-war military spending 19
Arends, Leslie C. (H/R) 68
Arnold, Laurence F. (H/D) 138
Ashai (Osaka and Tokyo newspapers) 30
Atherton, Ray 129
Atlanta Constitution 23, 130
Atlantic Conference 57, 98
Austin, Warren R. (S/R) 48
Australia: internment of citizens in Japan 34
Austria: number of citizens resident in U.S., 26–27

Baltimore Sun 22
Bates, Joe B. (H/D) 147
Bell, J. Jasper (H/D) 147
Bender, George H. (H/R) 63–64; every effort had been made to avoid war 146
Berge, Wendell (Assistant Attorney General) 27
Berlin 25, 32, 114
Biddle, Francis (Attorney General): announces arrest of Japanese 26; reasons for arrests of foreigners 28
Bilbo, Theodore G. (S/D) 52
Bill of Rights 28
Black Americans and the war 139; equal rights should be an obvious result of full participation 69

177

Index

Bloom, Sol (H/D): criticizes length of war resolution debate concerning Japan 58
Bolton, Frances P. (Mrs.) (H/R): role of industry in winning war 143–144
Bone, Homer T. (S/D) 52, 135
Boston 28
Boston Herald 130
Bradley, Frederick V. (H/R) 66
Brazil 123
Brewster, Ralph O. (S/R) 52
Brookhart, Smith W. (S/R; retired) 38
Brooks, Overton (H/D) 84
Bryson, Joseph R. (H/D) 77, 139–140
Buckler, J. Jasper (H/D) 147
Buffalo, New York 28
Byrne, William T. (H/D) 147
Byron, Katharine E. (H/D): personal family impact of the new war 59–60

California: number of Japanese in 26
Canada: German POWs in, 116; internment of nationals in Japan 34
Cannon, Arthur P. (H/D) 147
Capozzoli, Louis J. (H/D) 80–81
Capper, Arthur (S/R) 52
Caraway, Hattie W. (Mrs; S/D) 52
Casey, Joseph E. (H/R) 60
censorship 31
Central America: impact of a successful Japanese war upon 106
Chapman, Virgil M. (H/D) 86–86
Chavez, Dennis (S/D): initially hedges war support 15
Chicago 28; burning of Japanese consulate business papers 30
Chicago Daily News 23
Chicago Sun: editorial cartoons 138; Germany and Japan but two ends of one war-making monster "serpent" 25
Chicago Tribune 22–23; on shift of American public opinion toward war with Germany 108
Churchill, Winston (prime minister of Britain): anticipating war with Japan 9; "blood, sweat, and tears" 60
Ciano, Galeazzo (Italian Foreign Minister) 110, 122; description of Mussolini's speech declaring war 125; informed by Germans of Pearl Harbor attack 114; informs U.S. diplomat of Italian declaration of war 124
Civil Aeronautics Authority: grounds all civilian planes after Japanese attack 91
Clark, Bennett C. (S/D) 15
Cleveland 26
Cleveland Plain Dealer: Pearl Harbor proved oceans no definitive protection for U.S. 25–26
Cole, William F., Jr. (H/D): description of World War One experiences 79; old regimes must surrender power before a negotiated peace possible 79
Colonna, Ascanio dei principi (Italian ambassador to U.S.): uninformed by his government of war being declared on U.S., 129
Columbia Broadcasting System (radio) 38; monitored foreign broadcasts 120
Columbus (German ocean liner) 28
Congress: difference in how war declarations treated between Japan and Germany/Italy 131; inability to keep a secret 11; guarded by U.S. Marines 36; leaders meet with Roosevelt evening of attack 11; police security 92; Roosevelt keeping military strategy secret from 46–47; security for entering facilities 36
Congressional Medal of Honor 84
Congressional Record: expansion of remarks by members, 2, 161n51; interpreting speakers' remarks 3; remarks added by non-participants in the discussion 2
Connally, Thomas (Tom) T. (D/S): comments on war with Germany resolution 132; introduces war with Italy resolution 133; introduces war with Japan resolution 44; political background in Congress 47–48; presents war with Germany resolution to Senate 132; receiving copy of 1917 war declaration 21; recommends letting Germans take initiative in declaring war 12–13; secures entry to Congress for Chinese ambassador 36; suggests state of war statement rather than declaration of war with Japan 11;
Connecticut 28
Costello, John M. (H/D) 147; difficulty in reaching Washington from California in time for Japan war vote 90; remarks added to the *Congressional*

Index

Record due to arriving late for Japan war vote 78–79
Council of Versailles 65
Curley, Michael J. (Archbishop): joke on coming of war 12

D'Alesandro, Thomas, Jr. (H/D) 74, 138
D'Angell, Homer D. (H/R) 76–77
Decatur, Stephen 87
Delaney, John J. (H/D) 147, 148–149
Dietrich, Otto 113
Dimond, Anthony J. (H/D) 140
Dirksen, Everett M. (H/R) 63–64; attempts to get Rankin to change anti–Japan war vote, 95–96
Ditter, J. William. (H/R) 71
D.N.B. German news service 30, 31
Douglass, Frederick 139
Downs, DeRoy D. (H/D) 74
Dunn, James C. 129
Dutch East Indies 105
Dworshak, Henry C. (H/R) 96

Early, Stephen T. (Presidential Press Secretary): 4:40 P.M. press conference December 7th 10–11; on German and Italian declarations of war 130; Pearl Harbor information released through on December 7th 10
Eaton, Charles A. (H/R) 60
Eichelberger, Clark M. 24
Ellis, Clyde T. (H/D): unable to find transport to reach Washington in time for Japan war vote 91

Federal Bureau of Investigation (FBI): Japanese co-operation with in U.S. 33
Fight for Freedom 24
Finland 31
Fish, Hamilton (H/R): extremely hostile attitude toward FDR 56; later convinced Roosevelt conspired to get U.S. into a war with Japan 57; on Lend-Lease as making U.S. an enemy of Germany 107; long war probable 141; pre–Congressional debate statements on attack 14; volunteers for military duty 14, 57
Flanagan, John W., Jr. (H/D) 87
Florida 91
Floyd Benton Field (naval airport) 148
Forand, Aime (H/D) 75

Ford, Thomas F. (H/D): ideological aspects of the war 141–142
Fort Benning Infantry School 62
Fort Lincoln (North Dakota) internment camp 28
Fort Missoula (Montana) internment camp 28
Fort Stanton (New Mexico) internment camp 28
France: imperialism of 142

Gallup public opinion polls: on war danger with Japan 9
Gavagan, Joseph A. (H/D) 71
George, Walter F. (S/D): ponders possibility attack not authorized by Japanese government 15–16; war to be a long one, 16
Gerlach, Charles L. (H/R) 147
German-American Bund 33
Germany 105, 106; accused of seeking expansion in western hemisphere 49–50; American citizens arrested by 34; American discussion of whether it was behind Pearl Harbor 24–25; American press reaction to her declaring war 130; attacks on her submarines authorized before war broke out 57–58; attitude toward Italy 110; blames Roosevelt for Pacific War 104; citizens in U.S. arrested 26–29, 107; correspondents restricted in U.S. 30–31; decision to intervene in Japanese war with U.S. 113–115; expected Lend-Lease to end due to U.S. war with Japan 104; informs U.S. of war decision 127; initial reaction to Pearl Harbor 111–113; Lend-Lease as alienating Germany from U.S. 107; military advisers to Japan 25; navy ordered to attack American vessels 115; number of German citizens resident in U.S 26–27; post–Pearl Harbor reports filed by U.S. correspondents in 31; pre-war efforts by Japan to assure intervention in any war with U.S. 109; punitive peace sought for after war 85–86; rationale for arrests of its citizens in U.S. 27; restrictions on U.S. correspondents 31, 32; shared goals with Japan 106; submarines 116; text of war declaration against U.S. 127–128; U.S. House of Representatives

votes for war with 136; U.S. Senate votes for war with 131–132
Gibson, John S. (H/D) 87
Gillie, Robert A. 75
Glass, Carter (S/D) 151
Goebbels, Joseph (German Propaganda Minister): on inability of Americans to provide as much aid to European belligerents as previously 118–119
Goering, Hermann (Reich Marshall) 116, 117
Grant, George M. (H/D) 143
Great Britain: aid to as having reduced American resources for Pacific war 14–15; to benefit by Japanese attack on Pearl Harbor 100; blamed for scheming to provoke a Japanese-U.S. war 51; danger of war in Far East 57; as having economic incentive to drag U.S. into a Pacific war 16; House of Commons 35; imperialism of 142; internment of British citizens by and in Japan 34; Lend-Lease continued after war with Japan started 104; promised priority in anti–German war over that against Japanese 101; reaction to U.S. declaration of war with Germany and Italy 150; responsibility for U.S. involvement in World War One 94; should not be given war-aid priority over defeating Japan 102; U.S. would assist if attacked in Far East 57
Great Depression 45, 117
Greer (U.S.S.): attack on 57, 128
Guam 39
Guyer, Ulysses S. (H/R) 86

Halifax (Lord) (British ambassador to U.S.): interpretation of significance of Roosevelt's war speech of December 8th 40–41; observes Roosevelt's speech asking for war with Japan 36; observes Senate and House votes for war with Germany 137
Harris, Owen (H/D) 138
Harvey, Paul 2
Hawaii 41, 90; arrests of foreigners in 26; arrests of naturalized U.S. citizens in 28–29; fear of an invasion 42; non-voting representative in U.S. Congress 70; number of Japanese resident in 26–27; Oahu 39; *see also* Pearl Harbor

Hayden, Carl (S/D) 52
Hearst, William Randolph 101–102
Hiroshi, Oshima (Japanese Ambassador to Germany) 110
Hitler, Adolf 24, 25, 75, 84, 99, 100, 103, 106, 125, 143, 144; aggressive actions described 86; decides to intervene in Japan's war with U.S. 113–115; long-term plans against western hemisphere 105; miscalculation in declaring war on U.S. 101; speech to Reichstag announcing war with U.S. 115–118; why Hitler decided for war with U.S. 118–120; in World War One 117
Hobson, Henry (Bishop) 42
Hoffman, Clare E. (H/R): refuses to provide identification 36–37
Hofmann, Bernard 33
Holcomb, Thomas (Marines Major General) 38
Holman, Rufus C. (S/R) 52
Hong Kong 39
Honolulu (Hawaii) 39; civilian casualties 65
Hook, Frank E. (H/D) 66
Hoover, Herbert (former President): bad U.S. negotiating stance led to Japanese attack 13; leaves as open question issue of whether interventionists had been right 13; supports anti–Japan war decision 13
Hopkins, Harry 37; adds sentence to December 8th presidential address 41
Hori, Tomokazu (Japanese Cabinet spokesman): on foreign detainees 34
House Joint Resolution 254 54–55, 89
House of Commons 35
House of Representatives (U.S.): absentees from vote for war with Germany and Italy 147–149; call for smashing Japan's militaristic civilization 87; difference in how war vote with Germany and Italy approached versus that with Japan 137; discusses war with Japan resolution 54–88; galleries during vote for war with Germany and Italy 137; Naval Affairs Committee 91; post-vote denunciations of Germany 137–147; presence of children on floor to hear Roosevelt's December 8th speech 38; Senate form of war resolution

Index

against Japan substituted for House version 89; the sole voter against war with Japan 92–98; solemnity of war vote on Japan 79; those who missed voting on Japan war resolution 90–92; vote total on war with Germany resolution 136; vote total on war with Italy resolution 137; vote total on war with Japan resolution 88–90

House Resolution 51 authorizing joint session of Congress 36

Hull, Cordell (Secretary of State): on absurdity of the sneak attack 153n.4; accused of ill-advised diplomatic demands against Japan 13; press conference of December 9th 107; proposes major additions to FDR's war speech about Japan 41; public and private criticism of Japanese diplomats 21; receives final Japanese diplomatic note 39; snubs German diplomats 127; views German declaration of war as inevitable 103; wife 37

Hungary: number of citizens resident in U.S. 26–27

Iceland: U.S. seizure of 116

Ickes, Harold L. (U.S. cabinet member) 43

interventionists: attitude toward a Pacific war 9; Bishop Henry Hobson and 42; Committee to Defend America 24; deciding whether a two-front war still practical 6; Fight for Freedom group 24; Francis Miller and 42; pre-occupation with Europe rather than Pacific 5

isolationists *see* anti-interventionists

Italy 105, 106, 119; attitude of Germany toward 110; citizens in U.S. arrested, 28–29, 107; delay in formal response to Japan's war with U.S. 120–122; immigrants in Brazil 123; informs U.S. of war decision 127; low view of as a military force by U.S. 131; newspapers 121; number of Italian citizens resident in U.S. 26–27; post-Pearl Harbor reports filed by U.S. correspondents in 31; rationale for arrests of its citizens 27; restrictions on U.S. correspondents 31, 32; as subservient to German policy decisions 129, 130; U.S. House votes for war with 137; U.S. Senate votes for war with 133–134

Izac, Edouard V. M. (H/D) 84

Japan: citizens in U.S. arrested 26–29, 107; commitment to fair treatment of internees 34; Congressional call for smashing its militaristic civilization 87; correspondents restricted in U.S. 30; demonstrators outside embassy in U.S. 29; diplomatic mistakes in negotiating with 46, 58; diplomats deliver final message after Pearl Harbor attack begun 20; diplomats questioned by reporters 21; economic sanctions against 85, 162n.143; embassy and consulates in U.S. 29–30; emperor 39, 56, 64; encourages Germany to enter war 107; establishing exact time that war became official 90; export to of war-making supplies 80, final diplomatic note to U.S. did not declare war 20; German military advisers in 25; harsh peace treaty for demanded at end of war 87; imports from U.S. 20, 61; internment of foreigners 33–34; irrationality of it starting a war 22–23, 56–57, 67; negotiated peace with sought 101; newspapermen at White House day of attack 10–11; number of Japanese in U.S. 26; press 112; pre-war efforts to assure German intervention in any war with U.S. 109; priority in war sought over that involving Germany 101–102; public reaction to Japanese attack on Pearl Harbor 112; radio 112; reaction to U.S. declaration of war with Germany and Italy 150; shared goals with Germany and Italy 106; short war against anticipated 102; stigmatized by press and public for an "unprovoked" attack 20–22; taught imperialism by the example of the western powers 101; tense relations with prior to Pearl Harbor 6; U.S. citizens arrested by 33–34; U.S. embassy communications with Washington after attack 22; U.S. embassy receives Japanese declaration of war 21–22; U.S. House of Representatives: 54–88, 88–90; U.S. Senate: 44–51, 52–53;

value of Pacific targets to her economy and military strength 85; victory over useless unless Germany defeated as well 100; whether diplomats had prior knowledge of war plans 20
Japanese American Citizens' League 32
Jarman, Pete (H/D) 143
Jefferson, Thomas 73
Jenkins, Thomas A. (H/R): a fundamental of human history is war, 72–73
Jennings, John, Jr. (H/R) 84–85
Jews: extermination of justified by war becoming world wide 118; as using Roosevelt 116, 119
Johnson, Edwin C. (S/D): initially hedges war support 15
Johnson, Hiram (S/R) 100
Johnson, Luther A. (H/D) 58
Johnson, Lyndon B. (H/D): campaigns on pledge to enlist if war comes 62
Johnson, Ward (H/D) 147
Joint Resolution 116 (declaring war on Japan) 44
Justice Department 26

Kearny (U.S.S.): attack on 57–58, 128
Kelley, Augustine B. (H/D) 147, 148
Kelly, Edward A. (H/D) 64
Kennedy, Martin J. (H/D) 144–145
Kennedy, Michael J. (H/D) 79
Kent, F. R., Jr. (correspondent) 35
Keogh, Eugene J. (H/D) 140
Kerr, John H. (H/D) 147
KGU (radio station, Hawaii) 10
King, Samuel W. (H/R) 70, 96
Kirwan, Michael J (H/D) 147
Knutson, Harold (H/R) 96

LaFollette, Robert M., Jr. (S/P): challenges effort of late arriving member to be recorded as present for war vote 134–135; differences with other anti-interventionists 50; father's vote against previous war 50; opposed interventionism 50
LaGuardia, Fiorello H. (Mayor of New York City): claims Germany behind Pearl Harbor attack 104; hears Presidential war address of December 8th 38
Landon, Alf M. (former Republican presidential candidate): on supporting war 13
Larrabee, Michael J. (H/D) 147
Lawrence, David (columnist) 99
League of Nations 41; could have averted a second world war 85
Leahy, William D. (Admiral): on Hawaii attack being intentional 12; on success of attack implying major disaster 42
Lee, Josh (S/D) 135
Lend-Lease Act (1941) 47, 104, 107, 120
Libya 105
Lincoln, Abraham 58, 139
Lindbergh, Charles A.: diary entry on declaring war against Germany 133; effort to enter military rejected 18; initially dodges all comment on Japanese attack 17; on need to build up military facilities in the Philippines 155n.66; popular anti-war speaker 17
Lodge, Henry Cabot, Jr. (S/r) 48
Long, Breckinridge (Assistant Secretary of State) 42–43; accuses Hitler of long term plans against western hemisphere 104–105
Lorenz, Heinz 113
Los Angeles 28; airport 90; number of Japanese in 26
Los Angeles Japanese Cultural Society 32
Los Angeles Times 23, 130
Louisville (Kentucky) Courier Journal: Japan's war irretrievably linked with that of Germany's 25
Ludlow, Louis (H/D) 73–74

MacLeish, Archibald 42
Magnuson, Warren G. (H/D) 138
Malaya 39; attacked without warning 106
Manchuria 83
Mansfield, Joseph J. (H/D) 147
Marcantonio, Vito (H/A-L) 139
Marshall, George C. (General) 38
Martha's Vineyard: a home of Charles Lindbergh 17
Martin, Joseph W., Jr. (H/R; House Minority leader) 89; hopes for an unanimous pro–Japan war vote 56; on lack of partisan divisions over Japanese attack 12, 48–49; political background 55

Index

Mason, Noah W. (H/R) 148
McArdle, Joseph A. (H/D) 147, 148; difficulty in reaching Washington in time for Japan war vote, 90, 91
McCarran, Patrick (S/D) 52
McCormack, John D. (H/D): calls for immediate vote on Japan war resolution 88; endorses Japan war resolution 55; moves for immediate consideration of war with Germany resolution 136; moves to substitute Senate version of war with Germany resolution for that of the House 136; political background 54; role in substituting Senate version of war with Japan resolution for House's 89
McLaughlin, Charles F. (H/D) 65
McLean, Donald H. (H/R) 147
McNary, Charles L. (R/S; Senate Minority Leader): support of war resolution pledged 12
Mellet, Lowell: proposed changes in Presidential address 41
Meyer, John A. (H/D) 147
Miami 28
Michener, Earl C. (H/R): Japan had created the one situation in which he had always promised to support war 60
Midway Island 39
Miller, Francis 42
Miller, William ("Fishbait") (doorkeeper for U.S. House of Representatives) 96–97
Mitchell, Arthur W. (H/D) 68–69
Morocco 105
Moscow 113
Moser, Guy L. (H/D) 80
Mukaeda, Katsuma 32
Mundt, Karl E. (H/R) 83–84
Murdock, John R. (H/D) 148; stayed on West Coast during Japan war vote 91
Mussolini, Benito 103, 106, 143; complicity with Hitler in European war 86; his declaration of war mocked in U.S. 130–131; not supported by most Italians 138–139; promises aid to Japan if war came 122; reasons for intervention after Pacific war began 123; speech announcing Italian war with U.S. 124–125
Mutual Broadcasting System (radio) 10, 38, 104

National Airport (New York City) 38
National Broadcasting System (NBC radio): live broadcast of attack 10
National Guard 57, 70
Nelson, Donald M. (Director of Supply Priorities and Allocations Board) 104
Neutrality Act of 1935 80
New York City 26, 28; America First chapter 17–18; German language newspapers 33; harbor 149; National Airport 38; number of Japanese in 26; Times Square 38
New York Herald Tribune 28; explanation of Rankin's abstention on anti-German/Italy war votes 149; on sneak attack illustrating differences between Japan and U.S. 22
New York Journal-American 101–102
New York Post 130
New York Sun 130
New York Times: advertisements 24; cancels Japanese right to use its foreign communication lines 30; German influence on Japan's war decision unlikely 25
Newspapers: role in spreading attack information 35
Newsweek (magazine) 24–25
Niagara Falls, New York 28
9/11 attack and Pearl Harbor 1, 2
Norris, George W. (S/I): immediate threat demanded vote in favor of war with Japan 49; recognized war situation had drastically changed since World War One months before Pearl Harbor occurred 49–50; voted against World War One 49
Norton, Mary (H/D) 92
Nye, Gerald P. (S/R): skeptical of first Pearl Harbor reports, 51

O'Connor, James F. (H/D) 96, 145–146
O'Day, Caroline (H/D) 148
Ohmori, Kiagachiro 30
O'Leary, James A. (H/D) 148
O'Mahoney, Joseph C. (S/D) 48
Osmers, Frank C. (H/R) 148; successfully resisted FDR's policy of keeping Congressmen out of combat assignments 62
O'Toole, Donald L. (H/D) 144

Index

Pacific cable 1
Pagan, Bolivar (H/D) 74
Panama Canal Zone 74; arrests of foreigners in 26; danger to 105
Panay (U.S. gunboat): attacked by Japanese in Chinese waters 12; justified a U.S. declaration of war 80
Paris 32
Patterson, Eleanor ("Cissy") (editor of *Washington Times Herald*): wonders if FDR behind Japanese attack 17
Pearl Harbor: American discussion of whether Germany was behind Pearl Harbor 24–25, 68, 99, 104, 138; books on 5; casualties 39, 41–43; *Congressional Record* on 1–2; delay in stateside receipt of information and photos 1; distances involved required attack to be planned long in advance 39, 61, 71–72, 75; emotional turmoil at number of American losses 87; fear that it would distract attention from possibility of war with Germany 24; Hitler's view of 114–115, 120; humor about 12; initial Germany foreign ministry reaction to 112–113; initial popular German reaction to 111–112; Italian delay in reaction to 120, 121; Italian newspapers on attack 121–122; as justification for racism 65–66; limited data immediately available 15; navy's failures at 42–43; newspaper accounts 2; as proof that there was no longer a traditional "front line" in war 87; proved oceans no definitive protection for U.S. 25–26, 71; question of whether local commands responsibility for success of Japanese attack 82; rumors of German pilots involved 31; ship loses 43; shock at it being a target 6, 9–10, 42; strength of its defenses 63; *see also* Hawaii
Pegler, Westbrook (columnist) 99
Pepper, Claude (S/D): seeks simultaneous declaration of war with both Japan and Germany 100
Perkins, Frances (cabinet member): on steady arrival of new information on attack 11
Pfeifer, Joseph L. (H/D) 148
Pheiffer, William T. (H/R): no negotiated peace possible 141
Philadelphia 26

Philadelphia Inquirer 23, 130
Philippine Islands 39, 109
Pittsburgh, Pennsylvania (airport) 148
Plauche, Vance (H/D) 139
Plumley, Charles A. (H/R) 65–66
Poland: U.S. encouragement of 116
Poleti, Charles (Lieutenant Governor of New York) 33
Prohibition 93
Puerto Rico: non-voting member of House 74

radio (German) 111
radio (Italy) 120, 121, 124
radio (U.S.): audience for Roosevelt's December 9th speech to the nation 106; broadcast of Roosevelt's declaration of war request 10; estimated audience for president's "Day of Infamy" condemnation 38; role in spreading information about attack 35, 77; U.S. networks 38
Radio Corporation of America: refuses to send any foreign transmissions by Axis correspondents 31
Rafu Shimpo (Los Angeles Japanese language newspaper) 33
Rankin, Jeanette (H/R): attempts to delay roll call vote on Japan war resolution 88; attempts to immediately derail anti–Japan war resolution by sending it to committee 55; booed for voting against Japan war resolution 89; both Democrats and Republicans try to convince her to reverse anti–Japan war vote 96; Everett Dirksen attempts to get her to change anti–Japan war vote 95–96; Everett Dirksen attempts to get her to vote in favor of war with Germany and Italy 149; explaining her voting "present" rather than "no" on the anti–German/Italian war votes 149; home staters urge her to reverse anti–Japan war vote 97; immediate explanations for anti–Japanese war votes 96, 97; later placing of blame for war on FDR's intentional policies 97, 98; lobbyist for women's right to vote 92; personality of 96; pre-war efforts to curb FDR's leeway in involving U.S. in Europe 94; ran for House seat second time twenty odd years after first election 94; regarded

war over Pearl Harbor as no solution to the basic problem 96; took a front row seat during Japan war debate to assure her objections would not be overlooked 95; voted against World War One and faced massive criticism for decision by friends and foes alike 93–94; won House seat in first effort 93
Rankin, John E. (H/D) 65
Rayburn, Sam (D/H; House Speaker) 91; blocked effort to delay roll call vote on Japan war resolution 88; confident of full backing of House for an anti–Japanese war resolution 12; considered German declaration of war inevitable 107; explanation to constituents of why he voted for war with Japan 88–89
Reece, B. Carroll (H/R) 68
Reed, Chauncey W. (H/R) 88
Reed, Clyde M. (S/R) 92
Reed, Daniel A. (H/R) 67
Reichstag: Hitler's speech announcing war with U.S. 115–118
Reuben James (U.S.S.): sinking of, 128
Reynolds, Robert R. (S/D): demands more facts before declaration of war 16; factors leading to the attack 16; Japanese attack likely to lead to war with Germany 100
Rich, Robert F. (H/R) 72
Richmond (Virginia) News Leader 23, 131
Richmond (Virginia) Times Dispatch 23; on Jeanette Rankins' anti–Japan war vote 97
Rivers, L. Mendell (H/D) 70
Robinson, J. W. (H/D) 148
Rochester, New York 28
Rogers, Edith N. (H/R): insists there no gender difference in support of anti–Japan war 59; political career 59
Rolph, Thomas (H/R) 143
Romano, Francesco (Italian correspondent in U.S.) 120–121
Roosevelt, Eleanor: accompanies Franklin to hear his "Day of Infamy" speech 37; on U.S. government arrest policy 26
Roosevelt, Elliott: calls father seeking information on attack 11
Roosevelt, Franklin D.: accusations by Hitler against 116; balancing a Pacific only versus a two ocean war decision 6; broadcast of his declaration of war speech 10; Congressional lobbying of for anti–German war resolution 77; conspired to get U.S. into war in both Atlantic and Pacific 57–58, 98; "Day of Infamy" address to Congress 36–41; decides to let Germany take initiative in declaring war 102–104; dictates initial draft of war speech 11; executive order authorizing arrest of foreigners 26, 27; foreign policy praised 84; fundamental foreign policy mistakes 73–74; held back on war-making legislation he wanted before Pearl Harbor because of lack of support 19; keeping military strategy from Congress 47; loathed Congressman Hamilton Fish 56; locking Congress out of U.S.-Japan negotiating information 72; maintaining pre-war social programs in war-time 46–47; omissions in "Day of Infamy" address 41; press conferences 105; proposed changes in "Day of Infamy" speech 41; question of FDR and Washington level responsibility for success of attack 80; radio addresses 105–106; received and signed war with Japan resolution about four hours after his speech to Congress 89; rhetorically roasts Germany to provoke intervention 105–107; sends brief note to Congress informing it that Germany and Italy had declared war 129–130, 131 (text); signs declarations of war against Germany and Italy 150–151; speaks with son Elliott day of attack 11; *see also* White House
Roosevelt, James (Captain, U.S. Marines) 37
Rusk, Dean (later U.S. Secretary of State): intelligence data reviewed on Japanese targets 153n.3
Russia *see* Soviet Union

Sabath, Adolph J. (H/D) 85–86
St. Louis, Missouri 92
St. Louis Globe Democrat 130
Salisbury, Harrison E. (journalist): on newspeople's perception of war danger in December 9
San Francisco 28, 39, 91; Japanese

consulate nearly burns building down destroying its confidential papers, 30
San Francisco Chronicle 130
Sanders, Jared Y., Jr. (H/D) 71–72
Sarles, Ruth 43
Scanlon, Thomas E. (H/D) 148; World War One experiences 81
Schaefer, Edwin M. (H/D) 148
Schmidt, Paul (press spokesman for German Foreign Office) 31–32
Schwartz, H. H. (S/D) 52
Scott, Hugh D. (H/R) 75
Secret Service: guard president on way to Capitol Hill 37
Sell, Kurt G. (German newsman in U.S.): enquires about cancellation of press cards 30–31
Senate (U.S.): absence of members from vote on war against Germany and Italy 134–135; absence of members from vote on war against Japan 52–53; differences in how war resolutions with Japan and Germany/Italy treated 134; discusses declaring war on Japan 44–48; members serving and voting concerning war in both 1917 and 1941 49; off floor comments on declaring war on Japan 48–49; vote on declaring war with Japan 49–51
Shanley, James A. (H/D) 86
Sheridan, Henry B. (H/D) 148
Sherwood, Robert (Bob) 24, 37
Shih, Hu (Dr.) (Chinese ambassador to U.S.): visits Congress to hear Roosevelt's war declaration speech 36
Sikes, Robert L. F. (H/D): national unity vital to overcome great strength of enemy nations 142–143
Simpson, Richard M. (H/R) 73
Singapore 108, 109, 113
Smathers, William H. (S/D) 135
Smith, Joe L. (H/D) 148
South America: impact of a successful Japanese war upon 106
Soviet Union 10, 106, 108; atrocities in 140–141; December 1941 offensive 113; prisoners from 116; unexpected resiliency of forces 115
Spanish-American War 47, 63
Spencer, George L. (S/D) 52
Springer, Raymond S. (H/R) 76

Staats Zeitung und Herald (New York City German language newspaper) 33
Stark, Harold R. (Admiral; Chief of Naval Operations) 38; testifies to Senate committee 43
Starnes, Joe (H/D) 70
Steagal, Henry B. (H/D) 148
Stimson, Henry L. 103
Strempel, Heribert von 127
Sweeney, Martin L. (H/D) 64–65
Switzerland: embassy in Japan providing information on American detainees 34

Taft, Robert A. (S/R): pre-conflict concern over possibility of war with Japan 15
Tanaka, Togo 33
Thailand: attacked without warning 106
Thill, Lewis D. (H/R) 67
Thomas, Elbert D. (S/D) 23
Thomas, John (S/R) 52
Thomas, Norman (Socialist candidate for president) 100–101
Thompson, Dorothy (columnist): on shock at Pearl Harbor attack 10
Thomson, Hans (German diplomat in U.S.) 127, 129
Times Square (New York City) 38
Togo, Shigenori 150
Tojo, Hideki (Premier-General of Japan) 150
Tori, Shigenori (Japanese Foreign Minister) 126
Treadway, Allen T. (H/R): discusses World War One vote in Congress 71; quickness of action in declaring war on Germany and Italy 146
Tripartite Pact 24, 77, 128; as encouraging Japanese war with U.S. 16; German ambassador to Tokyo affirms his country would honor it in case of war 110; proposal to revise Pact 111; provisions of as to intervening in a war 108, 114, 122; Second Tripartite Pact 116, 125–126; whether original Pact required intervention against U.S. after Pearl Harbor 103, 120
Truman, Harry (S/D): difficulties in getting back to Washington in time for Japan war vote 91–92

Index

187

Truman, Margaret: account of attending "Day of Infamy" address 37–38; account of father's rush back to Washington for Japan war vote 91–92

Tully, Grace (presidential secretary): receives constant updates on Pearl Harbor attack 42; records president's preliminary draft of Japan war speech, 11

TWA Stratoliner 90

Tydings, Millard E. (S/D) 48, 135

United Nations 48

United Press 10

United States: American ambassador to Britain expected breakout of war 9; arrests German, Italian, and Japanese citizens in U.S. 26–29; efforts of domestic Germans, Italians, and Japanese to defuse hostility 32–33; exports to Japan 80; government officials encourage war with Germany 104–105; inability to grasp "two track" foreign policy concept 67–68; informed of war decision by Germany and Italy 127; internment of nationals by and in Japan 34; Italian-American enlistments in U.S. military 33; number of Axis citizens resident in country 26–27; number of Japanese in 26; price of food 29; public opinion on war danger with Japan 9; shift in American opinion on war with Germany 107–108; treatment of Japanese embassy and consulates 29–30; unifying results of the attack 23

Van Nuys, Frederick (S/D): appeals for calm in facing war-time decisions 48

Van Zandt, James E. (H/R): 1936 visit to Japan 81; recent active duty service with Navy at Pearl Harbor 82

Vandenberg, Arthur H. (R/S): defense of his pre-war anti-interventionist stance, 45–46; diary entry on war being declared against Germany 133; initial reaction to Japanese attack 13–14; political career 45; private opinions on Japanese assault 46–47; public statements in Senate on Japan 44–45; war convinced him of need for full U.S. involvement in international affairs afterwards 47

Vincent, Beverly M. (H/D): delay in reaching Washington for Japan war vote 90–91

von Ribbentropp (Germany Foreign Minister): attempts to bring Japan into war against Britain 108–109; dismisses Pearl Harbor attack report as American propaganda 111; evasive as to what aid would be given Japan 111; inability of America to produce good soldiers en masse 119; informed by Japanese ambassador of attack 114; pledge of support to Japan 110

Voorhis, H. Jerry (H/D): on American reaction to attack 77; need to preserve core religious, political, and social values in war-time 78; post-war policies essential to maintain peace 78

Vorys, John M. (H/R) 82–83

Vreeland, Albert (H/R): war service in the Pacific 62

Wadsworth, George 124

Wagner, Robert F. (S/D) 92, 135

Wake Island 39

Wallgren, Monrad C. (S/D) 52

Walsh, David I. (S/D) 15

Walter, Francis E. (H/D) 92

war: Japanese attacks required substantial advance planning 39; as a political decision 5

Washington, D.C.: police department assists Congressmen to reach Capitol Hill 90, 91; police escort for Jeanette Rankin after anti-Japan war vote 96; reaction to September 8th presidential motorcade 37

Washington, George 73, 139

Washington (D.C.) News: on U.S. exports to Japan 20

Washington Times Herald: "extra" edition on attack day 17

Welch, Richard J. (H/R) 148

Welles, Sumner 41

Wheeler, Burton K. (S/R): missed war vote with Germany and Italy 135; missed war vote with Japan 52; views Japanese attack as irrational 14; war to be a long one due to distances involved 14; would have filibustered any proposal for U.S. to initiate war with Germany 102

Whetstone, Dan (member of National Republican Committee) 97
White, Compton I. (H/D) 148
White House: December 7th evening cabinet meeting 43, 103; December 7th evening meeting with members of Congress 11, 48, 100, 103; guarded by U.S. Marines 36; Japanese newspapermen at on day of attack 10–11; public announcement of attack 10; release of details of attack 10; *see also* Roosevelt, Franklin D.
Wilkie, Wendell L. (former Republican Presidential candidate): certainty that U.S. would go to war 13
Wilson, Earl (H/R) 87–88
Wilson, Woodrow: as betraying promises for just peace 116
Wilson, Woodrow (Mrs.): attends December 8th presidential speech 37
Winant, John G. (ambassador to Britain) 150
Wisconsin Federation of German-American Societies 33
WNBC (radio; New York City) 104
Wolfenden, James (H/R) 148
Wolverton, Charles A. (H/R) 61; anti-interventionists had nothing to apologize for 145
Wood, Robert (head of America First): informed of Japanese attack by newspaperman 17; privately believed Roosevelt responsible for attack 17; receives reports on American loses in Hawaii 43; returns to active duty in military 18;
Woodruff, Roy O. (H/R): ultimate responsibility for the Hawaiian disaster 63; unprecedented length of remarks 63
World Trade Center 1
World War One 19, 26–27, 47, 90; British encourgement for gaining U.S. entry resented afterwards 94; British enthusiasm over American entry 150; Congressmen who had served in 57, 61, 63, 64, 68, 75, 76, 79–80, 81, 84; description of World War One war vote 71; Hitler in 117; senators present for votes in both world wars 49; significant vote against war 93

Young, Stephen M. (H/D) 74–75, 144

www.ingramcontent.com/pod-product-compliance
Lightning Source LLC
Chambersburg PA
CBHW032102300426
44116CB00007B/856